D1560120

IBM Mainframes
Architecture and Design

IBM Mainframes

Architecture and Design

N. S. Prasad

Intertext Publications
McGraw-Hill Book Company

New York St. Louis San Francisco Auckland Bogotá
Hamburg London Madrid Mexico Milan Montreal
New Delhi Panama Paris São Paulo
Singapore Sidney Tokyo Toronto

Library of Congress Catalog Card Number 88-83706

10 9 8 7 6 5 4 3 2 1

ISBN 0-07-050686-8

Intertext Publications/Multiscience Press, Inc.
One Lincoln Plaza
New York, NY 10023

McGraw-Hill Book Company
1221 Avenue of the Americas
New York, NY 10020

IBM is a trademark of International Business Machines Corporation

Composed in Ventura Publisher by Context, Inc.

Contents

Preface

IBM computers comprise more than 80 percent of mainframes in commercial use today. Ever since the introduction of the IBM 360 nearly a quarter of a century ago, IBM has dominated the large-scale computer market. The main reason for this domination is IBM's evolutionary approach toward systems architecture, which is defined in Lorin [1] as the architecture of hardware and software that constitutes a total system. From the user's point of view, compatibility of application programs is assured, even though architectures change because of technological advances and demands made by operating systems and other software. Two major extensions to the 360 architecture have been made (the 370 was introduced in 1970 and the 370/XA in 1981), and a third was recently announced (the ESA/370). Throughout this architectural evolution, the basic instruction set and conceptual machine present in the 360 architecture were kept, even though new ideas regarding memory, I/O management, and the use of multiple processors have been introduced.

During the past 25 years, many changes have taken place in the computing environment. When the 360 was introduced in 1964, most programs were run in the batch mode, and assembly language was widely used by application programmers. The current picture is different in many respects. On-line programs, distributed processing, networking, PC-to-mainframe linkage — these are common in today's environment. Also, the number of software layers surrounding an application program has increased significantly, contributing to the overall complexity of computation. Technology has changed drastically, making it possible to do millions of computations per second and to connect large numbers of processors in order to provide parallel processing capabilities.

IBM has successfully managed until now to achieve a compromise among conflicting challenges made by technology, software, and program compatibility. Today's IBM machines resemble the 360 machines, yet they are different — they execute 50 to 100 millions of instructions per second (as opposed to less than 500,000 instructions by some of the 360 models), and their instruction sets are exceedingly complex. The architecture became increasingly complex as it evolved, so that the descriptions of certain instructions run to many pages. The 360 architecture was clean, neat, and easy to understand. The 370 is more difficult and the 370/XA much more so. The complexity is attributable to the demands made by memory architecture, multiprocessing requirements, and the fact that functions previously provided by operating system routines are implemented in microcode.

OBJECTIVES OF THIS BOOK

The first objective of this book is to describe the principles of operation used by IBM mainframes during the past 25 years. IBM introduced the practice of building mainframes to conform to an architecture, which can be thought of as the specifications of a conceptual machine. The architecture itself is not seen as rigid and unchanging, but subject to periodic revisions and extensions. We describe the evolution of the 360 architecture into the 370 architecture and the evolution of the latter into the 370/XA architecture.

The second objective of this book is to describe machines (called models) that have been successful in the marketplace or have interesting features. The models described include the 3090, 308X, 9370, 438X and 3033. These models provide a range of processing power and design options.

The third objective is to provide an overview of the architecture and implementation of I/O subsystems and networks — in other words, the components of what is called systems architecture in Lorin [1].

The fourth objective is to give a critical appraisal of the various architectural and design concepts in the light of current-day thinking.

USES OF THIS BOOK

The intended uses of this book are threefold:

- It can be read by the general audience of computer professionals working on IBM mainframes, or used as a reference.
- It can be used as supplementary reading material in an assembly language course, since the instruction set is discussed in detail.
- It can be used as a supplementary text in a computer architecture course, since it describes the advantages and shortcomings of the pragmatic, cost/performance-ratio oriented attitude toward architecture, which is the view essentially adopted by IBM and other manufacturers regarding commercially used mainframes.

ORGANIZATION OF THIS BOOK

The book is organized into 15 chapters:

1. Introduction to IBM computers
2. Role of architecture in IBM mainframes
3. 360 architecture
4. 370 architecture
5. 370/XA architecture
6. ESA/370 architecture
7. Techniques used by IBM in the design of mainframes
8. 3033 processor design
9. 308X processor design
10. 3090 processor design
11. 4381 processor design
12. 9370 processor design
13. DASD subsystems implementation
14. Communication configurations
15. Review and concluding remarks

A list of references is provided at the end of each chapter, together with a list of additional sources of information, for those readers who wish to pursue the subject of that chapter.

The first two chapters of this book give an introduction to the architectural and design concepts of IBM computers in comparison to other architectures and conceptual models.

Chapters 3–6 describe the evolution of the architecture of IBM mainframes from the 360 to the ESA/370. We have tried to emphasize concepts without getting lost in details of specification. An appraisal of each architecture is given at the end of the relevant chapter.

Chapters 7–12 describe design concepts and specific implementations. Chapters 9 and 10 deal with the 308X and 3090 series, which are the most powerful among IBM mainframes. Chapters 11 and 12 describe smaller machines (the 4381 and 9370), which are used in midrange capacities.

Chapter 13 deals with direct access storage (DASD) subsystems and associated control units. Chapter 14 presents networking concepts and IBM's approach in integrating computers with different architectures into an architected system.

Chapter 15 is the concluding chapter and provides an assessment of the IBM mainframe environment.

ACKNOWLEDGMENTS

Of the many individuals who helped the author with this book, special mention should be made of Jay Ranade, editor of these series, for his unfailing support and commitment toward his authors and to Fred Pearl of Nynex Corporation for his invaluable help in critiquing the book manuscript. Special thanks are also due to Vida Dunie, who typed the original and several revisions of the manuscript with unfailing enthusiasm and cheerfulness.

REFERENCES

1. Lorin, H.; "Systems Architecture in Transition — An Overview, *IBM Systems Journal*, vol. 25, nos. 3/4, 1986.

1

Introduction to IBM Computers

This chapter is intended to provide background material pertaining to the evolution of computers in general and IBM computers in particular. In the process of doing so, various interrelated topics are discussed. The first topic is the evolutionary nature of computer architecture and design. Throughout the book this topic appears in one form or another. The second topic is conceptual models used in computers. A conceptual model is a level higher than architecture, which is one level higher than design. Many architectures use the same conceptual model, just as many designs use the same architecture. The third topic is the history of IBM mainframes in the past three decades. The last topic deals with IBM computers other than mainframes, some of which use very innovative architectural and design principles.

1.1 EVOLUTION OF COMPUTERS

The concept of a computer is evolutionary — and is still in the process of evolution. Most of the computers in use today, ranging from the personal computer (PC) to supercomputers capable of performing hundreds of millions operations in a second, have common characteristics:

• They are automatic, in the sense that no human intervention is necessary as the computer executes a task that is assigned to it, except in the case of machine failure or abnormal conditions.

- They are electronic, in the sense that the components used for computation and storage are electronic devices, such as transistors, and consequently high-speed computations are possible.
- They are digital (rather than analog) and use binary arithmetic and logical operations to convert input information into output information.
- They use the stored-program concept, in the sense that a program (which is a sequence of machine instructions) is stored and executed by the machine without the need for patch panels which, were used by the early electronic computers.
- They are general purpose as opposed to being dedicated or special-purpose machines and can perform a variety of functions (some more efficiently than others).

The origin of the digital computer as we know it today dates to the World War II years. During this period many one-of-a-kind experimental computers were built, such as:

- Mark I, which was the first automatic (nonelectronic) digital computer and used a sequence mechanism for controlling the automatic operation of the machine. Instructions were encoded on paper tape, and the paper tape was advanced after the execution of each instruction. Mark I was conceived by Howard Aiken at Harvard University and was implemented in collaboration with IBM. The primary use of Mark I was in the solution of defense-related problems, including the simulation of the first atomic bomb.
- ENIAC (Electronic Numerical Integrator and Computer), which was the first automatic electronic digital computer, in the sense that it used electronic components for performing calculations. Programming the computer was done by patch panel interconnection, and the computer had to be wired before executing a program. ENIAC was designed by John Mauchly and implemented by J. Presper Eckert. ENIAC was built at the Moore School of the University of Pennsylvania between 1943 and 1946. Its primary use was in the integration of ballistic equations.
- EDVAC (Electronic Discrete Variable Automatic Computer), which was the first automatic electronic digital stored program computer. EDVAC was developed at the Moore School also; and its design was influenced by the shortcomings of ENIAC. The most remarkable feature of EDVAC was the concept of the stored program. This concept is generally attributed to von Neumann, who was a consultant at Moore School. In a stored program machine, instructions

and data are stored together in a memory. This avoids the need for patch panel wiring, as required by ENIAC.

• WHIRLWIND I was developed in the late 1940s at the Massachusetts Institute of Technology under the direction of J. W. Forrester. It was a stored program 16-bit computer. It influenced subsequent hardware and software developments, such as magnetic core memories and operating systems, and can be regarded as a precursor of sorts to the early IBM and DEC computers.

The computer industry emerged in the 1950s. Eckert and Mauchly left the Moore School and started their own company, which built UNIVAC I. UNIVAC I is regarded as the first commercially successful computer. The company started by Eckert and Mauchly was acquired by Remington Rand, and several notable UNIVAC computers (such as the UNIVAC 1103 and 1103A) were subsequently built during the late 1950s. IBM also entered the field with the 700/7000 series. During the late 1950s and early 1960s, a number of companies were manufacturing both large and small computers. Some of them, such as RCA, dropped out of the industry; but others, such as IBM, NCR, Honeywell, and CDC, are still in the business. By the late 1960s, IBM had become the dominant vendor of mainframes (large-scale computers), primarily on account of the appeal of the 360 hardware and software architectures to data-processing managers of large-scale corporations.

The use of computers has changed greatly during the past three decades. Initially, computers were used only for scientific calculations, but they have gradually pervaded many aspects of the business world. One reason for this growth is technological, stemming from miniaturization of components and mass production of circuits. The other reason is the emergence of languages and software for a variety of applications.

1.2 CONCEPTUAL MODELS USED IN COMPUTERS

A conceptual model of a computer describes a hypothetical machine with well-defined operations. Such a machine views computation as a process that is performed by coordinating several components or subsystems. The same conceptual model may be used by several architectures (see Chapter 2). Examples of conceptual models are the von Neumann machine, the general purpose computer, and the dataflow computer. All these models plus a few others are discussed in this section.

1.2.1 Von Neumann Machine

The conceptual framework used by most computers today is generally attributed to the great mathematician John von Neumann. As mentioned previously, he was a consultant at the Moore School of the University of Pennsylvania, where he and his collaborators worked on the design of EDVAC, the first computer that used the stored-program concept. This concept postulates that instructions and data be stored together (rather than separately, as was the case in earlier machines) in a single memory unit. Later on in 1949, von Neumann and his collaborators at the Institute of Advanced Study (IAS) in Princeton came up with the specifications of a machine known as the IAS machine, or von Neumann machine. The von Neumann machine was the precursor of today's general purpose computer.

The von Neumann machine is schematically shown in Figure 1-1. The components of the machine are the following:

- Arithmetic/logical unit (ALU)
- Memory
- Input/output (I/O) units
- Control unit

The arithmetic/logical unit performs arithmetical operations such as addition, subtraction, multiplication, and division, and logical

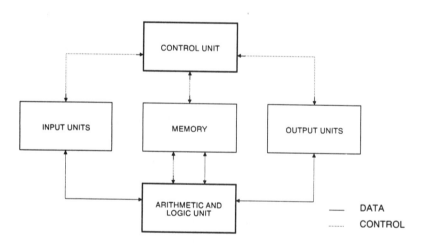

Figure 1-1 Schema for the von Neumann machine.

operations such as shifting, conjunction, disjunction, and complementation.

The memory is regarded as a linear array of cells numbered from 1 to n. It is used for storing instructions that comprise a program and data required for program execution. The data can be read from, stored, or modified in memory.

The input (output) units are used for receiving (sending) data from (to) the outside world. Note the data path in Figure 1-1. There is no direct path from an input or output unit to memory, and all data transfer is done via the arithmetic/logical unit.

The control unit, as its name implies, controls the machine. By control is meant the coordination of various units and the proper sequencing of instructions that is necessary before they are executed by the arithmetic/logical unit. Thus the control unit fetches an instruction, decodes it, and passes it on to the arithmetic/logical unit for execution.

The characteristics of the von Neumann machine are noted below:

- Both data and instructions are stored in memory, and no distinction is made between the two in terms of storage. Thus, instructions can be modified during program execution. Also, no distinction is made among various types of data (e.g., decimal, binary, floating point, character string).
- A program is viewed as a set of instructions that reside in memory. These instructions are executed in the physical sequence in which they appear in memory, except in the case of a branch instruction, which causes a new sequence starting with the instruction at the memory location specified by the branch. A program counter indicates the next instruction to be executed by the machine.
- Input/output is done by separate functional units. These transfer data to and from main memory via the arithmetic and logical units.
- The interpretation and sequential execution of instructions is done by a separately identified unit, control. The control unit fetches, decodes, and executes each instruction in sequence.

The advantages of the von Neumann machine are the following:

- It is conceptually easy to understand and to implement.
- It is well suited for implementing algorithms, which are traditionally written in terms of serial instructions with embedded loops and branches.

- In practice, it has proved itself to be a workable model for solving problems in scientific environments or for processing data in commercial environments.

The disadvantages of the von Neumann machine are the following:

- It does not make a distinction between instruction and data, as is done by most programming languages today.
- It does not make a distinction between various types of data (e.g., decimal, binary, floating point, character string), which is done by most programming languages today.
- Its execution logic is serial and hence cannot be used as a model when some or all the processing is done in parallel.
- Some researchers (e.g., Hills [1] and Backus [2]) claim that it can cause bottlenecks that adversely affect performance, because of its insistence on storing programs and data in memory. Their argument is that processors are much faster than memory these days and hence the storing and retrieval of instruction and data can slow down computation.

1.2.2   General Purpose Computer

A general purpose computer is a machine that can solve a wide variety of problems and operate in several different environments. It can function as a scientific machine, as a business machine, or as a communication processor, to name three common applications. Most computers in use today are general purpose computers. All general purpose computers have a number of features in common. These features evolved during the past four decades as a result of experimentation.

In this section, a conceptual model of the general purpose computer is presented. This model contains characteristics that are present in most general computers of today. This conceptual model contains two views, the programmer's view and the designer's view. The programmer's view is commonly called the architecture of the machine. The designer's view is the view of the hardware in terms of building blocks used for implementing the architecture.

Overview of the General Purpose Architecture

Conceptually, a general purpose machine has the following elements:

• Central Processing Unit (CPU)
• Memory
• I/O subsystem (called "channel" in IBM terminology).

The CPU executes instructions and interacts with memory and the I/O subsystem. The I/O subsystem performs the actual read/write operations relating to I/O units such as disks, terminals, and printers. Data is transferred between memory and I/O units by the I/O subsystem. At the end of an I/O operation the CPU is notified that the I/O operation has been completed by an interruption from the I/O subsystem. The interruption mechanism is an integral part in the design of the general purpose computer. Its essential function is to replace the currently executing program in the CPU by a new program for handling the event causing the interruption. The specific means of accomplishing this function varies among computers (see Chapters 3, 4, and 5 for details on how interruptions are handled by IBM computers).

The conceptual view of the CPU is that of a machine with an instruction set and a set of objects (also called entities, as in Rao and Rosenfeld [3]) that can be manipulated by instructions. These objects can be registers, memory locations, program counters, timers, I/O units, etc. In the 360 CPU described in Chapter 3, the instruction set operates on the following objects:

• Registers
• Memory
• Program status word
• Storage key
• Channels

The number of objects increases in the case of the 370 and the 370/XA, because more sophisticated concepts are used in the areas of hardware and programming.

The conceptual view of the machine is the view generally offered to programmers. Programmers are classified as application (or "problem") programmers and systems programmers. The former write application programs (solve specific problems); their view is limited to what is necessary for writing such programs. The systems programmers write operating systems, compilers, access methods, on-line monitors, etc.; their view generally encompasses the entire conceptual view.

In addition to the conceptual view of the CPU, there is a generally accepted implementation view, which is different from the conceptual view. Under the implementation view, the CPU consists of the following components:

- Instruction fetching unit
- Instruction execution unit
- Cache (or high-speed buffer)
- Control unit

The actual characteristics and functions of these components vary from machine to machine (see Chapters 7–12 for the implementation details of these components on various IBM machines).

Instruction Set

An instruction consists of two parts:

- Operation code
- Operand(s)

The execution of an instruction yields a result (which may replace an operand) and a condition code. The condition code is stored in a status register. The status register may not exist independently and can be combined with another component. In the IBM 360 architecture, the status register is combined with the program counter and the combination is called the program status word.

The instruction set for general purpose machines includes the following:

- Arithmetic instructions
- Logical (or boolean) instructions
- Move instructions
- Branch (or jump) instructions
- Comparison instructions
- I/O instructions
- Control instructions

The operands for these instructions can be any of the objects mentioned earlier, such as registers, memory, etc.

Registers

Registers are an integral part of the general purpose architecture. They are generally implemented using high-speed circuit elements, physically close to the arithmetic and logic circuits of the CPU to minimize delays. They were initially introduced for performance reasons and subsequently became standard architectural features.

In the general purpose environment, registers serve a variety of functions. They can be used in arithmetic operations as accumulators, in shift operations as shift registers, and for addressing memory. The last function serves to reduce the total size of instructions in a program because fewer bits are needed to specify a register (e.g., 4) than to specify storage locations (e.g., 24).

The registers can be used to address memory in a number of ways. For example, a register can be designated as a "base" register in an instruction. The instruction can also contain a "displacement." The contents of the base register are added to the displacement to get the actual address of the operand. It is also common for an instruction to contain an "index" register, in addition to the base register. The address is then obtained as a sum of the contents of the base and index registers and the displacement.

The number of registers used by an architecture varies. The 360 used 16 general purpose registers. The 370, on the other hand, uses 16 general registers and 16 control registers. Some of the newer machines use as many as 1,024 registers (see later discussion on RISC computers).

Program Counter

The role of the program status word (or program counter) varies from computer to computer. It can take on the functions of the status register in addition to being a program counter and also can display the condition code after an instruction is executed. For computers with several modes of operation (as in the case of the 370 machine), it can contain a code indicating the mode of operation that is currently being used. It can indicate a "state" of the computer, the states being designated as "supervisor," "problem," etc. One of its major roles, however, is in relation to interruption. The program counter contains the address of the next executable instruction. After an interruption, the contents of the program counter is saved in a pre-assigned location in memory, and a new program counter is loaded from another pre-assigned location in memory.

Memory

As in the von Neumann machine, memory consists of cells numbered from 1 to n. The cell can be a byte (as in the case of the IBM 370 architecture) or a word. Each cell can be read from or written to. The address of a cell is specified as part of an instruction, usually using a base register number, a displacement, and perhaps an index register number as well. It is also common to use two or more schemes for addressing a location in memory. For example, one can have a real addressing scheme wherein the addresses used in instructions directly correspond to memory locations. Or, one can have a virtual addressing scheme in which the addresses used in instructions do not directly correspond to memory locations but are fictitious or virtual addresses. These virtual addresses are translated into real addresses for memory locations before an instruction is executed. As can be imagined, this process involves maintaining tables of real and virtual addresses and subsequently searching them. The maintenance of tables is usually done by the operating system, but the look-up is done by hardware.

I/O Subsystem

The function of the I/O subsystem is to

• decode an I/O instruction,
• interact with I/O units,
• transfer data between the I/O unit and memory, and
• interrupt the CPU on completion of the I/O operation.

In the IBM 360 and 370 architectures, I/O subsystems are called channels. The 360 and 370 architectures specify elaborate rules regarding the interactions between CPU, channel, and memory. In the 370/XA architecture, an I/O subsystem is called a channel subsystem and is a computer that manages channels.

Channels are not used by computers such as the VAX machines or the INTEL 8080 processors used in PCs. Instead, these computers use a bus architecture, wherein CPU, memory, and I/O units are connected to a bus. The functions of the bus are two-fold:

- to provide data transfer capabilities among various components connected the bus, such as CPU, memory, I/O units
- to provide a protocol by which various requests for the use of the bus by the components are handled in an orderly and methodical manner.

Conceptual Versus Implementation Aspects

It seems to be the consensus among architects of general purpose computers that certain functions pertain to architecture and certain other functions pertain to implementation.

The architecture, as mentioned before, specifies an abstract machine with an instruction set. These specifications provide the programmer with a view limited to serial program execution. Many other activities that take place in the computer are not allowed to be seen by the programmer. Examples of these activities are given in the following paragraphs.

The execution of an instruction consists of many steps, such as fetching it from memory, decoding it, etc. Separate registers and microcoded programs handle these functions, using the pipelined techniques discussed in Chapter 7. These are invisible to the programmer who uses the machine. There are varying degrees of parallelism in instruction execution, but from the programmer's point of view instruction execution is always serial.

Almost all modern computers use a storage hierarchy concept, which is dictated by technology. The most recent IBM mainframes use three levels of memory:

- Cache (high-speed buffer)
- Main storage (memory)
- Expanded storage.

The cache is a high-speed semiconductor memory with an access time that can be as low as 15 nanoseconds, depending on the model. Main storage uses slower semiconductor memory with access time of 300–350 nanoseconds. Expanded storage is electronic storage, slower and cheaper than main storage. The movement of data between the three levels of storage has been the subject of considerable study and experimentation. At present the accepted approach among most architects is that the cache operations should be hidden from the programmer's view of the machine. However, this approach is challenged by the architects of the HP Spectrum series (Birnbaum and Worley [4]).

Control Function and Microprogramming

The control function in the von Neumann machine has its counterpart in general purpose computers. This function is partly implemented by hardware and partly by microprograms. A microprogram resides in a control store, which is usually regarded as distinct from memory. The control store is organized into control words. A microprogram consists of a set of microinstructions. A microinstruction, in turn, consists of a set of microoperations. A microoperation can be regarded as the most basic or primitive activity that takes place inside a computer.

A control word contains one microinstruction. If each microinstruction specifies one or a few microoperations, such microprogramming, is called vertical. If, on the other hand, several microoperations are

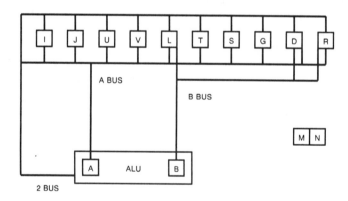

(b) Internal Structure of System 360/30

NEXT ADDRESS	CM	CU	CA	CB	CD	CF	CC

(b) Micro Instruction

Figure 1-2 System 360/50

specified, then the microprogramming is called horizontal. In either case, microinstructions are executed one at a time. In the case of horizontal microprogramming, several microoperations are executed in parallel, during one machine cycle.

In Figure 1-2 we give an example of a small microprogrammed computer in the 360 family, the System 360/30. The simplified design of the computer is shown in Figure 1-2(a). It consists of an arithmetic/logic unit (ALU) connected to 10 external registers via 2 internal registers, A and B. A Z-bus delivers the output of the ALU to an external register. The inputs to the ALU are sent from a pair of the external registers via the buses A and B. The address of the memory location to be fetched is placed in a memory address register (MAR) and the actual contents of the memory location in a memory data register (MDR). The MAR is a pair of registers indicated by M and N. They are chosen from the external registers. The R register is designated as the MDR. The machine has a local store that is not accessible by the 360 instruction set. All paths and registers are only eight bytes wide. A simplified version of the microword, omitting certain fields used by this machine is given in Figure 1-2(b). The CM field specifies the value for the pair M, N. The CU field indicates whether the reference is to memory or to local store. The CA and CB fields specify the numbers of the input registers to the ALU, and CD indicates the output register. CC specifies the type of operation to be carried out by the ALU (e.g., ADD, AND, OR, XOR).

The foregoing example is used to illustrate the gap between the instruction set and the physical organization of a machine. In this case, every 360 instruction is interpreted on the 360/30 machine by writing a set of microinstructions for each instruction. The execution of the instruction is done in a manner similar to the execution of a high-level language by an interpreter. The instruction is decoded into microinstructions, and each microinstruction is executed by the machine.

Review of Concepts Used in the General Purpose Architecture

The general purpose architecture is evolutionary. It is derived from the cumulative experience of computer architects and engineers over the past four decades. It is based on a number of concepts, some of which are obvious, but others may not be. These concepts are summarized in the following paragraphs.

First of all, there are underlying assumptions regarding the functions or uses of the general purpose computer:

- The computer is used for executing scientific or commercial programs written in high-level algorithmic languages such as COBOL, PL/1, FORTRAN, PASCAL, or "C."
- The I/O operations that are commonly performed are record-oriented; i.e., a data record (whether from a terminal or a disk) is fetched, one at a time; modifications are made to it, and it is returned to its source or stored in some other I/O unit.
- The interface with the user is a terminal; the computer runs multiple programs concurrently, especially in a business environment where transaction processing takes place.

Second, there is the concept of pragmatism, namely, that the best engineering design is the one that is simple and makes optimal use of resources. The general purpose architecture makes no pretensions to intellectual elegance. It does not give any insight into human problem-solving and does not address the question of its own limits. It is meant to solve certain classes of problems efficiently and, to its credit, it must be said that it has been doing that well.

The third concept has to do with the view of the programming environment. It is tacitly assumed that this environment consists of two layers, namely, an operating system acting as a shell or outermost layer, and programs constituting the innermost layer.

The fourth concept has to do with hiding certain functions from the programmer by making them inaccessible. Basically, the attitude taken by architects of general purpose computers is that certain functions should not be made available even to the operating system and are classified as implementation details of no interest to the programmer.

Recent Developments in General Purpose Computer Architecture

During the past decade, many questions have been raised about the fundamental assumptions involved in the architecture of general purpose computers, such as the following:

- What should the instruction set consist of? Should there be more instructions or fewer instructions?
- Should the assembly language provided as part of the architecture be the language for writing software? Or should there be another language, one level higher than the assembly language?
- Should there be fewer registers or more registers?
- Should the cache be hidden from the programmer? Should there be two caches, one for instructions and one for data?

The computers that are widely used today (e.g., IBM, VAX) have instruction sets that are characterized by large size, richness, and complexity. They are called complex instruction set computers (CISCs). They contain instructions for performing operating system functions and for supporting high-level language compilers.

One of the more interesting approaches toward computer design is the Reduced Instruction Set Computer (RISC) approach, pioneered by IBM's 801 project (see Radin [5]), and work at the University of California at Berkeley (Patterson [6]). The RISC approach, in its pure form, uses only register instructions for computation. Thus, the only instructions that access memory are load and store instructions for moving data between memory and registers. As a consequence, the following advantages arise:

• The number of instructions are reduced. As an example, the RISC computer in Patterson [7] has 31 instructions.
• All instructions are the same size, and there is no need for instructions with varying lengths.
• Because instruction-processing logic is simplified, a CPU can be implemented on a single VLSI (very large-scale integration) chip, and an instruction can be executed in one processor cycle.
• Because instructions can be executed in one cycle, there is no need for microcode.
• Because the instruction set is simple, it is possible to provide a highly efficient compiler for an advanced language. The language PL.8 (which is similar to PL/1) is mentioned in Radin [5].

The RISC designers provide more registers than are available in conventional computers. Sets of registers called windows are assigned to programs, and frequent load and store operations are avoided.

It is not practical to implement RISC in its pure form, and the successful commercial computers that use RISC have instruction set sizes larger than the 31 instructions mentioned in Patterson [7]. One such computer, the IBM RT PC, is described briefly in the section on IBM small systems.

1.2.3 Parallel Machines

At present there is no commonly accepted conceptual model of a parallel machine. For example, in the implementation of high-speed general purpose computers, many functions are done concurrently using pipelining (see Chapters 7–12). Also, the IBM 370 architecture allows multiple CPUs to share a common main storage and channels, and allows vector processing. But these are regarded as extensions of the von Neumann architecture rather than as a departure from it. So then, what is a truly parallel machine?

One view is that a large number of von Neumann machines, each having its own memory, interconnected to each other via a fast medium constitutes a parallel machine. The most frequently discussed implementation of this conceptual machine is the Connection Machine, which has 65,536 processors, each with 4K bits of memory (Hills [1]). The Connection Machine has two parts, a front-end machine and an array of small processors. The front-end processor has a general purpose architecture (e.g., it can be a VAX). The memory of each local processor can be randomly accessed by the front end, in a parallel mode if necessary. As a program is executed on the front-end processor, instructions are passed to all processors and are executed by the processors that are free. This approach is commonly referred to as Single Instruction Stream Multiple Processing (SIMP). The key feature of the Connection Machine is the high-speed network (called the Cosmic Cube) that connects the processors.

Another view is that of a dataflow machine, where hundreds of functional units perform primitive arithmetic and logical operations concurrently. The dataflow model has been around for a few years, and prototypes have been built (Arvind [8], Gurd [9]). It is sometimes classified as a parallel model and sometimes as a functional model. The model conceptually can be explained best by data flow graphs. The graph for the expressions $A = B + C$, $D = E + F$, $G = (A + D) * (A - D)$ is given in Figure 1-3. Any arithmetic or logical expression can be represented by a dataflow graph. The model uses a unique terminology. Data values are carried by tokens (packets), which flow along arcs. Computation is done by nodes. When all input arcs for a node have tokens, the node fires (carries out the computation). The dataflow model is predicated on performing a number of parallel computations concurrently. It becomes fairly complicated when data dependencies are included. The interested reader is invited to look into Arvind [8], Gurd [9], and Veen [10].

It is common to associate "granularity" with parallelism. Thus "coarse grain" usually refers to multiple processors executing independent tasks but sharing common resources, such as memory and input/output channels. Medium grain usually refers to machines that can execute parts of a task independently and synchronize the results. Fine grain usually refers to machines with multiple processors that can break up an instruction into components, execute them independently of each other, and synchronize the results (Serlin [11]).

IBM mainframes do not support parallel architecture in the medium grain or fine grain sense. True, the 3090 series has a vector processing facility that provides vector arithmetic capability. This is not regarded as true parallel processing by IBM but as an extension of pipelining concepts.

Two IBM projects for development of parallel computers have appeared in the literature, the GF11 project and the RP3 project. Both are research projects, and their commercial viability is not yet proven. The GF11 project uses up to 576 von Neumann processors controlled by a central processor. The processors communicate with each other using a permutation network called the Memphis switch. The RP3 consists of up to 512 processors that share a common memory and a high-speed network.

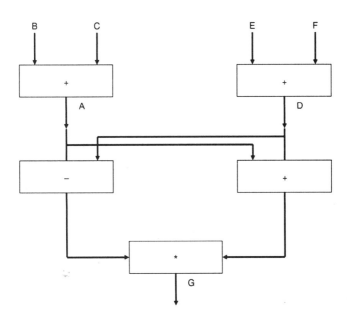

Figure 1-3 Dataflow graph.

1.2.4 Other Models

We shall discuss briefly a few other conceptual models for computers. Most of these are either specifications on paper or one-of-a-kind prototypes. It is difficult to evaluate these models in terms of their future impact on the computing environment.

Logic as a programming language has been the subject of research in the past decade. The language PROLOG uses a variant of logic called Horn clauses. There have been proposals for machines that implement PROLOG as a machine language. The concept has been further refined into sequential versus parallel machines that execute PROLOG instructions (Tick and Warren [12], Li and Wah [13]).

The functional model was proposed by Backus [2] as an alternative to the von Neumann model. The model is tied to the concept of programming by functions. A program itself is regarded as a mathematical function, obtained as a composite of several primitive functions. Examples of functional programming languages are LISP, Backus's FP, and others (Vegdahl [14]). The advantages of the functional model are ease of detection of parallelism and ease of verification. The disadvantages are the difficulty in dealing with inherently sequential computational procedures. For more on this topic, the reader is referred to [14].

1.3 EVOLUTION OF IBM MAINFRAMES

As mentioned previously, the earliest automatic digital computer was Mark 1, which was built by IBM in 1943 under the direction of Howard Aiken. It read its instructions from punched tape and did powerful scientific calculations during the second world war. Its components were mechanical and electromechanical, but not electronic.

Electronic digital computers are grouped into generations on the basis of the underlying technology. The first generation used vacuum tubes as active elements, the second generation used transistors, the third used integrated circuits, the fourth used very large-scale integration (VLSI), and the fifth proposes to use a more powerful version of VLSI with a high density of transistors (e.g., 10 million) per chip. Among first-generation computers were IBM's 650, which used a magnetic drum storage for memory, and the 701, which used magnetic core memory. Among second-generation computers were IBM's 1401 and 1410 machines and the IBM Stretch (7030) computer, which was a very powerful machine for its time. The third generation dates from the introduction of the IBM 360. The 370 and 370/XA computers that followed the 360 years later are usually classified as later third-generation computers.

In Table 1-1, the evolution of IBM mainframes is shown, with appropriate dates. The word "lines" is often used in describing the earlier computer families. Following is a list of various lines in the early 1950s and 1960s (Tucker [15]):

• The 701 line (comprising the 701, 704, 709, 7090, 7094 and 7094-11), used primarily for scientific applications.

Table 1-1 Evolution of IBM Mainframes

YEAR	COMPUTER	COMMENTS
1946–53	IBM 701, 702	These early first-generation computers used electrostatic storage.
1953–59	IBM 650, 704, 705, 709	These are late first-generation computers. The 650 used magnetic drum storage for main memory. The 704, 705, and 709 used magnetic core memory.
1959–64	IBM 7030, 7080, 1400 series	These second-generation computers used transistors.
1964–69	IBM 360 series	These ushered in the third generation of computers. The 360 provided a line of computers with a common architecture. The early machines used solid logic technology (SLT) whereby transistor chips were mounted on 1/2" square ceramic modules that contained one or two circuits.
1969–80	IBM 370 series	These introduced virtual storage and a sophisticated operating system, the Multiple Virtual Storage operating system. There were no major departures from the 360 architecture.
1981	IBM 370/XA series	This series resulted from further extensions of the 360 architecture.

- The 702 line (comprising the 702, 705 and 7080) and the 7070 line (comprising the 7070 and 7074), used primarily for large commercial applications.
- The 1401 line (comprising the 1401, 1410 and 7010), primarily for small commercial applications.
- The 7030 (also known as STRETCH) which, as mentioned before, was a very powerful machine for its time.

Note the dichotomies "scientific" versus "commercial" and "large" versus "small" in the foregoing classifications. Scientific computers required floating-point arithmetic and were word oriented. Commercial computers required decimal arithmetic and character manipulation capability and were byte oriented. The "small" versus "large" classification was a matter of the power of the CPU, the size of available main memory, and the capability of handling a large number of peripherals. The advent of the 360 did away with these dichotomies.

1.3.1   360 Computers

The first 360 computer was announced in April 1964. The phrase "computer architecture" was first used in the 360 context but is attributed to the earlier 8000 project (Gifford and Spector [16]). Machines in the 360 series varied in speed and circuitry, but they had the same architecture; i.e., they used the same instruction set, operating systems, and input/output devices. Both upward and downward compatibility were provided; i.e., programs running on the lower end machines could also run on the higher-end machines and vice versa.

The 360 series were an enormous success in the commercial data-processing environment. Part of the success was due to the development of systems software such as multiprogramming operating systems; telecommunications and transaction-processing systems such as Basic Telecommunications Access Method (BTAM) and Customer Information Control System (CICS); database software such as Information Management System (IMS). CICS and IMS are still widely used and show no sign of obsolescence. The success of the 360 was also due to its architecture. The ability to replace a computer with a more powerful one without having to rewrite programs was appreciated by many data processing managers and professionals.

The 360 architecture provided versatile, general purpose machines. They were designed for operation in both commercial and scientific environments. The instruction set provided for both scientific com-

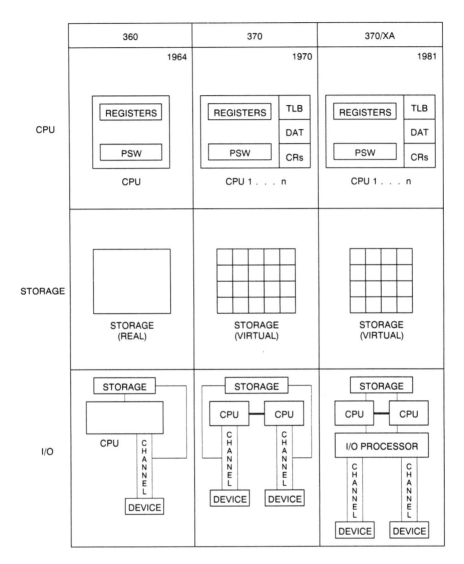

Figure 1-4 Architectural evolution of 360 series.

putation (e.g., floating-point arithmetic) and commercial data processing (e.g., decimal arithmetic). The architecture was simple and easy to understand. From a programmer's point of view, a 360 machine consisted of a single central processing unit (CPU), main storage where programs and data resided, and input/output devices including terminals, printers, and disk and tape units (see Figure 1-4). The level of complexity in the implementation of the machines, however, was far from simple. The architecture demanded that basically dissimilar machines should execute the same instruction set; this was mostly achieved by means of microcode.

Some of the notable models in the 360 series were the Models 30, 65, 67, 75 and 85 (see Table 7-2). The Model 30 was the smallest of the series; its data path was one byte wide, compared to eight bytes used in most machines today. The packed decimal format, which compresses two digits into one byte and which was part of the 360 architecture, is directly attributable to the limited data-transfer capability of this model [16]. Whereas the Model 30 implemented the 360 architecture via microprogramming, the top-of-the-line Model 75 was implemented using hardware. The Model 65 is remarkable because it is an ancestor to the present-day 3090 series [15]. Various models followed the 65, each using advanced technology for circuits and storage and having increased parallelism in instruction-fetching, decoding, and execution via pipelining. The Model 85, for example, was the first to incorporate a cache. Essentially, the cache implementation consisted of using a small, fast storage as part of the processor to hold recently referenced contents of main storage. The Model 67, a derivative of Model 65, used virtual storage implementation even though the 360 architecture did not include the virtual storage concept (which is regarded as part of the 370 architecture).

1.3.2   370 Computers

The 360 architecture was found to be inadequate for the processing demands of the commercial world. More and more enterprises were converting batch programs to on-line systems. Operating systems more sophisticated than those provided by the 360 were required to handle multiprogramming environments that required fast response at the terminal. Another factor was the introduction of multiple CPUs to speed up processing. The 370 architecture was introduced to solve these problems. It was not a radical departure from the 360 architecture. Essentially, the 360 instruction set and input/output concepts were kept, but enhancements to storage made the architecture more complex. A highly sophisticated operating system, Multiple Virtual Storage (MVS), was also introduced. The operating system used the concepts of virtual storage and multiple CPU operation that were introduced as part of the 370 architecture. IBM also introduced new software such as Virtual Telecommunications Management (VTAM) to manage telecommunications processing, and Virtual

Storage Access Method (VSAM) to manage files. CICS and IMS were rewritten for the new architecture. In Figure 1-4, the architectural differences between the 360 and the 370 are illustrated schematically.

Virtual storage, which is the major architectural concept that distinguishes the 370 from the 360, grew out of the recognition that using real storage addresses for programs caused problems in downward compatibility from high-end machines with large main storage to the low-end machines with small main storage. It also caused serious operational difficulties for on-line programs and degraded response times. The 370 architecture provided an elegant way of handling these problems (see Chapter 4 for details).

The early 370 machines were small machines that consisted of several microprogrammed processors in a single compact package. One processor executed instructions, another interfaced with disk drives, and a third acted as a communications processor to which terminals could be directly attached. At the high end of the line were the 370/168 and IBM 3033. Currently, the 370 architecture is supported by the 438X series, by the 9370 series, and by the 308X and 3090 series. It is by no means an obsolete architecture, even though the large IBM mainframes currently in vogue are built according to the 370/XA architectural specifications. The currently available 370 machines can be grouped into the following lines:

• Small to medium: The 9370 series, described in Chapter 9
• Medium to large: The IBM 438X series, which also conform to the 370/XA architecture
• Large: The IBM 308X and 3090 series, designed to conform to the 370/XA architecture but can also operate as 370 models

1.3.3   370/XA Computers

As in the case of the 360, the 370 architecture was found inadequate to cope with the processing demands made in the commercial world, and major extensions were required. These architectural extensions removed storage constraints and input/output performance bottlenecks, and introduced cleaner concepts for input/output processing and interaction between multiple CPUs. The 370/XA (XA stands for Extended Architecture) instruction set contains new instructions for I/O operations and the introduction of an I/O processor. The architectural differences between the 370 and the 370/XA are the following:

- The 370/XA supports multiprocessing in a true sense, as opposed to the 370, which supported dual processing (multiprocessing with two computers).
- The 370/XA uses a larger address, comprising 31 bits as opposed to the 24 bits supported by the 370 architecture.
- The 370/XA uses more sophisticated I/O principles of operations, which results in better performance.

The 370/XA computers are the most powerful IBM mainframes available today. Among them are the 308X series and the 3090 series, which are discussed in Chapters 9 and 10.

1.3.4 370/ESA Computers

The ESA architecture was announced only recently; its differences from the 370/XA architecture have not yet been published by IBM. In Chapter 6, this architecture is discussed briefly.

1.4 OTHER IBM COMPUTERS OF INTEREST

There are many IBM computers that use interesting and innovative architectural principles. They have been developed for use in small business environments, scientific computation, and artificial intelligence applications.

1.4.1 IBM Small Systems

These systems were designed to meet the requirements of small business users or for special applications that were not contemplated by the mainframe architecture. Their main characteristics are noted below:
- They do not use the IBM mainframe architecture.
- They do not support the I/O volumes and data transfer rates found in the mainframes.
- They are cheaper than the mainframes.

Some of them have innovative architectural and design features. In this context, the following quote is appropriate:

"For many years, the sheer power, complexity, and technological sophistication of large mainframe computer systems overshadowed the novel architectures and design features of small systems. Nevertheless, the challenges of developing competitive small computer systems are equally great and have commanded equally high levels of innovation and exploitation of advanced technology.... In fact, in order to meet their marketplace requirements, IBM's small systems have often employed advanced architectures, design features and technologies prior to their use in larger systems." (Waldecker and Woon [17])

A few noteworthy examples are briefly discussed in the following paragraphs.

The System 32, a small, single-user oriented computer system, was introduced in 1975. It implemented large portions of its operating system in microcode, instead of assembly language. This approach was subsequently used by the System 36 and System 38 computers and also in IBM mainframes.

The System 38 is a computer suited for a small to medium enterprise or for departmental computing. Its novel architectural features are the use of single-level storage and the compaction of the arithmetic instruction set. Under single-level storage, no distinction is made between main storage and secondary storage (e.g., disks). Thus, main storage and secondary storage are addressable in the same manner. The instruction set is made compact by having only one instruction for performing a function. Thus, there is a single instruction for addition, called ADD. The operands for the instruction are defined in a separate program dictionary. The dictionary contains characteristics of operands such as type and length. We contrast this capability to the 360 architecture's separate instruction for each type in Chapter 3.

The IBM RT Personal Computer uses the RISC architecture and a sophisticated virtual storage management system. It has 16 registers and 118 instructions. Most instructions are executed in one cycle. It supports a very powerful compiler for PL.8, on the assumption that most software for the machine will be developed using a high-level language [17]. Its uses are those of a work station in an office environment (Henry [18]).

1.4.2 Projects

IBM projects abound in many areas of computer architecture. The following are noteworthy and are briefly mentioned.

The IBM 801 project pioneered the use of the reduced instruction set computer (RISC) approach. Its architectural proposals are interesting and are described in Radin [5].

The AIK-0 computer for artificial intelligence application is among the first of its kind. It is a parallel computer that has instructions geared for PROLOG execution (Diel et al. [19]). It is meant for use by expert systems.

The RP-3 and GF-11 projects, which use experimental parallel machines, were mentioned earlier in this chapter.

REFERENCES

1. Hills, D.W.: "The Connection Machine," The MIT Press, 1985.
2. Backus, J.: "Can Programming Be Liberated From the von Neumann Style? A Functional Style and Its Algebra of Programs," *Communications of the ACM*, vol. 21, August 1978.
3. Rao, G. S., and P.L. Rosenfeld: "Integration of Machine Organization and Control Program Design — Review and Direction," *IBM Journal of Research and Development*, vol. 27, no. 3, May 1983.
4. Birnbaum, J., and W.S. Worley: "Beyond RISC: High-precision Architecture," in "IEEE Reduced Instruction Set Computers (Tutorial)" *Computer Society* order no. 713, 1986.
5. Radin, G.: "The 801 Minicomputer," *IBM Journal of Research and Development*, vol. 27, no. 3, May 1983.
6. Patterson, D.: "Reduced Instruction Set Computers," *Communications of the ACM*, vol. 28, no. 1, January 1985.
7. Patterson, D., and C.H. Sequin: "A VLSI RISC," *Computer*, September 1982.
8. Arvind and D.E. Culler: "Dataflow Architectures" *Annual Review of Computer Science*, vol. 1, Annual Review Inc., Palo Alto, California, 1986.
9. Gurd, J.R., C.C. Kirkham, and I. Watson: "The Manchester Prototype Dataflow Computer," *Communications of the ACM*, vol. 28, no. 1, January 1985.
10. Veen, A.H.: "Dataflow Machine Architecture," *ACM Computing Surveys*, vol. 18, no. 4, December 1986.

11. Serlin, O.: "Parallel Processing: Fact or Fancy?," *Datamation*, December 1985.
12. Tick E., and D.H.D. Warren: "Toward a Pipelined Prolog Processor," *New Generation Computing*, vol. 2, OHMSHA, Ltd. and Springer-Verlag, 1984.
13. Li, G., and B.W. Wah: "MANIP-2: A Multicomputer Architecture for Evaluating Logic Programs," *Proc. Intl. Conf. on Parallel Processing*, IEEE, 1985.
14. Vegdahl, S.R.: "A Survey of Proposed Architectures for the Execution of Functional Languages," *IEEE Transactions on Computers*, vol. C-23, no. 12, December 1984.
15. Tucker, S.G.: "The IBM 3090 System: An Overview," *IBM Systems Journal*, vol. 25, no. 1, 1986.
16. Gifford, D., and A. Spector: "Case Study: IBM's System/360-370 Architecture," *Communications of the ACM*, vol. 30, no. 4, 1987. (This is a transcript of an interview with 370 architects Richard Case and Andris Padegs.)
17. Waldecker, D.E., and P.Y. Woon: "ROMP/MMU Technology Introduction," *IBM RT Personal Computer Technology*, IBM Publication No. SA 23-1057, 1986.
18. Henry, G.G.: "IBM Small System Architecture and Design — Past, Present and Future," *IBM Systems Journal*, vol. 25, nos. 3/4, 1986.
19. Diel, H., N. Lenz, and Welsch: "An Experimental Computer Architecture Supporting Expert Systems and Logic Programming," *IBM Journal of Research and Development*, vol. 30, no. 1, January 1986.

ADDITIONAL READING

Interesting articles and historical sketches pertaining to the evolution of computers in general are contained in the following:

Ralston, A., and C.L. Meek (eds.): *The Encyclopedia of Computer Science*, Petrocelli/Charter, 1976.

For the evolution of early IBM computers, see the following:

Bashe, C.J., L.R. Johnson, J.H. Palmer, and E.W. Pugh: *IBM's Early Computers*, The MIT Press, 1986.

Tucker S.G.: "The IBM 3090 System: An Overview," *IBM Systems Journal*, vol. 25, no. 1, 1986.

For tutorials and original papers in computer architecture, the following publications by the IEEE Computer Society are recommended:

"Computer Architecture" (Tutorial), *The Computer Society of IEEE*, Computer Society Order No. 704, 1987.

"Advanced Computer Architecture" (Tutorial), *The Computer Society of IEEE*, Computer Society Order No. 667, 1986.

"Reduced Instruction Set Computers" (Tutorial), *The Computer Society of the IEEE*, Computer Society Order No. 713, 1986.

2

Role of Architecture in IBM Mainframes

IBM mainframes were the first to use the principle that various models introduced by a computer manufacturer should conform to the architecture laid down by the manufacturer. The following quotation from Patterson [1] is appropriate in this context:

"The IBM System/360, first introduced in 1964, was the real beginning of modern architecture. Although computers in the System/360 'family' provided a different level of performance for a different price, all ran identical software. The System/360 originated the distinction between computer architecture — the abstract structure of a computer that a machine language programmer needs to know to write programs — and the hardware implementation of that structure. Before the System/360, architectural trade-offs were determined by the effect on price and performance of a single implementation; henceforth, architectural trade-offs became more esoteric. The consequences of single implementations could no longer be sufficient to settle an argument about instruction set design. Microprogramming was the primary technological innovation behind this marketing concept. Microprogramming relied on a small control memory and was an elegant way of building the processor control unit for an instruction set."

The foregoing quotation highlights a number of points. The first point is that before the 360 there was no concept of a family of computers with varying price/performance characteristics that provided program compatibility. The second is that without the advent of microprogramming such compatibility would not have been feasible, because the lower-priced models would not have been able to emulate the hardware functions performed by the higher-priced models. The third is the role of the architect as the guiding force in the development of the new models as opposed to the computer designer, who no longer is given a free hand in building new models.

2.1 VARIOUS DEFINTIONS OF COMPUTER ARCHITECTURE

It has been pointed out in Lorin [2] that the word "architecture" is often used informally and with a qualifying word before it. In the literature on computers there are frequent references to von Neumann architecture, parallel architecture, dataflow architecture, etc., all of which embrace a conceptual model as well as an architecture (namely, a set of specifications for one or more classes of intended users). It is also common to speak of memory architecture, I/O architecture, and the architecture of other functional units of a computer, such as disk drives.

Since our primary focus is the architecture pertaining to IBM mainframes, our conceptual model will be that of the general purpose computer. Even here, there are problems with respect to the definition of architecture. The earlier definitions took a narrow view of architecture, as evidenced by the following quotations:

"Computer architecture embraces the art and science of assembling logical elements into a computing device. As normally conceived, a computer architect accepts from a logical designer units such as adders, stacks, memory modules and tape drives; puts them together so that they form a computer; and turns this over to a systems programmer, who then constructs an operating system for the machine. This should not be construed as being a passive role. The computer architect is responsible for (and indeed, is almost the only one in a position to accomplish) the ideas interchanged between the two groups. He must bring software problems to the attention of the hardware types and hardware potentialities to the attention of the software types." (Foster [3])

"The [computer] architecture specification covers all functions of the machine that are observable by a program. It either specifies the action the machine performs or states that the action is unpredictable." (Case and Padegs [4])

The current view of architecture, as stated by Lorin [2], Dasgupta [5], Myers [6], and others tends toward presenting architecture in terms of interacting hierarchical levels or layers. Thus, Dasgupta states:

"Basically a computer system consists of a number of interacting components organized or constructed as a hierarchy of levels, where each level may consist of several components. The boundaries between levels of construction constitute the interfaces within the system. Thus . . . we may define architecture as a discipline that includes (1) the decisions concerning the precise distribution of functions across interfaces and (2) the specification of the logical structure of these interfaces." [5]

In Figure 2-1, the various levels or layers and the interfaces between them are shown. Each level may see multiple levels beneath it. The lowest level is the digital level, consisting of the hardware of a computer. The next level is the microcode required to implement the instruction set. The "fatness" of the microcode level is based on the functions that are to be implemented in microcode as opposed to hardware. The next level is the operating system (also called "control program" by IBM) software level. The interface between this level and the two levels beneath it is the instruction set of the computer, the specification of which is traditionally regarded as the primary function of computer architecture.

The view of architecture presented in this book is along the following lines:

• An architecture describes a conceptual machine. The conceptual machine uses a model of computation called the conceptual model. Many architectures use the same conceptual model.
• The machine consists of interacting subsystems, such as one or more CPUs, I/O processors or channels, and a global memory shared amongst these.
• The interacting subsystems are complex and have architectures of their own. Thus we use the word architecture in the context of a subsystem and speak of "CPU architecture," "storage architecture," and "I/O architecture," even though these phrases are not used in the context of mainframe architecture by IBM (but Lorin [2] does

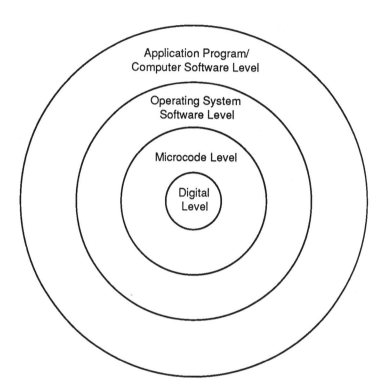

Figure 2-1 Layers in a computing system.

extend the use of the word architecture to delineate subsystems architecture).

- Instruction sets are available to various users, who might be operating system designers, compiler designers, application developers, etc.
- Various models of a computer are viewed as implementations of the same architecture; although their designs may vary, they produce similar results when the same program is executed.

2.2 CLASSIFICATION SCHEMES FOR ARCHITECTURES

Computer architectures are classified in many ways and the following are bases for commonly used classifications:

- A conceptual model (e.g., serial computers, parallel computers).

- A technique used to implement a conceptual model (e.g., pipelined computers, dataflow computers).
- A philosophy on which the instruction set is based (e.g., reduced instruction set computers, high-level language computers, complex instruction set computers).
- A combination of instruction stream types and data instruction stream types, such as single instruction single data stream (SISD) computers, single instruction multiple data stream (SIMD) computers, multiple instruction single data stream (MISD) computers, and multiple instruction multiple data stream (MIMD) computers. (Flynn [7]
- The number of CPUs used by the computer. If only one CPU is used, the computer is called a uniprocessor. If more than one CPU is used, the computer is called a multiprocessor. A further subclassification is used on the basis of the functionality of each processor. If, in a multiple processor environment, all processors have the same functionality, then the multiprocessors are called symmetrical. Otherwise, they are asymmetrical.

In the context of IBM mainframes, the classification schemes can overlap, in some cases. All IBM mainframes are general purpose computers, and the conceptual model calls for serial program execution. The modern IBM computers are mostly pipelined but the extent of pipelining varies, as described in later chapters of this book. The earlier IBM machines supported only one CPU but the current mainframes have multiple CPUs. The current machines also have separate I/O processors. If the I/O processors are excluded, the multiprocessing is symmetrical. If they are included, the multiprocessing is asymmetrical. The multiple symmetrical CPUs work on a "single image" principle. Under this principle, the various CPUs use a single copy of the operating system, share memory and work concurrently on independent units of work assigned by the operating system (in other words, each CPU executes an operating system task independently of other CPUs).

2.3 DEFINITION OF ARCHITECTURE USED BY IBM

In IBM 370 Principles of Operations [8], the architecture of a computer is defined as "its attributes as seen by the programmer; that is, the conceptual structure and functional behavior as distinct from the organization of the data flow, the logical design, the physical design, and the performance of any particular implementation.

Several dissimilar machine implementations may conform to a single architecture. When programs running on different machine implementations produce the results that are defined by a single architecture, the implementations are considered to be compatible." [8]

The foregoing definition is motivated by the following practical considerations. A wide variety of computers are available under a given architecture. There are significant differences in the implementation of the slower low-priced models as opposed to the faster high-priced models. Because programs have to be compatible between various models, they have to be written in a common language, using the same rules for interaction among various components. Thus, the two aspects of a computer, functionality and performance, are separated into architecture and implementation.

2.3.1   Methodology for Architectural Specifications

The Principles of Operations for the 360, 370, and 370/XA [8, 9, 10] follow a uniform format. The architectural specifications can be grouped as follows:

- The interacting subsystems (the CPU, storage, and I/O processors) are individually described in detail, and their interactions are also given in detail.
- A description of the conceptual machine on which the architecture is based and program execution on that machine (including details on branching and interruptions) is given.
- The representation of data storage and the data types (e.g., decimal, binary, and floating point numbers) used by instructions are described in detail.
- The instructions are classified as general, decimal, floating point, and control, and a description of each instruction is given in English, along with the results of its execution and conditions that cause exceptional results.

However, a few concepts are missing in these specifications. One is a complete description of the interaction between the operating system and the instruction set. But this is available (though not in easily understandable form) in the IBM manuals for the operating system. It should also be mentioned that there are several operating systems for IBM systems, but for the present-day mainframes the MVS/XA operating system appears to be generally accepted as the standard. Another is a description of how single image multiprocessing is truly achieved. It is a joint effort on the part of the architecture, operating system, and implementation techniques. The architecture, for example, does not dwell on the function of the cache, which plays a vital role in single-image systems.

2.3.2 Audience for the Architectural Specifications

A number of groups are interested in the architectural specifications. The first group, as mentioned before, is the team of designers who are in charge of designing a machine for a given price/performance ratio. This group, among other things, decides what functions should be implemented in hardware as opposed to microcode.

Another audience for architecture specifications is the team of programmers who write operating systems for computers. The relationship between a computer and its operating system has been an evolutionary one. Many architectural changes have been instigated by problems faced by operating system designers, and vice versa. We discuss this relationship in detail in several places in this book.

A third audience for architecture specifications is the team of programmers who write compilers for programming languages. Major changes in architecture have come about as a result of the need for optimization of compiled object code. This topic is also discussed in various sections in this book.

2.3.3 Methodology Used for Architectural Specifications

The methodology used in specification of architecture is a topic that has received very little attention in the literature on computer architecture. In practice, English is commonly used for architectural specification. The IBM 370 Principles of Operation, which contains the architectural specifications for the 370, is written entirely in English. The advantages in using English are ease of comprehension and clarity of presentation. The disadvantages are lack of formalism and the potential for misinterpretation. At one time APL was considered as a vehicle for description of the architecture but English was chosen over APL. (Gifford and Spector [11])

2.4 IMPORTANCE ATTRIBUTED TO ARCHITECTURE BY IBM

By having an architecture, it was possible to dissociate the instruction set from the internal workings of any particular machine. In the words of System/370 architect Andris Padegs in [11], "If you build a single machine, there is always a temptation to optimize the architecture for the machine you are building. If you are building a collection of machines from low to high performance, you are forced to take a broader view." Thus, the instruction set was designed on the basis of analysis of sequences of instructions that appeared to be commonly used by computers in specific business or scientific environments. Architectural decisions are reached as a result of interactions by various interested groups. Again in the words of Andris Padegs [11], "The XA architecture was developed by a couple of teams of people, each specializing in a certain area, such as channels, virtual machines and addressing. Each team consisted of a half a dozen people and included one or two architects, along with machine designers, programmers and planners. The architects were in charge of the final conclusion and would probably be considered the leaders. A design would start with a consideration of what the programmers wanted and what the engineers could provide. A memo would then be written stating one possibility for extending the architecture. The memo would initially be only a few pages long, but over time it would be revised to include more detail. Any conflicts that arose were negotiated and eventually a group proposal resulted. Finally, any incompatibility between the proposals generated by different teams were resolved."

2.4.1 Models Within an Architectural Framework

A model is a specific implementation within the framework of an architecture. Usually a model is designed to conform to price/ performance objectives and the terms "low end" and "high end" are used to describe the low and high limits of the price/performance spectrum. The parameters that increase performance, such as pipelining, cache, and hardware circuits for executing instructions (as opposed to microcoding) are viewed as design, as opposed to architectural, considerations.

All models that conform to the same architecture have the property of program compatibility. By program compatibility is meant that the operating system and other software can run on all models without the need for changes to these programs. This requires that all models use the same instruction set and follow the same conventions in regard to I/O operations, interruptions, and other parameters that affect program execution.

2.5   EVOLUTION IN IBM MAINFRAME ARCHITECTURE

The past two decades have shown that an architecture is not a set of static rules, frozen for all time. Changes are made to the architecture by adding new instructions or concepts. Often, new models introduce features not present in the architecture. Three examples to illustrate this point are given:

- The System 360 Model 67 had the dynamic address translation capability that is not present in the 360 architecture. It was released in 1966, four years prior to the announcement of the 370 architecture, which included dynamic address translation as part of virtual storage management. The features of dynamic address translation present in the Model 67 were modified before incorporation into the 370 architecture.
- The 360 and 370 architectures specified 24-bit addressing and the 370/XA specifies 31-bit addressing. Actually, in the later versions of the 3033 model of the 370, extra address bits were provided to increase the addressability of real storage from 16 MB provided in the 370 architecture to 64 MB.
- The 3081 introduced the concept of a separate I/O processor before the 370/XA architecture formally defined the channel subsystem.

One of the interesting aspects of the 360 architecture was that it did not anticipate its own longevity. By 1970 the original 360 architecture was not functioning in a number of areas and had to be changed; it was replaced by the 370 architecture. Likewise, the 370 architecture was replaced by the 370/XA architecture in 1981. It is likely that the 370/XA architecture will be replaced by the 370/ESA in the near future.

When does a set of extensions to an old architecture trigger a new architecture? The instruction set used by the problem programmer is pretty much the same for the 360, 370, and 370/XA architectures. The number of registers is also the same. So why are the 370 and 370/XA called new architectures? The answer is probably that the cumulative impact of certain extensions requires the ushering in of a new architecture rather than continuing with the old. This appears to be the philosophy of the architects of the 360, 370 and 370/XA.

A related issue is compatibility among the various architectures. One of the primary concerns of the IBM mainframe architects was to provide means of running program's written for an earlier architecture on a machine using the current architecture. The solution implemented for this purpose is that of "modes," i.e., dual architectures. A 370 computer can run in the 360 mode or 370 mode. A 370/XA computer can run in the 370 mode or 370/XA mode. The mode of operation can be selected initially, or a 370 program can be interpretively executed by a 370/XA machine.

2.6   CONCLUDING REMARKS

We shall conclude this chapter with a brief survey of the factors that influence computer architecture. These factors can be divided into three classes: economic, technical, and accumulation of knowledge and experience. The economic factors are cost-effectiveness and marketing considerations, such as the notion of a family of computers varying in price and performance. The technical factors are the innovations in the fabrication of logic circuits, such as large-scale integration (LSI) and very large-scale integration (VLSI). The accumulation of knowledge and experience in theoretical as well as practical computation make it possible to look at new ways of integrating the requirements from various disciplines (e.g., operating systems, communications software, data base management systems, etc.) into the architecture of the general purpose computer.

REFERENCES

1. Patterson, D.: "Reduced Instruction Set Computers," *Communications of the ACM*, vol. 28, no. 1, 1985.
2. Lorin, H.: "Systems Architecture in Transition — An Overview," *IBM Systems Journal*, vol. 25, nos. 3/4, 1986.
3. Foster, C.: "Computer Architecture," in Encyclopedia of Computer Science, Ralston, A. and C. Meek (eds.), Petrocelli/ Charter, 1976.
4. Case, R., and A. Padegs: "Architecture of the IBM System/370," *Communications of the ACM*, vol. 21, no. 1, 1978.
5. Dasgupta, S.: "Some Aspects of High Level Microprogramming," *ACM Computing Surveys*, vol. 12, no. 3, 1980.

6. Myers, G.: "Advances in Computer Architecture," John Wiley & Sons, 1982.
7. Flynn, M.J.: "Some Computer Organizations and Their Effectiveness," *IEEE Transactions on Computers,* vol. C-21, no. 9, September 1972.
8. IBM 370 Principles of Operation, Order No. GA 22-7000.
9. IBM 370/XA Principles of Operation, Order No. SA 22-7085.
10. IBM System 360 Principles of Operation, Order No. GA 22-6821.
11. Gifford, D., and A. Spector: "Case Study: IBM's System/360-370 Architecture," *Communications of the ACM*, vol. 30, no. 4, 1987. (This is a transcript of an interview with Richard Case and Andris Padegs.)

3

360 Architecture

The IBM 360 machines (as mentioned before) were the first computers to use architectural concepts. Now, after 23 years, the 360 architecture does not seem exciting in comparison to newer architectures. But it should not be forgotten that it has been a widely imitated architecture and that many concepts introduced by it have become standards in the industry. (One example is the use of the byte as the unit of transmission of data.) In this chapter the 360 architecture is described in detail, because large portions of it are used by the 370 and 370/XA architectures.

3.1 COMPUTER ORGANIZATION

In the IBM System/360 Principles of Operation [1], the phrase "system structure" is used. The word "organization" is used here instead, in the same sense that it is used in the IBM System/370 Principles of Operation [2] and the IBM System/370 XA Principles of Operation [3]. By organization is meant the overall structure, functional description of components, and specification of interaction between the components of the conceptual machine described in the architecture.

The conceptual machine is illustrated schematically in Figure 3-1. It consists of the following components:

• Central Processing Unit (CPU)
• Main Storage

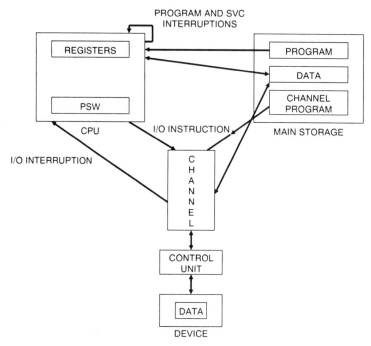

Figure 3-1 Schema for the 360 conceptual machine.

- Channel(s)
- Control Unit(s)
- Device(s)

These components and their interaction are described briefly next.

3.1.1 CPU

The main functions of the CPU are (1) program execution and (2) interruption handling. A program is a sequence of instructions taken from the instruction set specified by the architecture. Instructions are executed in the sequence in which they appear in a program, except when such sequence is modified by a branch instruction or when an interruption causes the CPU to suspend temporarily the execution of the current program and to execute an interruption-handling program. Interruptions are caused by a set of specified events (e.g., completion of an I/O operation); and the architecture assigns a code to each event that causes an interruption. The interruption-handling program makes use of this code in processing the interruption. By processing an interruption is meant identifying the source of the interruption and taking steps for resolution of the condition that caused the interruption (e.g., notification of a waiting program that an I/O operation started by it has been completed).

The CPU interacts with main storage and channels in performing these functions. It fetches instructions and data from main storage during program execution, and modifies main storage if an instruction calls for such modification. It initiates an I/O operation by means of a START I/O instruction. The channel then takes charge of the operation, leaving the CPU free to execute other instructions. When the I/O operation is complete or has reached a predefined stage, the channel interrupts the CPU (there may be several interruptions during an I/O operation).

3.1.2 Main Storage

The term "main storage" is used to denote physical memory containing instructions and data. Main storage is addressable by an instruction. It is distinct from the local storage used by a CPU, comprising registers and Program Status Word (PSW). It is also distinct from the storage used by microcode located in the computer, called control storage. The reason for emphasizing this distinction is that in some models, registers, Program Status Word and control storage may be housed in the physical memory that holds main storage.

The architecture regards main storage as a set of contiguous physical locations that have sequential addresses. These locations are accessed by the CPU during program execution, and by the channel when it performs an I/O operation.

3.1.3 Channel

The function of a channel is to perform all control and data transfer operations that arise during an I/O operation. The channel interacts with the CPU, main storage, and control units. Data transfer always takes the following physical path:

Main Storage+++Channel+++Control Unit+++Device

where the +++ symbol denotes bidirectional transfer. The CPU initiates an I/O operation by means of an I/O instruction, and the channel functions independently of the CPU from that point onwards. An I/O operation involves control operations (e.g., positioning the read/write head of a disk unit on a specific track) as well as data transfer operations (e.g., reading a record from a disk). The channel executes its functions under the control of a channel program, which is a set of instructions contained in channel command words (CCWs).

3.1.4 Control Unit

The function of a control unit is to act as an intermediary between device and channel. Usually several devices are connected to a control unit and several control units are connected to a channel. The interaction between channel and control unit and between control unit and device varies greatly according to device types.

3.1.5 Device

By a device is meant a peripheral unit that stores, transmits, or receives data and is connected to the channel via a control unit. Examples of devices are disks, card readers, terminals, printers, and similar peripheral equipment used in data storage and transfer. Usually several devices are connected to a control unit which, in turn, is connected to a channel.

3.2 CPU ARCHITECTURE

The function of the CPU is to fetch an instruction from main storage, decode it, fetch operands of the instruction from main storage if necessary, and execute the instruction. In the 360, an instruction is executed in its entirety and is not interruptible. An instruction can be 2, 4, or 6 bytes in length. It works on objects such as registers, bytes in main storage, the Program Status Word (PSW), storage keys, etc. Instructions occupy contiguous locations in storage. The address of the next serial instruction, which is obtained by adding the length of the current instruction to the address of the current instruction, is contained in the PSW. The next serial instruction is executed after the current instruction, except when branching or an interruption takes place at the end of the current instruction. The instruction set of the 360 provides for many types of branches. If a branch is to be taken, the branch address will replace the next instruction address in the PSW. In the case of an interruption, the contents of the PSW are replaced by contents of a specified location in main storage. This location varies according to the class of interruption. The PSW now contains a new address and it is implicitly understood that this is the address of a routine that handles the interruption.

The 360 architecture divides programs into two classes:

• Supervisor program (the operating system)
• Problem program (any program other than the supervisor, such as an application program).

Only the supervisor program is allowed to execute certain instructions, called privileged instructions. These instructions include I/O instructions and a few others described later in this chapter. The problem program can request the services of the supervisor program by means of the Supervisor Call (SVC) instruction, which causes an interruption. The SVC instruction contains a numeric code (0–255) that specifies the action to be taken by the operating system. The numeric code is used by the operating system to branch to the routine that performs the appropriate function.

It was originally assumed by the 360 architects that there would be only one operating system, which was given the name OS 360. In practice, it was found that the smaller models needed a disk-oriented operating system (DOS). Also OS 360 had two versions based on whether a fixed or variable number of concurrently programmed tasks were supported. Thus OS/MFT was an operating system using multiprogramming with a fixed number of tasks. It was succeeded by OS/MVT which used multiprogramming with a variable number of tasks.

3.2.1 Program Status Word (PSW)

The Program Status Word is a doubleword, its format is shown in Figure 3-2. It cannot be read from or modified or written to by a problem program, except for the field containing the condition code, which is available on a read-only basis. The supervisor program cannot read the PSW but can modify the contents of the PSW by means of the LOAD PSW instruction. The functions and uses of the PSW and the fields that are relevant to each function or use are described next.

SYSTEM MASK	KEY	AMWP	INTERRUPTION CODE
0	8		16 31

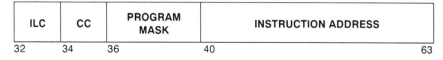

ILC	CC	PROGRAM MASK	INSTRUCTION ADDRESS
32	34	36 40	63

A   — ASCII FLAG   M — MACHINE CHECK MASK
W   — WAIT STATE   P — PROBLEM STATE
ILC — INSTRUCTION LENGTH CODE   CC— CONDITION CODE

Figure 3-2 PSW format.

Instruction Execution

The PSW contains the address of the next serial instruction in the Instruction Address field. This field is 24 bits long, since the 360 architecture uses 24-bit addresses. The length of the current instruction is given in the Instruction Length Code (ILC) field, which is 2 bits in length. This length is given in halfwords (2 bytes) and, as pointed out before, an instruction can be 1, 2, or 3 halfwords long. The execution of an instruction can cause a condition code to be set. The Condition Code (CC) field is 2 bits long and the values (0–3) are used for specifying conditions. For example, the ADD instruction can set the following values for the condition code:

0 — sum is zero
1 — sum is less than zero
2 — sum is greater than zero
3 — overflow has taken place

The BRANCH ON CONDITION instruction can be used to branch to a new instruction based on the value of the condition code.

Interruption Action

The current PSW is replaced by a new one after interruption. The Interruption Code (IC) field of the new PSW identifies the source or cause of an interruption. The following fields of the PSW are used for enabling or disabling interruptions from various sources:

System Mask — Channels, external signal
Machine Check Mask — Machine error
Program Mask — Program

Interruptions are discussed later in this chapter.

State of the CPU

The state of the CPU is stored in two one-bit fields, namely Wait State field (W) and Problem State field (P). The CPU is put in a wait state when W is set to one, and is in a running state if it is set to zero. The CPU will execute programs only in a running state and not in a wait state.

The CPU is in the problem state when P is set to one, and is in the supervisor state if it is set to zero. Problem programs can be run only when P is set to one, and supervisory programs can be run only when P is set to zero.

Storage Protection

The Key field contains a 4-bit key that is used for storage protection. Its use is described under storage architecture.

ASCII vs. EBCDIC

For decimal arithmetic operations, the sign or zone code can be generated according to ASCII or EBCDIC conventions. The A field, which is one bit long, specifies whether the results should be in ASCII or EBCDIC. IBM uses EBCDIC, normally, the ASCII capability is provided for compatibility only. When A is set to zero EBCDIC is used, and when A is set to one ASCII is used.

Note that this capability was discontinued in the 370 and 370/XA architectures.

3.2.2 Registers

The architecture provides for 16 general registers and 4 floating-point registers. The general registers are identified by the numbers 0 to 15 (see Figure 3-3). The floating-point registers are numbered 0, 2,

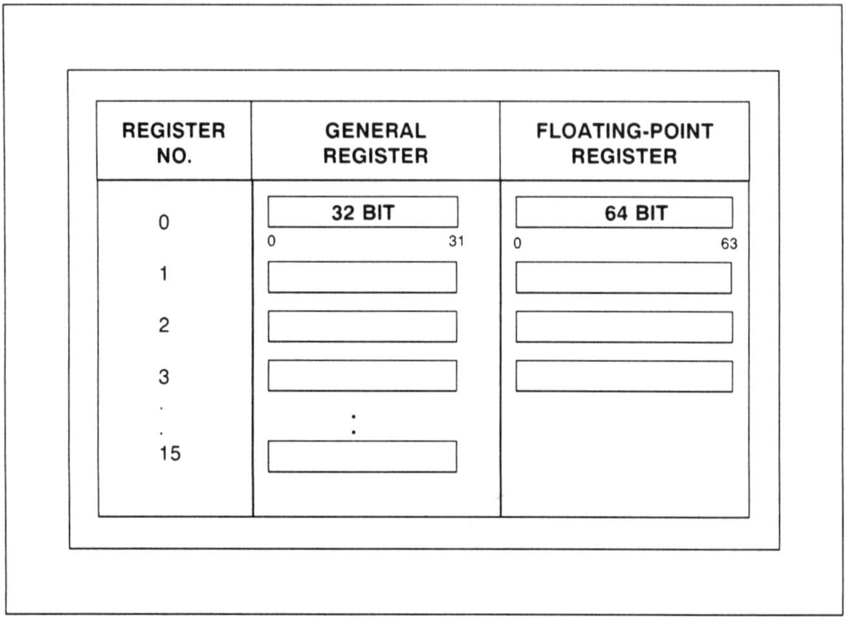

REGISTER NO.	GENERAL REGISTER	FLOATING-POINT REGISTER
0	32 BIT 0 31	64 BIT 0 63
1		
2		
3		
. . . 15	.	

Figure 3-3 Registers.

4, and 6. The general registers are each one fullword (32 bits) in length and the floating-point registers are doublewords (64 bits) in length.

General registers can be used to specify operands in binary arithmetic and logical instructions. The RR instructions generally use two registers, whereas the RX and RS instructions generally use three registers. An instruction requires less in storage space if it uses registers, since only 4 bits are used to identify a register as opposed to 24 bits required for a storage address. The registers are also used for address generation. One register is designated as base and another as an index in RX instructions.

Floating-point registers are used to specify operands in floating-point instructions. The RR instructions use two floating-point registers, and the RX instructions use one floating-point register and two general registers for address generation.

3.2.3   Interruptions

Interruptions are divided into five classes, as listed:

• Program Interruption

- SVC Interruption
- External Interruption
- Machine Check Interruption
- I/O Interruption

Each of these will be discussed separately. However, certain general remarks are applicable to all of them:

- An interruption action consists in storing the current PSW in a doubleword in storage designated for that class of interruption (usually called old PSW for that class of interruption) and loading the PSW with the contents of a doubleword in storage designated for that class of interruption (usually called new PSW for that class of interruption); the architecture requires that the swapping of the contents of the PSW is done automatically (by hardware).
- An interruption is called "pending" if an interruption action is not taken immediately.
- An interruption action takes place after the execution of the current instruction; i.e., an instruction is not interrupted in the middle of its execution.
- Unless it is masked, an interruption is accepted immediately after the current instruction is executed; by masking, the CPU is disabled for that interruption; i.e., no action is taken against the interruption until the mask is cleared.

  When it is not masked, an interruption is accepted after an instruction has normally completed its execution or has been abnormally terminated (e.g., due to error or malfunction). The word "completed" is used to describe normal completion. The word "termination" is used to specify abnormal completion with unpredictable results stored and unpredictable condition codes set in the PSW. The word "suppressed" is used to specify abnormal completion, with results similar to no operation (the condition code is not changed, and no results are stored).
- When there are multiple pending interruptions, the machine check interruption has the highest priority. Program or SVC interruptions have the next highest priority and are followed by external and I/O interruptions.

Program Interruption

A program interruption is caused by improper specification or use of an instruction or data, or abnormal conditions arising during instruction execution.

In the course of its execution by the CPU, an instruction is fetched, decoded, and then executed. During any of these operations, exceptions (errors or abnormal situations) may be detected. Typical exceptions follow:

- The operation code in the instruction is invalid (operation exception).
- A privileged instruction is executed in the problem state (privileged operation exception).
- An address is encountered that is beyond the limit of the installed main storage (addressing exception).
- A data field or an instruction is not on an integral boundary (specification exception).
- Overflow occurs in binary arithmetic (fixed-point overflow exception).

An instruction may generate one or more of the foregoing exceptions, but only one program interruption takes place. The instruction itself may be suppressed, terminated, or completed as a result of the interruption.

The current PSW is stored in address 40, and a new PSW is fetched from location 104. Certain types of exceptions, such as fixed-point overflow, decimal overflow, etc., can be disabled for interruption by setting bits to zero in the Program Mask field of the PSW. Operation, privileged operation, addressing and specification exceptions cannot be disabled from generating interruptions. The Interruption Code in the PSW contains the cause of the interruption.

Supervisor Call (SVC) Interruption

Execution of the SVC instruction triggers the SVC interruption. The SVC instruction is used for requesting the supervisor (the operating system) to perform services such as starting an I/O operation, obtaining storage, etc. The SVC instruction can be executed in the problem state or the supervisory state. The instruction specifies as an operand an 8-bit code, which is used to indicate a specific function that is to be performed by the supervisor. There can be 256 such functions.

The old PSW is stored at location 32 and a new PSW is fetched from location 96. The 8-bit code in the SVC instruction is in the Interruption Code field of the old PSW.

External Interruption

The sources of external interruption are the timer, the interrupt key of the operator's console, and any hardware unit defined as an external unit. Up to six lines can be connected to the CPU for receiving signals from an external unit.

The CPU can be disabled for external interruption by setting the system mask bit 7 to zero. The old PSW is stored in location 24, and a new PSW is fetched from location 88. The source of the interruption is identified in the Interruption Code (IC) field of the PSW.

Machine Check Interruption

When a computer malfunctions, the malfunction is indicated by the machine checkout signal. This causes an interruption, and the currently executing instruction is terminated. The old PSW is stored in location 48 and the Interruption Code (IC) field of the old PSW identifies the type of malfunction. The "state" of the CPU (contents of registers and PSW) is copied into main storage, starting from location 128. The new PSW is loaded from location 112. Machine check interruptions can be masked.

I/O Interruption

An I/O interruption is caused by a channel during an I/O operation. The interruption causes the old PSW to be stored at location 56 and a new PSW to be loaded from location 120. The interruption action takes place only after the current instruction is completed. The architecture supports seven channels; bits 0–6 of the System Mask field of the PSW can be used to disable the CPU from an interruption from one or more of the channels. I/O interruption is discussed in detail later in this chapter.

3.3 STORAGE ARCHITECTURE

The 360 storage architecture is straightforward. Our discussion will cover the following topics:

- Organization of storage
- Data representation
- Storage protection
- Serialization of storage access
- Reserved locations in storage.

3.3.1 Organization

At the lowest level, storage is organized as bytes, which are units of eight bits (plus a ninth bit for parity checking). The 8 bits provide for 256-bit configurations. The Extended Binary-Coded-Decimal Interchange Code (EBCDIC) is used by IBM for internal representation of graphic and control characters, by bit configurations.

Each byte is individually addressable. The addresses range from 0 to 2^{24} - 1. Thus, the bytes in storage can be viewed as a string of numbers 0, 1, 2, ... n where n is the size of the installed main storage which is less than or equal to 2^{24} - 1.

Instructions use data types such as binary numbers, decimal numbers, bit strings, byte strings (character strings), etc. These can be of fixed or variable length. Binary arithmetic uses 2 or 4 bytes, but decimal instructions use a variable number of bytes. When a group of bytes is used in an instruction, the number of bytes in the group is specified either implicitly or explicitly. The group is addressed by using the lowest address of the bytes in the group (usually noted as the address of the leftmost byte in the group). The bytes in a group always have consecutive addresses.

A halfword is a group of 2 bytes, a fullword or word is a group of 4 bytes, and a doubleword is a group of 8 bytes (see Figure 3-4). These should be located on an integral boundary for that group; i.e., the address of a halfword should be a multiple of 2, of a fullword a multiple of 4, and of a doubleword a multiple of 8. Another way of saying this is that the address of a halfword should always have its lowest bit equal to zero, a fullword should have its two low-order bits set to zero and a doubleword should have its three low-order bits set to zero.

The bits in a byte, halfword, fullword, etc., are numbered 0–7, 0–15, 0–31, etc., from left to right. The bits are not individually addressable.

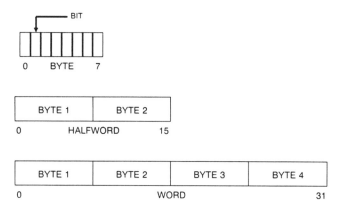

Figure 3-4 Byte, halfword, word.

3.3.2 Data Representation

A group of bytes in main storage can represent an instruction or data. If it is an instruction, the following rules apply:

• It should reside on an integral boundary for a halfword.
• The first byte should contain the instruction code (op code).

If the first rule is violated, a specification exception arises and a program interruption occurs. If the second rule is violated, an operation exception arises and a program interruption occurs. The instruction is not executed in either case.

Data types are divided into several subtypes as shown in Figure 3-5. At the highest level, a group of bytes can be any of the following types:

• Arithmetic
• Character
• Logical
• Address

Each type is briefly discussed next.

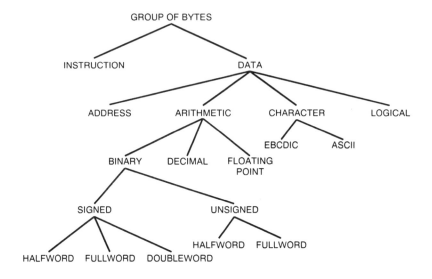

Figure 3-5 Data types and subtypes.

Arithmetic Data

Arithmetic data is classified as binary, decimal, and floating point. The binary representation can be signed or unsigned. In the signed format, a fullword binary number consists of a sign bit (bit 0) and a 31-bit binary integer; a halfword binary number consists of a sign bit (bit 0) and a 15-bit binary integer. Negative binary numbers are kept in two's complement notation by inverting each bit of the corresponding positive binary number and adding one. In the unsigned format, bit 0 does not denote the sign. A fullword unsigned binary number is a 32-bit binary integer, and a halfword unsigned binary number is a 16-bit binary integer (see Figure 3-6).

Decimal digits 0 through 9 are represented in binary coded decimal (BCD) form by 4 bits, ranging from 0000 through 1001. The sign codes for "+" and "-" are usually 1100 and 1101. Alternate sign codes (1010, 1110 and 1111 for "+" and 1011 for "-") are also accepted in input data but are not used in forming outputs. The two decimal formats are packed and zoned. In the packed format, two decimal digits are stored per byte with the sign in the rightmost four bits of the rightmost byte (see Figure 3-7). The number of decimal digits can vary from 1 to 31. In the zoned format, each byte contains a digit

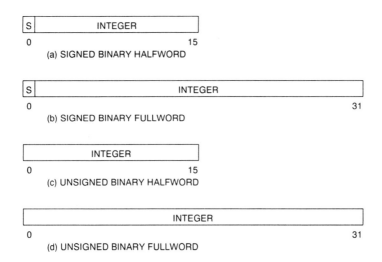

Figure 3-6 Binary arithmetic representation.

and a zone field "1111" (equivalent to hexadecimal "F") except for the rightmost byte which contains a sign instead of the zone code.

Floating point numbers are represented in short, long or extended formats (see Figure 3-8). A number is represented by two parts, a characteristic and a fraction. These terms are defined later in this chapter, under floating-point arithmetic.

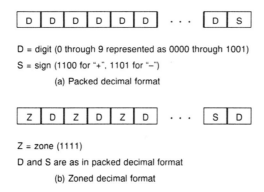

Figure 3-7 Decimal number representation.

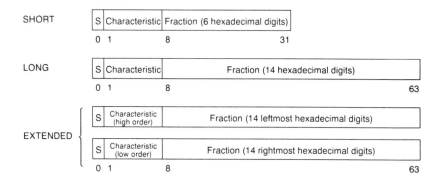

Figure 3-8 Floating-point formats.

Character Data

Characters are represented using the Extended Binary Coded Decimal Interchange Code (EBCDIC) and also the USA Standard Code for Information Interchange (USASCII). The 8 bits in a byte yield 256 bit configurations. These bit configurations are used in representing alphabetic or numeral characters and other symbols used with terminals and other I/O devices. EBCDIC is the standard code for IBM mainframes and USASCII, although supported by the 360, has been dropped from the 370 and 370/XA architectures. In what follows we shall discuss only the EBCDIC representation. The 8 bits in a byte are divided into two sets of 4 bits, each of which represents a hexadecimal number (0 through F). The decimal numbers 0–9 are represented by the hexadecimal numbers "F0" to "F9." The characters A–I are represented by hexadecimal numbers "C1"–"C8," J to R by "D1"–"D8" and S through Z by "E2"–"E8." Representations are provided for other keyboard characters, and for communication control characters.

Logical Data

Logical data types are bytes or strings of bytes, viewed as bit strings. The operations performed on these types are shifting and boolean operations such as AND, OR, and XOR.

	24-bit Address	
0	8	31

Figure 3-9 Address representation.

Address Data

The 360 uses 24-bit addresses. An address is always an unsigned positive integer, comprising three bytes. When an address is stored in a register, bits 0–7 of the register are set to zeros and bits 8–31 contain the 24-bit address (see Figure 3-9).

3.3.3 Storage Protection

Storage protection is an orderly approach for preventing unauthorized access to or destruction of programs or data in storage. The architecture provides a simple mechanism for storage protection by means of keys.

Storage is divided into blocks of 2K bytes. Each block has a storage key associated with it. The storage key is 5 bits in length. The instruction SET STORAGE KEY can assign a 5-bit storage key to a 2K byte block. The instruction INSERT STORAGE KEY can be used to retrieve the storage key associated with a block. Storage keys are stored in a separate hardware unit.

Protection is achieved by matching the storage key with another key supplied by the program or channel that reads from or writes to the 2K block. This latter key is called a protection key and is four bits in length. The two keys match when the four high-order bits of the storage key are equal to the protection key or when the protection key is zero. The low-order bit of the storage key specifies whether or not reading from the storage block is to be protected also.

The protection key for the current instruction is stored in the PSW in the key field. The matching of this key with the storage key is done by the hardware (see Figure 3-10). If the keys do not match, a protection violation condition arises and a program interruption takes place.

The protection key for a channel is provided in the Channel Address Word (CAW) discussed later. The storage protection action for

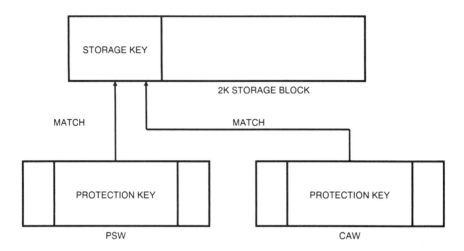

Figure 3-10 Storage protection.

a channel is similar to that described above. The CAW key is matched against the storage key and, if there is no match, an error condition is generated as described later.

3.3.4 Serialization

The rules for serial access to main storage are fairly straightforward. Channels and CPU access main storage independently of each other. If a CPU and channel access the same storage location, the channel has priority over the CPU and the accessing is done in sequence, with the channel first and the CPU next.

An instruction TEST AND SET is provided for granting serial access to common storage areas used by multiple programs. This instruction reads a byte and sets a flag and locks the storage location during the read and write phases of the instruction.

3.4   INPUT/OUTPUT ARCHITECTURE

The I/O architecture of the 360 series provides a common framework in which the same peripheral device (e.g., a 2314 disk drive) can be connected to any 360 model, and the same general principles are applied to input/output operations regardless of the specific device (e.g., tape, terminal).

3.4.1 Principles of I/O Operations

An input/output operation is regarded as a unit of work that is distributed among the following components:

- CPU
- Channel
- Control Unit
- Device

A program initiates an I/O operation by means of the START I/O instruction. The execution of this instruction is a cooperative operation by the abovementioned components (see Figure 3-11). The channel executes a channel program consisting of Channel Command Words (CCWs) in main storage. The channel fetches a CCW and passes it to the control unit, which in turn passes it to the device. The CCW contains orders to be performed by the device address for transferring data and other information.

A channel is logically viewed as consisting of one or more subchannels. A subchannel can be thought of as the memory resources of the channel needed for conducting an I/O operation. A subchannel may be dedicated to servicing only a particular device or may be shared among many devices.

An I/O operation has three phases, namely:

- Initiation
- Continuation
- Termination

The START I/O instruction, as mentioned before, initiates an I/O operation. The operand of the START I/O instruction specifies the

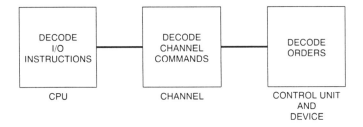

Figure 3-11 Allocation of I/O functions.

address of the channel, control unit, and I/O device. As part of the execution of the instruction, the channel signals the control unit and device to test their availability. If either the channel, device, or control unit is not available, a condition code is set in the PSW and the I/O operation is abandoned. The Channel Address Word (CAW) is fetched by the channel from storage. The CAW contains the address of the first CCW of the channel program that is to be executed by the channel. The CCW is read by the channel, and the operation specified by the CCW is initiated. A condition code of 0 is set in the PSW to indicate successful initiation and the CPU is free to execute the next instruction.

During the continuation phase, the channel executes in sequence the Channel Command Words (CCWs) that comprise the channel program. It also passes orders to the device, and these are executed by the device.

The completion of the I/O operation results in an I/O interruption initiated by the channel. The detailed status of the I/O operation is contained in the Channel Status Word (CSW).

The interaction between CPU, main storage, channel, control unit, and device is schematically illustrated in Figure 3-12. A program issues a Start I/O instruction for starting an I/O operation. The program that does this is usually the operating system's I/O Supervisor. Before issuing the Start I/O instruction, a channel program has to be created and loaded in storage. The Channel Address Word (CAW), which is a fixed location in storage, contains the address of the first CCW. The channel fetches the first CCW from storage, decodes it, selects the control unit and device (whose addresses are specified as operands in the Start I/O instruction), and sends the control unit the command code contained in the CCW. The control unit responds with an initial status byte to the channel, which the channel, in turn, presents to the CPU as a condition code. The Start I/O operation ends after the setting of the condition code, and the CPU is free to execute other instructions. The I/O operation, however, is not yet complete, and the channel fetches the remaining CCWs from main storage, one at a time. It decodes each CCW and issues commands to the control unit. The commands can be for controlling a device (e.g., positioning the read/write head of a disk) or for data transfer (e.g., reading or writing a record from a disk). Data transfer takes place between device and main storage, with the channel and control unit providing a path for the data transfer. When the last CCW in the channel program has been executed, the channel presents the CPU with an I/O interruption to indicate completion of the I/O operation. The interruption handler routine passes control to the I/O Supervisor

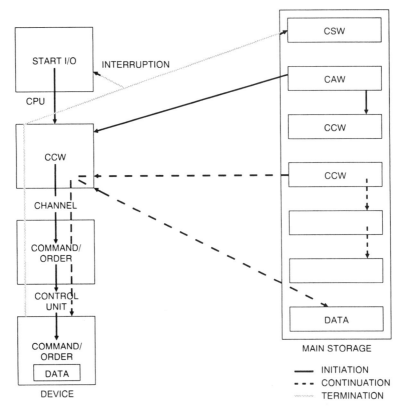

Figure 3-12 Phases in an I/O operation.

module of the operating system, which in turn, passes control to the program that requested the I/O operation.

3.4.2 Channel Programs

A channel can be regarded as a special purpose computer capable of performing only one function, the execution of I/O operations. To perform this function, the channel needs a program, which is called the channel program. It is the responsibility of the system programmer who writes an access method (which is part of the operating system) to create a channel program.

A channel program consists of one or more Channel Command Words (CCWs). Each CCW occupies a doubleword location in storage. The CCWs have consecutive addresses. The channel fetches a CCW, decodes it, and executes it. Execution consists of passing the CCW to the control unit and device for performing the required operation. After the required operation is performed, the channel executes the CCW in the next contiguous location, if the last CCW contains a chaining flag. It is possible to branch to a noncontiguous CCW by using a transfer-in-channel command. By using command chaining and the TRANSFER in CHANNEL command it is possible to perform branching and looping within a channel program.

Format of a CCW

The format of a CCW is shown in Figure 3-13. A CCW contains the following information:

- A command to a device or the channel to perform a function (COMMAND CODE)
- A main storage address from (or to) which data is transferred to (or from) a device (DATA ADDRESS)
- The number of bytes of data to be transferred between main storage and device (BYTE COUNT)
- A set of flags to indicate the presence or absence of the following:
  — command chaining
  — data chaining
  — program controlled interruption
  — skipping
  — suppress length indication.

The above terms are explained below.

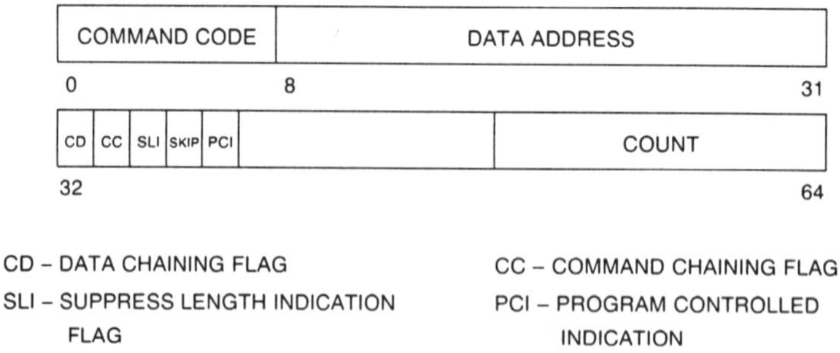

COMMAND CODE	DATA ADDRESS
0 8	31

CD	CC	SLI	SKIP	PCI		COUNT
32						64

CD – DATA CHAINING FLAG   CC – COMMAND CHAINING FLAG
SLI – SUPPRESS LENGTH INDICATION   PCI – PROGRAM CONTROLLED
     FLAG   INDICATION

Figure 3-13 Format of the CCW.

Command

There are six commands, namely READ, WRITE, READ BACK-WARD, CONTROL, SENSE, and TRANSFER IN CHANNEL. Each command has an 8-bit code associated with it. The command code uses the lower-order bits to indicate the command and the higher-order bits as modifier bits (indicated by M) for device-specific operations.

The READ command (MMMMMM10) causes data to be read from the device to a storage address indicated by the Data Address field. The WRITE command (MMMMMM01) causes data to be written to the device from the storage address indicated by the Data Address field. Both READ and WRITE transfer the number of bytes specified by the Byte Count field. The READ BACKWARD command is applicable to tape drives and reads data in a backward direction.

The CONTROL command (MMMMMM11) is used to convey device-specific orders by setting the modifier bits or by specifying a data address containing the orders in the Data Address field. Examples of orders are the rewinding of a tape, skipping a line on a printer or positioning the moving head of a disk.

The SENSE command is used for obtaining device-specific status. Examples of such status are file-protected condition of a magnetic tape and stacker-full condition of a card reader.

The TRANSFER IN CHANNEL command is used for branching to a CCW in a location specified by the Data Address field. Normally, the channel executes the next CCW in sequence. A TRANSFER IN CHANNEL is like a branch, in the sense that the next sequential instruction is not executed and a branch instruction is executed instead.

Command Chaining (CC)

Command chaining is used to execute a channel program containing several CCWs using a single START I/O (SIO) instruction (see Figure 3-14). When command chaining is indicated in a CCW, the next CCW is fetched by the channel from the doubleword location that follows the address of the current CCW, after execution of the current CCW. Command chaining is the means for serial execution of CCWs in a channel program. Branching is done by the TRANSFER IN CHANNEL command described earlier.

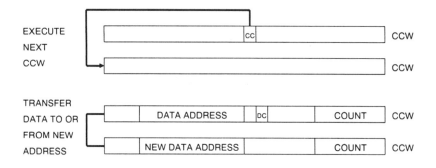

Figure 3-14 Command chaining (CC) and data chaining (DC).

Data Chaining (DC)

Data chaining is used to transfer data to or from noncontiguous locations (see Figure 3-14) in storage. When the data chaining flag is on, a new CCW is fetched from the next successive location after all the data specified by the byte count field of the current CCW has been transferred. The command field of the new CCW is ignored (unless it is a transfer in channel command), and data transfer takes place using the address specified by the CCW until the byte count specified by the new CCW is reached.

Program Controlled Interruption (PCI)

During execution of an I/O operation using several CCWs it may be desirable to have interruptions at intermediate stages of the I/O operation. A PCI flag in a CCW causes a CPU interruption. This intermediate interruption does not in any way affect the execution of the current I/O operation, but is a means of notifying the CPU of the progress of the current I/O operation.

The following remarks are in order:

1. A channel normally interrupts the CPU after completion of an I/O operation.
2. The PCI flag in a CCW causes an interruption during or after execution of that CCW. The time of interruption is not precisely defined in the architecture.
3. PCI can be used to monitor the progress of an I/O operation.

Skip

This flag suppresses the data transfer to main storage during the execution of a read, read backward, or sense operation. When combined with data chaining, skipping is useful in selectively transferring blocks of data to storage.

Suppress Length Indication (SLI)

This flag indicates whether an incorrect length condition is to be indicated at the end of an operation.

To summarize, the following are the main characteristics of a channel program:

- A channel program consists of a collection of chained channel command words (CCWs).
- The address of the first CCW is in the channel address word (CAW). The channel fetches the first CCW, decodes it and executes it; if command chaining is indicated, the next CCW is fetched, decoded and executed and the process is continued until the last CCW (i.e., a CCW that neither contains a transfer-in-channel command and nor has a chaining indicator) is processed.
- Branching is provided by the TRANSFER IN CHANNEL command.

Example of a Channel Program

Suppose it is desired to read a record with a specific ID from a disk drive. The following steps are involved in such an operation:

1. Place the read/write head above the track that contains the record to be read (known as a SEEK operation).
2. Read the ID of a record in the track and compare it with the specified ID (a SEARCH ID operation).
3. If the comparison is unequal, then go to step (2); if the comparison is equal, then go to step (4).
4. Read the contents of the record.

The actual channel program consists of the commands shown in Figure 3-15. These commands are discussed in Chapter 13. After a SEARCH ID operation, the device notifies the channel whether the

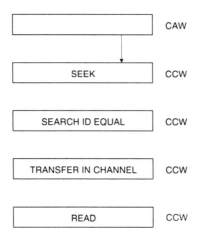

Figure 3-15 Channel program.

comparison was equal or unequal. In the case of an equal comparison, the channel fetches the CCW containing the READ command (i.e., it skips the CCW immediately following the one containing the SEARCH ID EQUAL). In the case of an unequal comparison, the channel executes the next CCW that contains the TRANSFER IN CHANNEL command that loops back to the CCW containing the SEARCH ID EQUAL command.

3.4.3   Unit Status

A device accepts orders from a channel. After the order is executed by the device, status is presented to the channel. It is important to understand the various types of status associated with devices and control units.

Device End

The device end status indicates that the device has completed the order and is ready for another order.

Unit Check

The unit check status indicates that the I/O device or control unit has detected an unusual condition. Details regarding the condition that caused the unit check are usually available by means of a SENSE command.

Unit Exception

The unit exception status includes an exception condition on a device operation, such as recognition of a tape mark.

Channel End

The channel end status indicates that the channel has performed its part successfully in an I/O operation and that the device or control unit no longer needs it. A channel end is not indicated in unsuccessful operations.

Control Unit End

The control unit end status indicates that the control unit has completed the order and is ready for another order.

Busy

The busy status indicates that the device or control unit is executing a previous order (or it has initiated a pending interruption).

Status Modifier

The status modifier is generated by a device when it cannot provide its status in answer to the TEST I/O instruction.

Attention

The device generates attention when it needs the services of an access method. In the case of a terminal, for example, the attention is generated when an operator hits an "enter" or "return" key to initiate data transfer from a terminal. The attention status causes an interruption and the consequent execution of a program to service the device.

3.4.4   Types of Channels

The architecture specifies two types of channels:

• Selector
• Byte multiplexer

The byte multiplexer channel is generally used for connecting low-speed devices (printer, card reader, card punch) while the selector channel is used for connecting high-speed devices (disks and high speed tapes). The word "multiplexer" denotes an important characteristic of byte multiplexer channels, namely, the concurrent execution of I/O operations pertaining to multiple devices. The selector channel, on the other hand, performs only one I/O operation at a time and is dedicated to the device for the duration of the operation.

Selector Channels

These channels are used for high-speed data transfer from devices such as tapes and disk drives. Several devices can be connected to a channel. The channel is dedicated to a device from start to end of the channel program, even during the execution of channel commands that do not cause data transfer to take place. This feature of the selector channel made it obsolete and the 370 architecture introduced a block multiplexer channel which is widely used today. In the case of the block multiplexer channel the device disconnects from the channel when the device is performing control functions such as positioning a read/write head.

The characteristics of the selector channel are summarized below:

1.   The channel performs only one I/O operation at a time.
2.   The channel is attached to a device for the entire duration of I/O operation. It has only one subchannel.
3.   The channel is used in connection with high-speed tape drives and direct access storage devices (DASD).
4.   The channel is replaced by the block multiplexer channel introduced in the 370 architecture.

Byte Multiplexer Channels

A byte multiplexer channel is used for connecting low-speed devices like card readers, card punches and printers. The channel is not dedicated to any single device while performing an I/O operation, unlike the selector channel. I/O operations pertaining to several devices are overlapped.

The characteristics of the byte multiplexer channel are summarized below:

1. The channel multiplexes I/O operations (it performs overlapping I/O operations).
2. The channel is used to attach card reader, printer, card punch, terminals, and other low-speed devices.
3. The channel interleaves bytes from several devices during the course of data transfer.
4. The channel is part of the 360 architecture, but is supported by the 370 and 370/XA architectures.
5. The channel can contain shared or nonshared subchannels.

3.4.5 I/O Instructions

The System 360 uses four I/O instructions, namely START I/O, TEST I/O, HALT I/O and TEST CHANNEL. The I/O instructions use the SI format. The I field is ignored. The B and D fields indirectly specify the addresses of the channel, subchannel, control unit and device as follows (see Figure 3-16). {B1} is added to D1 to obtain a word. The third byte of the word is used as a channel address. Thus, up to 256 channel addresses are possible even though the architecture permits only 7 channels. Only channel addresses 0–6 are valid, and any address beyond 6 is invalid. The fourth byte is used for device identification. It can consist of a subchannel, control unit, and device number. The numbering system is intricate — we will not go into details here. The motivation is to identify a device by specifying an I/O path, namely, channel, subchannel, control unit, and device.

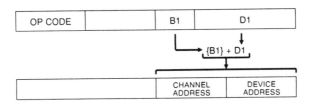

Figure 3-16 Instruction format and its interpretation.

Thus device selection consists of selecting a channel, a subchannel (which may be shared or nonshared) within a channel, a control unit connected to the channel, and a device connected to the control unit.

The START I/O instruction initiates an I/O operation. This instruction ties up the CPU until the addressed device is selected and the I/O operation is initiated. The channel selects a device by sending the device address to all control units attached to it. One of these control units recognizes the address and responds affirmatively. The I/O operation is initiated by the channel fetching CAW and the first CCW. A condition code is set in the PSW to indicate whether or not the I/O operation is initiated.

The TEST I/O instruction is used to test the availability of the addressed channel, subchannel, and device. The setting of the condition code indicates whether they are available, busy, operational, or not operational. The channel status word is sometimes stored for providing further details.

The architecture assigns "states" to a channel, subchannel, and device. The states are indicated by the letters "A," "I," "W," and "N." The interpretation of these letters is as follows: "A" when applied to channel, subchannel, or device indicates that the item is available. "N" means it is not operational. "W" means that the item is "working," i.e., it is performing another I/O operation. "I" means that the item is ready to interrupt. The phrase "interruption pending" has the following interpretation:

- In the case of a channel, the interruption is immediately available.
- In the case of a subchannel, the information for the CSW is available.
- In the case of a device, it is ready to pass on an interruption condition to the channel.

THE HALT I/O instruction halts the I/O operation at the addressed device. The addressed device is selected and signals are sent to terminate the current operation.

The TEST CHANNEL instruction tests the state of the addressed channel. The condition code indicates whether the channel is available, busy, not operational, etc.

3.4.6 I/O Interruption

The action taken on I/O interruption is illustrated schematically in Figures 3-17 and 3-18. The hardware stores the old PSW in real

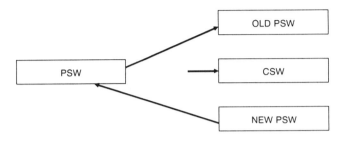

Figure 3-17 Interruption hardware action.

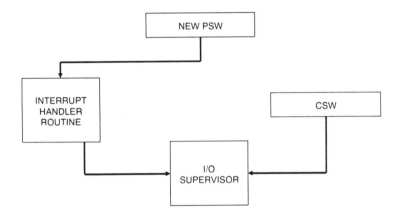

Figure 3-18 Interrupt software action.

storage locations 56–63, loads the new PSW from locations 120–127, and stores additional information in a Channel Status Word in locations 64–71. The old PSW contains the interruption-causing channel and device address in bit positions 16–31.

The new PSW contains the address of the I/O interruption handler which is an operating system routine. The details of interruption handling depend on the operating system, but, in general, the following actions take place:

- Error-handling operations are performed if an error in the I/O operation is indicated.
- If there are no errors, the program that initiated the I/O operation is notified of the completion of the I/O operation.

Channel Status Word (CSW)

The format of the CSW is shown in Figure 3-19. The CSW is a doubleword and is always stored at location 64. The key field contains a 4-bit storage protection key. The CCW address field gives an address that is equal to the address of the last CCW used plus 8 bytes.

Bits 48–63 show the residual count of bytes transferred as of the last CCW used. Bits 32–47 show status of the device and channel. They comprise 2 bytes, the first byte sent by the device or control unit to the channel over the I/O interface and presented in the CSW without modification, and the second byte generated by the channel. The first byte is called Unit Status byte, and the second byte is called Channel Status byte. The Unit Status byte contains a flag for unit status conditions such as channel end, device end, etc. The Channel Status byte consists of a flag for program-controlled interruption, protection violation, chaining check, etc.

To sum up, I/O interruptions can be initiated by a device or channel in a variety of situations, and the Channel Status Word (CSW) contains flag bits indicating the conditions associated with the interruption. At the end of an I/O operation, the control unit and device present the channel with an indication that it has successfully executed the channel program by means of channel end, device end, and control unit end. The channel requests an interruption at this stage. An attention interruption is initiated by a device (or control unit) to indicate that it has unsolicited data to send to a program. The program is notified by the I/O Supervisor that it should start an I/O operation for reading from the device. An example of a device that uses the attention interruption is the locally attached terminal, which requests this interruption when the attention key is depressed.

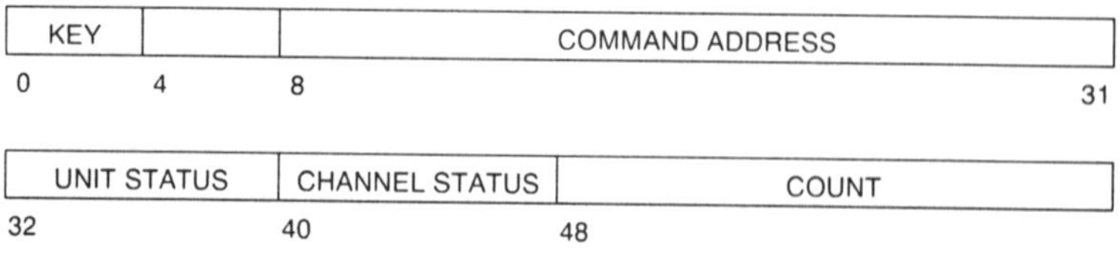

KEY		COMMAND ADDRESS
0	4	8 31

UNIT STATUS	CHANNEL STATUS	COUNT
32	40 48	

Figure 3-19 Format of the CSW.

The channel can initiate an interruption in other situations, some of which are listed below:

• When a CCW contains a program-controlled interruption (PCI) flag, the channel presents an interruption request. (PCI is used to periodically check the progress of complex I/O operations, such as loading a program from disk to main storage.)
• When the channel encounters program checks or protection checks.

The indicators presented by the channel for various interruption types are summarized in Table 3-1.

3.5 INSTRUCTION SET

The instruction set of the 360 is relatively easy to understand for someone who is familiar with the machine language of a general purpose computer, but can be difficult for someone who has not had exposure in this area. The complexity of the instruction set arises from the fact that the instruction set has been built to accommodate many views regarding the basic function of the machine. The 360 is a decimal machine and a binary machine and a floating-point machine, with separate instructions for arithmetic operations for

Table 3-1 Commonly Used Interruption Flags

EVENT	FLAGS
I/O COMPLETION	
— AT CHANNEL	CHANNEL END
— AT DEVICE	DEVICE END
— AT CONTROL UNIT	CONTROL UNIT END
I/O ERROR	
— AT CHANNEL	CHANNEL CONTROL CHECK
— AT DEVICE	UNIT CHECK
— AT CONTROL UNIT	INTERFACE CONTROL CHECK
ATTENTION	ATTENTION
PROGRAM CONTROLLED INTERRUPTION	PCI

each machine. The instruction format for decimal addition is not the same as that for binary addition, because decimal addition does not use registers. Floating-point arithmetic uses its own set of registers, and special conventions in regard to numbering registers have to be followed.

In a higher-level language, the rules for working with the language are easy to grasp; but complex instruction sets in general do not lend themselves to formal treatment. Each instruction, more or less, has its own set of rules and conditions. Thus learning the instruction set means learning the rules applicable to each instruction instead of a few general rules.

An instruction can be two, four, or six bytes in length and has to be on a halfword boundary. The instructions should be located contiguously in main storage. An instruction is divided into several fields. The first field refers to the operation code (op code). The other fields refer directly or indirectly to any of the following:

• The number of a register (general, floating point)
• A storage address
• A data item (called "immediate operand")
• A mask (a string of bits)
• A number (e.g., to indicate shifting of bits)

The interpretation of an instruction (the semantics of its operation) specifies whether or not the operands are to be generated directly or indirectly. For example, in LOAD ADDRESS, the operand is an address and this address is placed in a register, with the first eight bits of the register set to zero. In LOAD, on the other hand, the operand is the contents of an address specified by registers. Thus, the operand can be interpreted in several ways, depending on the instruction.

An instruction can generate a program interruption. For each instruction, the architecture lists the conditions that can cause a program interruption.

The condition code in the PSW is used to show the diagnosis, or sometimes (as in the case of COMPARE) the result of execution, of an instruction. The condition code can have four values (settings), numbered 0–3. Not all instructions set condition codes. The interpretation of the condition code can vary with the instruction. For example, a 0 value of the condition code means "operands are equal" in the COMPARE DECIMAL instruction and "result is zero" in an ADD instruction. The BRANCH ON CONDITION is used to branch to an address depending on the value of the condition code.

3.5.1 Instruction Formats

A format, in the normal use of the word, denotes the layout and physical organization of data. When applied to instructions, it carries extra semantics, and there is a potential for misunderstanding. The architecture defines five formats (see Figure 3-20):

- Register to register (RR)
- Register to storage, indexed (RX)
- Register to storage (RS)
- Storage to storage (SS)
- Storage and immediate operand (SI)

An RR instruction has three fields, namely OPCODE, R1, and R2. The OPCODE is one byte long. R1 and R2 are four bits in length and may denote general registers or floating-point registers. In the case of certain instructions, neither R1 and R2 refer to registers. Examples are the SVC instruction where the R1 and R2 fields are combined to form an SVC code whose ranges is 0–255, or the BRANCH ON CONDITION instruction, where R1 does not refer to a register but to the value of a condition. Hence, care must be taken in interpreting RR instructions, because the fields R1 and R2 can denote things other than registers. However, normally R1 and R2 refer to registers whose contents are the first and second operands of the instruction.

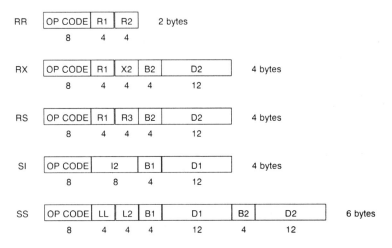

Figure 3-20 Instruction formats.

An RX instruction has five fields, namely, OPCODE, R1, X2, B2, D2. R1 may denote a register as before. B2 and X2 are each 4 bits in length and may denote registers. B stands for "base" and X stands for "index." The D2 field is 12 bits in length and is called the displacement. The contents of register B2 is called the base address. The displacement field D2 can contain a number from 0 to 4,095. The contents of R1 is the first operand. The contents of registers B2 and X2 are added to the D2 field to generate the address of a second operand.

An RS instruction has five fields, namely, OPCODE, R1, R3, B2, D2. It can have three operands, as in the BRANCH ON INDEX HIGH instruction. The operands are the contents of registers R1, R3, and the contents of the address generated by adding the base address to the D2 field. The shift instructions are also in the RS format, but the interpretation of the fields is different. The R3 field is not used. The contents of register B2 added to the D2 field is used for generating the number of bits for shifting the contents of register R1.

An SI instruction has four fields, namely, OPCODE, I2, B1 and D1. I2 is eight bits in length. The I stands for "immediate." The sum of the contents of register B1 with D1 is the address of the first operand. The contents of the I2 field is used as the second operand. The SI instruction format is used in a different way by the I/O instructions, and the I field is ignored.

An SS instruction has seven fields, namely, OPCODE, L1, L2, B1, D1, B2, D2. The symbol L denotes length of an operand. The L1 and L2 fields are both four bits in length. Some instructions using the SS format perform operations on two operands of length L1 and L2, starting at addresses generated from B1, D1 and B2, D2. L1 and L2 are sometimes combined into an L field, where L indicates the length of both operands. Examples are MOVE and COMPARE. Other instructions such as TRANSLATE or EDIT use the SS format in a completely different manner, as described later.

3.5.2 Interpretation of Instructions

The 360 Principles of Operation uses a tuple to denote an instruction. The tuple is divided into fields based on the format of the instruction. Some fields may be omitted, combined, or renamed. The value of a field may also be interpreted in several ways, depending on the instruction. For example, the tuple 18 01 02 is an instruction in the RR format that loads the contents of register 2 into register 1.

The tuple 1C 02 04 is also an instruction in the RR format and it multiplies the contents of register 03 with the contents of register 04 and stores the result in the pair of registers 02 and 03. Note that 03 is not mentioned explicitly in the tuple, even though it contains the multiplier. This is only one of several instances where an instruction is interpreted according to special rules instead of general rules.

The 360 Principles of Operation uses the terms "first operand," "second operand," etc., to indicate contents of R1, R2, etc., and the terms "first operand location," "second operand location" to indicate R1, R2, etc. We, also, shall use this terminology. But sometimes we shall use braces { } for indicating the contents of a register or storage location. We shall also be using IBM assembler conventions in letting D1(B1), D2(B2), and D2(X2, B2) stand for {{B1}+D1}, {{B2}+D2}, and {{B2}+{X2}+D2} in operand address generation (see Table 3-2). The use of zero in a B or X field needs special mention because it indicates that the field is not used in address generation. Thus D1(0) means not {{0}+D1} but {D1}, because 0 is to be interpreted as "value not applicable."

For many instructions having two operands, the result is placed in the first operand location — i.e., the execution of the instruction ends in the destructive replacement of the first operand with the result of the instruction. We call this the normal pattern of execution to avoid repeatedly describing this sequence of events. Examples of

Table 3-2 Operand Address Generation

Interpretation of first operand			
FORMAT	FIRST OPERAND	FIRST OPERAND LOCATION	FIRST OPERAND LENGTH IN BYTES
RR	{R1}	R1	4
RX	{R1}	R1	4
RS	{R1}	R1	4
SI	{{B1}+ D1}	{B1} + D1	1
SS	{{B1} + D1}	{B1} + D1	L or L1

Interpretation of second operand			
FORMAT	SECOND OPERAND	SECOND OPERAND LOCATION	SECOND OPERAND LENGTH IN BYTES
RR	{R2}	R2	4
RX	{{B2} + {X2} + D2}	{B2} + {X2} + D2	4
RX	{{B2} + D2}	{B2} + D2	4
SI	I2	–	1
SS	{{B2} + D2}	{B2} + D2	L or L2

normal pattern of execution are addition, subtraction, conjunction, and disjunction. Examples of non-normal patterns of execution are the SVC, branch, and I/O instructions.

In the following paragraphs, we give brief descriptions of most of the 360 instructions. We have not tried to give a complete and exhaustive treatment of the instruction set. The interested user can consult 360 Principles of Operations [1] for further reference.

3.5.3   Instruction Classification

The following classification is used in the 360 Principles of Operation:

• Fixed-point arithmetic instructions
• Decimal arithmetic instructions
• Floating-point arithmetic instructions
• Logical operations
• Branching instructions
• Status switching instructions (e.g., changing the PSW)
• I/O instructions

The following classification is used in the 370 Principles of Operation:

• General instructions
• Decimal instructions
• Floating-point instructions
• Control instructions (instructions used by the operating system)
• I/O instructions

We shall adopt a different classification scheme, using a tree structure with many levels, as shown in Figure 3-21. At the highest level, the instruction set is divided into two subsets, namely, supervisor (or privileged) and problem (or application). The supervisor instructions are further classified by the object referred to by the instruction, such as PSW, storage key, channel, etc. The problem program instructions are grouped by functions, namely:

• Arithmetic instructions
• Conversion instructions
• Data movement instructions
• Logical instructions

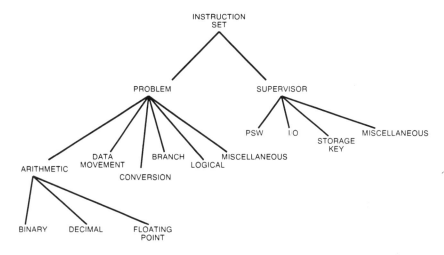

Figure 3-21 Instruction classification.

- Branch instructions
- Miscellaneous instructions

These functions are further decomposed at the next level. For example, arithmetic instructions are decomposed into binary, decimal, and floating-point instructions. Each of these again is decomposed into subtypes to which they are applicable (e.g., signed integer, unsigned integer, etc.).

3.5.4   Arithmetic Instructions

The following arithmetic operations are provided in the instruction set:

- Addition
- Subtraction
- Multiplication
- Division
- Comparison
- Negation
- Complementation
- Absolute value formation
- Shifting
- Conversion

However, these are not provided for all arithmetic data types (the instruction set is not orthogonal with respect to arithmetic data types). In Table 3-3, the instructions and the applicable data types are shown.

The data types can be classified at the highest level as follows:

• Signed binary integer (SB)
• Unsigned binary integer (UB)
• Decimal integer (D)
• Floating-point number (F).

The signed binary integer is broken into subtypes along the following lines (see Figure 3-22):

• 32-bit signed integers (fullword)
• 16-bit signed integers (halfword)
• 64-bit signed integers (doubleword)

An unsigned binary integer is subtyped as follows:

• 32-bit unsigned integers (fullword)
• 16-bit unsigned integers (halfword)

Table 3-3 Arithmetic Operations vs. Data Types

OPERATIONS	VALID DATA TYPES FOR OPERANDS AND RESULTS
ADDITION	SB, UB, D, F
SUBTRACTION	SB, UB, D, F
MULTIPLICATION	SB, D, F
DIVISION	SB, D, F
COMPARISON	SB, UB, D, F
COMPLEMENTATION	SB, F
ABSOLUTE VALUE	SB, F
SHIFTING	SB, UB
CONVERSION	SB, D

SB — Signed binary   UB — Unsigned binary
D — Decimal   F — Floating point

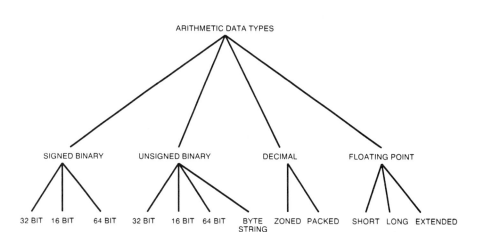

Figure 3-22 Arithmetic data subtypes.

• Byte strings of up to 256 bytes in length.

  A decimal number is subtyped along the following lines:

• Packed
• Zoned

  A floating point number is subtyped as shown below:

• Short (fullword)
• Long (doubleword)
• Extended (quadword)

Binary Arithmetic Instructions

The following binary representation conventions are used in the 360 architecture:
• For signed binary integers, bit 0 indicates the sign, a value of zero denoting "+" and a value of one denoting "-."
• Negative binary integers use two's complement notation; the actual implementation of the two's complement notation is done by inverting (substituting a zero for one and vice versa) each bit of the corresponding positive binary integer and adding 1 to the result. For example, -26 is represented as a negative 16-bit integer:

```
+26     0  000  0000  0001  1010
invert  1  111  1111  1110  0101
add 1                           1
-26     1  111  1111  1110  0110
```

- The bits between the sign bit and the leftmost significant bit are the same as the sign bit for both positive and negative integers; thus, when a halfword integer is converted as a fullword integer, the sign bit is propagated to fill the low bit positions (the same applies to shifting to the right).
- For unsigned binary integers, there is no sign bit per se, and all bits are used for representing the integer. The integer is always treated as a positive integer.

In Table 3-4, the binary arithmetic instructions are shown with applicability to specific subtypes. In Table 3-5 the actual 360 instructions are shown. Condition codes are set for some instructions. To facilitate the understanding of the logic behind the setting of the condition code, we have introduced the concept of types in condition

Table 3-4 Binary Arithmetic Operations by Subtypes

OPERAND 1	OPERAND 2	RESULT 1	RESULT 2	CC SETTING TYPE	INSTRUCTIONS
32 SB	32 SB	32 SB		1	ADD. SUBTRACT
32 SB	32 SB			3	COMPARE
32 SB		32 SB		1	LOAD COMPLEMENT. LOAD AND TEST. LOAD POSITIVE. LOAD NEGATIVE. SHIFT RIGHT SINGLE. SHIFT LEFT SINGLE
32 SB	32 SB	64 SB		N/A	MULTIPLY
32 SB	16 SB	32 SB		1	ADD. SUBSTRACT
32 SB	16 SB			3	COMPARE
32 SB	16 SB	32 SB		N/A	MULTIPLY
64 SB	32 SB	32 SB	32 SB	N/A	DIVIDE
64 SB		64 SB		1	SHIFT RIGHT DOUBLE. SHIFT LEFT DOUBLE
16 SB		32 SB		1	LOAD HALFWORD
32 UB	32 UB	32 UB		2	ADD. SUBTRACT

SB — signed binary

code setting. Type 1 is used commonly with signed binary, decimal, and floating-point arithmetic. It has the following interpretation:

- 0 means that result is 0.
- 1 means that result is less than 0.
- 2 means that result is greater than 0.
- 3 means that overflow has occurred.

Type 2 is used in unsigned binary arithmetic. It has the following interpretation:

- 0 means that result is 0.
- 1 means that result is not 0.
- 2 means that result is 0 and a bit has been carried.
- 3 means that result is not 0 and a bit has been carried.

Type 3 is used in conjunction with the comparison instruction. Its interpretation is the following:

- 0 means that both operands are equal.
- 1 means that the first operand is less than the second operand.
- 2 means that the first operand is greater than the second operand.

Referring to Table 3-4, the binary operations applicable to 32-bit signed integers are the following:

- Addition
- Subtraction
- Multiplication
- Division
- Comparison.

The result is a 32-bit signed integer for the first two operations and is placed in R1. For multiplication, the result is a 64-bit signed integer and is placed in the consecutively numbered registers R1 and R1 + 1. R1 must be an even number (otherwise a specification exception is recognized). The actual multiplier is {R1 + 1}. In the case of division, the first operand is a 64-bit signed integer placed in consecutively numbered registers R1 and R1 + 1 (R1 must be even). The operation has two results, a remainder (placed in R1) and a quotient (placed in R2). Both are 32-bit signed integers. In the case of comparison, the result is placed in the condition code. Type 3 interpretation is used.

Table 3-5 Binary Instructions

OPERATION	INSTRUCTIONS	MNEMONIC	FORMAT	CONDITION CODE SETTING TYPE
ADD	ADD	AR	RR	1
	ADD	A	RX	1
	ADD HALFWORD	AH	RX	1
	ADD LOGICAL	ALR	RR	2
	ADD LOGICAL	AL	RX	2
SUBTRACT	SUBTRACT	SR	RR	1
	SUBTRACT	S	RX	1
	SUBSTRACT HALFWORD	SH	RX	1
	SUBTRACT LOGICAL	SLR	RR	2
	SUBTRACT LOGICAL	SL	RX	2
MULTIPLY	MULTIPLY	MR	RR	
	MULTIPLY	M	RX	
	MULTIPLY HALFWORD	MH	RX	
DIVIDE	DIVIDE	DR	RX	
	DIVIDE	D	RR	
LOAD	LOAD HALFWORD	LH	RX	
	LOAD AND TEST	LTR	RR	1
	LOAD COMPLEMENT	LCR	RR	1
	LOAD POSITIVE	LPR	RR	1
	LOAD NEGATIVE	LNR	RR	1
STORE	STORE HALFWORD	STH	RR	
SHIFT	SHIFT LEFT SINGLE	SLA	RS	1
	SHIFT LEFT DOUBLE	SLDA	RS	1
	SHIFT RIGHT SINGLE	SRA	RS	1
	SHIFT RIGHT DOUBLE	SRDA	RS	1
COMPARE	COMPARE	CR	RR	3
	COMPARE	C	RX	3
	COMPARE HALFWORD	CH	RX	3
	COMPARE LOGICAL	CLR	RR	3
	COMPARE LOGICAL	CL	RX	3
	COMPARE LOGICAL	CLI	SI	3
	COMPARE LOGICAL	CLC	SS	3

The unary operations applicable to 32-bit signed integers are the following:

• Complementation
• Absolute value formation

- Negation
- Right shift
- Left shift.

A type 1 condition code setting takes place after each of the foregoing instructions. The LOAD COMPLEMENT instruction places the 2's complement of {R2} in R1. The LOAD POSITIVE instruction places the absolute value of {R2} in R1. The LOAD NEGATIVE instruction places -{R2} in R1. The shift instructions have the RS format, but the R3 field is ignored. R1 contains the operand that is to be shifted n bits to the right or to the left. The number of bits n is indicated by the low-order 6 bits of the sum of {B2} and D2. B2 and D2 fields are not used for address generation. If B2 is 0, then it is ignored and only D2 is used. The maximum value of n is 63. In the case of SHIFT RIGHT SINGLE, bits 1–31 are shifted n places to the right and the value of the sign bit is placed in the vacated bit positions. If n is between 31 and 63, the resulting value is either -1 or 0, depending on the sign of the operand. The SHIFT LEFT SINGLE instruction shifts bits 1–31 n places to the left and bit value zero is placed in each vacated bit position.

It is also possible to do the following arithmetic operations when the first operand is a 32-bit signed integer and the second operand is a 16-bit signed integer:

- Addition (ADD HALFWORD)
- Subtraction (SUBTRACT HALFWORD)
- Multiplication (MULTIPLY HALFWORD)
- Comparison (COMPARE HALFWORD).

The result is a 32-bit signed integer. These operations can be useful in compiling high-level languages such as PL/1 or FORTRAN, where the abovementioned operations are used in many situations. The only unary operation permitted on 16-bit signed integers is the LOAD HALFWORD instruction, which is equivalent to a conversion to the 32-bit signed integer format.

The unary operations permitted on 64-bit signed integers are the following:

- Shift left double
- Shift right double.

These operations are similar to the shift operations on 32-bit signed integers. The operand is contained in two consecutive registers R1 and R1+1 (where R1 is even), and the result is contained in the two registers. The number of bits to be shifted is specified in the lower six bits of the sum of {B2} and D2, as in the case of shift left single and shift right single.

The arithmetic operations provided for 32-bit unsigned binary integers are the following:

• Addition
• Subtraction.

The result is an unsigned 32-bit integer and the condition code setting type is 2.

The comparison instruction for unsigned binary integers (COMPARE LOGICAL) views the operands as byte strings of variable length. The CLR instruction specifies a length of four bytes for each operand. The CLI instruction compares a single byte given as data (i.e., with the instruction) to a byte in storage. The CLC instruction compares two arbitrary strings of length L + 1, where L is less than or equal to 255 bytes. The comparison instruction can be used to compare characters represented in EBCDIC. The collating sequence used in EBCDIC puts the alphabetical characters A–Z in ascending sequence. The condition code setting type is 3, which is the same as for algebraic comparison.

Decimal Arithmetic Instructions

As mentioned previously, decimal arithmetic uses two formats, packed and zoned. The arithmetic instructions are applicable to the packed format. A packed decimal integer can be from 1 to 31 digits (or 1 to 16 bytes) in length. Each byte contains two digits encoded in binary form, except for the last (or rightmost) byte, which contains a digit plus a sign code. A decimal integer is represented as one or more entire bytes. Hence, the number of digits in a decimal integer is always odd, because the last byte can hold only one digit. If the number of significant digits in a decimal integer is even, a leading zero has to be inserted to make it odd.

The following conventions apply to decimal arithmetic:

• The operands need not have the same length, the shorter operand is expanded to the same length as the longer operand by inserting leading zeros during instruction execution.
• The operands should not overlap at all, but the first and second operand can be the same.

Table 3-6 Decimal instructions

INSTRUCTION	MNEMONIC	FORMAT	CONDITION CODE SETTING TYPE
ADD DECIMAL	AP	SS	1
SUBTRACT DECIMAL	SP	SS	1
MULTIPLY DECIMAL	MP	SS	N/A
DIVIDE DECIMAL	DP	SS	N/A
ZERO AND ADD	CP	SS	1
COMPARE DECIMAL	ZAP	SS	3

Table 3-7 Decimal Arithmetic Operations

OPERAND 1	OPERAND 2	RESULT 1	RESULT 2	CC SETTING TYPE	INSTRUCTIONS
$D(L_1)$	$D(L2)$	$D(L_1)$		1	ADD DECIMAL, ZERO AND ADD, SUBTRACT
$D(L_1)$	$D(L_2)$	$D(L_1-L_2-1)$	$D(L_2+1)$		DIVIDE
$D(L_1)$	$D(L_2)$	$D(L_1)$			MULTIPLY
$D(L_1)$	$D(L_2)$			3	COMPARE

- The binary codes for digits and signs are checked during instruction execution, and a data specification will be recognized in case of incorrect codes, followed by program interruption.
- The instructions use the storage to storage (SS) format. The length of operands are specified by L1 and L2, which vary from 0 to 15. The true lengths are L1 + 1 and L2 + 1, and can be from 1 to 16 bytes.

In Table 3-6 the packed decimal arithmetic instructions and their formats are shown. In Table 3-7, the lengths of the operands and the results are shown together with condition codes. The following instructions store the result in the first operand location (the length of the result is the same as that of the first operand):

- ADD DECIMAL
- SUBTRACT DECIMAL
- MULTIPLY DECIMAL
- ZERO AND ADD.

In the case of the ADD DECIMAL instruction, the two operands are added and the sum is placed in the first operand location. Type 1 condition code setting is used to indicate overflow. The SUBTRACT DECIMAL operation works the same way. The ZERO AND ADD instruction is equivalent to an addition of the second operand to zero.

The MULTIPLY DECIMAL instruction multiplies two operands of length L1 and L2. The length L2 of the second operand should not exceed 7 bytes (15 digits), and L2 should also be less than L1. The first operand must have high-order zeros at least equal to two times L2. All these conditions are checked during instruction execution, and a specification or data exception is recognized if violations occur.

In the case of the DIVIDE DECIMAL instruction, the first operand is divided by the second operand. The quotient and the remainder are placed in the location of the first operand in that order. The length of the quotient is L1-L2 bytes, and that of the remainder is L2 bytes. L2 should be less than seven and also less than L1; otherwise, a specification exception is recognized.

Floating-Point Arithmetic

In floating-point arithmetic, a number is represented in hexadecimal arithmetic and has two parts, namely:

- A fraction
- An exponent

For example, the number 1 can be represented as $(1/16) \times 16^1$, in which case 1/16 is the fraction and 1 is the exponent. The numbers are represented in three formats, namely:

- Short (fullword)
- Long (doubleword)
- Extended (quadruple word)

The exponent is represented in excess 64 format (i.e., the exponent is added to 64); this representation is called the characteristic. The fields for characteristics and fractions under the above three formats were illustrated in Figure 3-8.

A floating-point number is said to be normalized if the fraction does not contain leading zeros. For example, 1 can be represented as 0.1×16^1 or $.01 \times 16^2$. The first representation is normalized.

Most instructions normalize the result and are called "normalized" instructions. However, there are a few instructions that do not normalize the result and are called "unnormalized" instructions.

The following general remarks apply to floating-point instructions:

• The floating-point instructions have RR or RX format. In the RR format, both R1 and R2 fields contain the number of a floating-point register. In general, R1 and R2 should be multiples of 2, i.e., 0, 2, 4, or 6 for short and long operands, and 0 or 4 for extended operands. In the RX format, R1 refers to a floating-point register and the preceding remarks apply. The B and X fields refer to general registers.

• An operation may result in an exponent overflow (i.e., the characteristic of the result is larger than the size of the characteristic field) or exponent underflow (i.e., the characteristic is less than zero). The overflow condition is not indicated in the condition code setting, as in the case of binary or decimal arithmetic, but create exceptions resulting in program interruption (unless the interruption is masked).

• The result of an operation may be such that the fraction is zero, in which case a significance exception is generated.

The following mnemonic is used in an instruction to indicate the format that is applicable to it:

E, U — short normalized, short unnormalized
D, W — long normalized, long unnormalized
X — extended normalized

The floating-point instructions are shown in Table 3-8. The normalized instructions are shown in Table 3-9. The following instructions use the same formats (long, short) for both operands and result:

• ADD NORMALIZED
• SUBTRACT NORMALIZED

Table 3-8 Floating-Point Operations

OPERATION	NAME	MNEMONIC	FORMAT	CONDITION CODE SETTING TYPE
ADD	ADD NORMALIZED SHORT	AER	RR	1
	ADD NORMALIZED SHORT	AE	RX	1
	ADD NORMALIZED LONG	ADR	RR	1
	ADD NORMALIZED LONG	AD	RX	1
	ADD NORMALIZED EXTENDED	AXR	RR	1
SUBTRACT	SUBTRACT NORMALIZED SHORT	SEX	RR	1
	SUBTRACT NORMALIZED SHORT	SE	RR	1
	SUBTRACT NORMALIZED LONG	SDR	RR	1
	SUBTRACT NORMALIZED LONG	SD	RR	1
	SUBTRACT NORMALIZED EXTENDED	SXR	RR	1
MULTIPLY	MULTIPLY SHORT	MER	RR	
	MULTIPLY SHORT	ME	RR	
	MULTIPLY LONG	MDR	RR	
	MULTIPLY LONG	MD	RR	
	MULTIPLY EXTENDED	MXR	RR	
	MULTIPLY LONG EXTENDED	MXDR	RR	
	MULTIPLY LONG EXTENDED	MXD	RX	
DIVIDE	DIVIDE SHORT	DER	RX	
	DIVIDE SHORT	DE	RR	
	DIVIDE LONG	DDR	RX	
	DIVIDE LONG	DD	RR	
COMPARE	COMPARE SHORT	CER	RX	3
	COMPARE SHORT	CE	RR	3
	COMPARE LONG	CDR	RX	3
	COMPARE LONG	CD	RR	3
LOAD	LOAD SHORT	LER	RX	
	LOAD SHORT	LE	RR	
	LOAD LONG	LDR	RX	
	LOAD LONG	LD	RR	
	LOAD AND TEST SHORT	LTER	RX	1
	LOAD AND TEST LONG	LTDR	RR	1
	LOAD COMPLEMENT SHORT	LCER	RR	1
	LOAD COMPLEMENT LONG	LCDR	RX	1
	LOAD POSITIVE SHORT	LPER	RR	1
	LOAD POSITIVE LONG	LPDR	RX	1
	LOAD NEGATIVE SHORT	LNER	RR	1
	LOAD NEGATIVE LONG	LNDR	RR	1
	LOAD ROUNDED (EXTENDED TO LONG)	LRDR	RR	
	LOAD ROUNDED (EXTENDED TO SHORT)	LRER	RR	
HALVE	HALVE SHORT	HER	RR	
	HALVE LONG	HDR	RR	
STORE	STORE SHORT	STE	RX	
	STORE LONG	STD	RX	
ADD	ADD UNNORMALIZED SHORT	AUR	RR	1
	ADD UNNORMALIZED SHORT	AU	RX	1
	ADD UNNORMALIZED LONG	AWR	RR	1
	ADD UNNORMALIZED LONG	AW	RX	1
SUBTRACT	SUBTRACT UNNORMALIZED SHORT	SER	RR	1
	SUBTRACT UNNORMALIZED SHORT	SE	RX	1
	SUBTRACT UNNORMALIZED LONG	SUR	RR	1
	SUBTRACT UNNORMALIZED LONG	SU	RX	1

Table 3-9 Normalized Floating-Point Instructions

O₁	O₂	R₁	R₂	CONDITION CODE TYPE SETTING	INSTRUCTIONS
S	S	S		1	ADD NORMALIZED, SUBTRACT NORMALIZED
S	S	S			MULTIPLY, DIVIDE
S	S			3	COMPARE
S		S		1	HALVE
L	L	L		1	ADD NORMALIZED, SUBTRACT NORMALIZED
L	L	L			MULTIPLY, DIVIDE
L	L			3	COMPARE
L		L			HALVE
E	E	E		1	ADD NORMALIZED, SUBTRACT NORMALIZED
L		S			LOAD ROUNDED
E		L			LOAD ROUNDED
S	S	L			MULTIPLY
L	L	E			MULTIPLY

S — Short   L — Long   E — Extended

- MULTIPLY
- DIVIDE

The result is normalized and stored at the first operand location. Note that division generates only one result, namely the quotient.

The COMPARE instruction uses normalized subtraction to determine if the first operand is equal to, less than, or greater than the second operand, and the condition code setting is of type 3.

The unary instruction HALVE divides the operand in R2 by 2 and the normalized result is placed in R1.

For extended formats, only the following instructions are available:

- ADD NORMALIZED
- SUBTRACT NORMALIZED

The result can be in a format different from that of the operands in the case of the MULTIPLY instruction. Thus, the operands can be in short format and the result can be in long format; or, the operands can be in long format and the result can be in extended format.

The unnormalized instructions are shown in Table 3-10. The following operations using two operands are available:

Table 3-10 Unnormalized Floating-Point Instructions

O₁	O₂	R₁	R₂	CONDITION CODE TYPE SETTING	INSTRUCTIONS
S	S	S		1	ADD UNNORMALIZED, SUBTRACT UNNORMALIZED
S		S			LOAD, STORE
S		S		1	LOAD AND TEST, LOAD COMPLEMENT, LOAD POSITIVE, LOAD NEGATIVE
L	L	L		1	ADD UNNORMALIZED, SUBTRACT UNNORMALIZED
L		L			LOAD, STORE
L		L		1	LOAD AND TEST, LOAD COMPLEMENT, LOAD POSITIVE, LOAD NEGATIVE
L		S			LOAD ROUNDED
E		L			LOAD ROUNDED

S — Short   L — Long   E — Extended

- ADD UNNORMALIZED
- SUBTRACT UNNORMALIZED

The unnormalized result has the same format as the operands and is placed in the first operand location.

The following unary operations store the result without normalization:

- LOAD
- LOAD AND TEST
- LOAD COMPLEMENT
- LOAD NEGATIVE
- LOAD POSITIVE
- LOAD ROUNDED
- STORE

The LOAD instructions are in the RR format and the R1 and R2 fields should indicate 0, 2, 4, or 6. LOAD copies the contents of R2 into R1. LOAD AND TEST is the same as LOAD, except that the condition code setting is type 1. LOAD COMPLEMENT inverts the sign bit. LOAD NEGATIVE sets the sign bit to value 1 and LOAD POSITIVE sets it to value 0.

The instruction LOAD ROUNDED converts a long operand into a short operand, or an extended operand into a long operand.

3.5.5 Conversion Instructions

The architecture provides instructions for converting one data type into another type, required by languages such as COBOL and PL/1. The conversion is schematically illustrated in Figure 3-23. The conversion of floating-point numbers from extended to long and long to short (the LOAD ROUNDED instruction) is not shown in the diagram.

The conversion instructions are given in Table 3-11. Table 3-12 shows the data types of the operand and the result. The CONVERT TO BINARY instruction converts a 15-digit decimal (8 bytes) into a 32-bit signed binary integer. The CONVERT TO DECIMAL instruction performs the reverse operation. The PACK instruction converts a zoned decimal number L1 bytes in length to a packed decimal representation L2 bytes in length. If L2 is not long enough to contain all the digits, the result will be truncated. The UNPACK instruction performs the reverse operation. The EDIT instruction is used for converting a packed decimal into zoned format for display purposes. Thus, the number 51246 can be edited as 5,124.6 by providing an appropriate edit mask, or pattern, to be used in conjunction with the

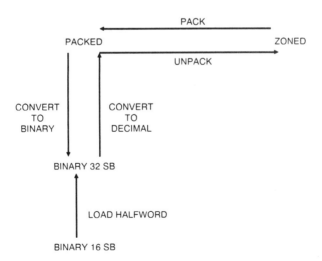

Figure 3-23 Conversion of types.

Table 3-11 Conversion Instructions

INSTRUCTION	MNEMONIC	FORMAT
CONVERT TO BINARY	CV	RX
CONVERT TO DECIMAL	CVD	RX
PACK	PACK	SS
UNPACK	UNPACK	SS
EDIT	ED	SS
EDIT AND MARK	EDMK	SS

Table 3-12 Type of Operand and Result

O_1	R_1	CONDITION CODE SETTING TYPE	INSTRUCTION
DP(8)	32 SB		CONVERT TO BINARY
32 SB	DP(8)		CONVERT TO DECIMAL
DZ(L_1)	DP(L_2)		PACK
DP(L_1)	DZ(L_2)		UNPACK
DP(L)	DZ(M)		EDIT
DP(L)	DZ(M)		EDIT AND MARK

EDIT instruction. The EDIT AND MARK instruction performs the same function as the EDIT instruction but can also insert a currency symbol ($ sign) in front of a packed decimal number.

3.5.6 Data Movement Instructions

The data movement instructions are classified as follows:

- LOAD instructions that move data from storage into registers
- STORE instructions that move data from one or more registers into storage
- MOVE instructions that move data from one storage location into another.

These instructions do not convert the data from one type to another. Thus, the LOAD HALFWORD instruction which converts a 16-bit signed integer into a 32-bit signed integer is not discussed here but under arithmetic instructions.

In general, instructions are available for loading, storing, or moving a byte or a group of bytes (with some exceptions). Table 3-13 lists the data movement instructions. In Table 3-14, the number of bytes moved by these instructions is shown. The instructions that pertain to moving a single byte are MOVE IMMEDIATE, INSERT CHARACTER, and STORE CHARACTER. The MOVE IMMEDIATE instruction is an immediate instruction, and the data contained in the instruction is moved to a location in storage. The STORE CHARACTER instruction moves the rightmost byte (bits 24–31) from R1 into a location at the address D2 (B2, X2). INSERT CHARACTER performs the reverse operation.

The STORE HALFWORD instruction moves the two rightmost bytes (bits 16–31) from R1 into the location at the address D2 (B2, X2). The LOAD HALFWORD instruction (which is not shown in Figure 3-36) moves two bytes from storage into R1, but propagates the sign bit and hence alters the contents of R1.

The LOAD and STORE instructions transfer four bytes from storage to register and register to storage, respectively. The LOAD instruction comes in two formats, namely, RR and RX. In the RR format, it is used for loading R1 with {R2}.

The LOAD MULTIPLE instruction is used for loading up to 16 registers with the contents of contiguous storage locations. It is in the RS format. The registers R1 and R3 indicate the beginning and ending of registers to be loaded. A register sequence 0, 1, 2, ... 15, 0, 1 ... is used. For example, if R1 = 7 and R3 = 1, then the registers 7, 8, 9, 10, 11, 12, 13, 14, 15, 0, and 1 are loaded. The starting address

Table 3-13 Data Movement Instructions

INSTRUCTION	MNEMONIC	FORMAT
LOAD	LR	RR
LOAD	L	RX
LOAD MULTIPLE	LM	RS
STORE	ST	RX
STORE HALFWORD	STH	RX
STORE MULTIPLE	STH	RS
INSERT CHARACTER	IC	RX
STORE CHARACTER	STC	RX
MOVE	MVI	SI
MOVE	MVC	SS
MOVE NUMERICS	MVN	SS
MOVE ZONE	MVZ	SS

Table 3-14 Number of Bytes Moved

OPERAND 1	RESULT	INSTRUCTION
1	1	MOVE IMMEDIATE, INSERT CHARACTER, STORE CHARACTER
2	2	STORE HALFWORD
4	4	LOAD, STORE
$n \times 4$	$n \times 4$	LOAD MULTIPLE, STORE MULTIPLE
L	L	MOVE CHARACTER, MOVE NUMERICS, MOVE ZONES, MOVE INTO OFFSET

in storage is given by the second operand. The STORE MULTIPLE instruction uses the same logic except that data is moved from registers to storage. These instructions may be used in saving (restoring) sets of registers (say 0–15) before (after) calls to subroutines.

The MOVE instruction (MVC) is in the SS format. It moves the contents of L + 1 bytes starting with location D1(B1) into L + 1 bytes starting with location D2(B2). The L field is one byte long; hence, its maximum value is 255.

The MOVE NUMERICS instruction moves the right half (bits 4–7) of each byte of the second operand into the corresponding byte in the first operand. Both operands are of equal length. The MOVE ZONE moves the left half of each byte of the second operand into the corresponding byte in the first operand. These instructions are useful in extracting or inserting numeric or zone fields in decimal integers using the zoned decimal format.

3.5.7 Logical and Bit Level Instructions

These instructions (see Tables 3-15 and 3-16) are grouped under the following headings:

• Boolean instructions
• Nonnumerical Comparisons instructions
• Shift instructions
• Bit-testing instructions

The boolean instructions perform boolean operations. The operands vary depending on the format. There are three boolean operations provided, namely, AND, OR, and EXCLUSIVE OR. These operations

Table 3-15 Logical Instructions

INSTRUCTION	MNEMONIC	FORMAT	CONDITION CODE SETTING TYPE
AND	NR	RR	4
AND	N	RX	4
AND	NI	SI	4
AND	NC	SS	4
OR	OR	RR	4
OR	O	RX	4
OR	OI	SI	4
OR	OS	SS	4
EXCLUSIVE OR	XR	R	4
EXCLUSIVE OR	X	RS	4
EXCLUSIVE OR	XI	SI	4
EXCLUSIVE OR	XS	SS	4
TEST UNDER MASK	TM	SI	
SHIFT LEFT SINGLE LOGICAL	SLL	RS	N/A
SHIFT LEFT DOUBLE LOGICAL	SLDL	RS	N/A
SHIFT RIGHT SINGLE LOGICAL	SRL	RS	N/A
SHIFT RIGHT DOUBLE LOGICAL	SRDL	RS	N/A

Table 3-16 Logical and Boolean Instructions

O$_1$	O$_2$	R$_1$	CONDITION CODE SETTING TYPE	INSTRUCTIONS
BYTE	BYTE	BYTE	4	AND, OR, EXCLUSIVE OR
4 BYTES	4 BYTES	4 BYTES	4	AND, OR, EXCLUSIVE OR
L BYTES	L BYTES	L BYTES	4	AND, OR, EXCLUSIVE OR
BYTE	BYTE			TEST UNDER MASK
4 BYTES		4 BYTES	N/A	SHIFT LEFT LOGICAL, SHIFT RIGHT LOGICAL
8 BYTES		8 BYTES	N/A	SHIFT LEFT LOGICAL DOUBLE, SHIFT RIGHT LOGICAL DOUBLE

Table 3-17 Logical Operations

BIT VALUES		LOGICAL OPERATION		
FIRST	SECOND	AND	OR	XOR
0	0	0	0	0
0	1	0	1	1
1	0	0	1	1
1	1	1	1	0

are performed on two operands of equal length on a bit-by-bit basis. The rules for the operations are given in Table 3-17.

The boolean instructions are available in RR, RX, SI, and SS formats. In the RR format {R1} and {R2} are the operands, and the operation is done on two 32-bit words. In the RX format, {R1} is the first operand and the second operand is {{B2} + {X2} + D2}. The operation is done on two 32-bit words. In the SI format, the operation is done at a byte level. The first operand is a byte in storage having the address {B1} + D1, and the second operand is immediate data in the I2 field. In the SS format, the operands are two byte strings having identical lengths. The operands can overlap. If they do, the result appears as though the operation was done for each byte and immediately stored. The result of the operation is stored at the location of the first operand. The condition code has two values, a 0 indicating that the operation has resulted in all zeros, and a 1 indicating that the result contains at least 1.

The shift logical instructions have the same format as the shift instructions discussed under binary arithmetic operations. The difference between the two is that the operand to be shifted is no longer viewed as a binary integer. All bits (including the sign bit, i.e., bit zero) participate in the shift operation. Zeros are supplied to the vacated bit positions.

The TEST UNDER MASK instruction is used for testing whether or not one or more bits of a byte in storage are ones. This is in the SI format and I field contains a one-byte mask. A mask bit of one indicates that the corresponding bit of the byte in storage is to be tested. If all the bits thus tested are 0, a condition code of 0 is set. When all the bits thus tested are 1, a condition code of 3 is set. Otherwise (in case of mixed results), the condition code is set to 1. Thus, if a mask bit pattern is "00000001," and the byte in storage contains a 1 in the rightmost position the condition code will be set to 3. If the byte contains a 0 in the rightmost position, the condition code will be set to 0.

3.5.8 Branch Instructions

As mentioned previously, the instructions in a program are normally executed under the assumption that they occupy successive locations in storage. Under this sequence, the next instruction occupies the storage locations succeeding the current instruction. The address field of the PSW contains the address of the next instruction, which is obtained by adding the length of the current instruction in bytes to the address of the current instruction.

A branch instruction can change the preceding sequence by substituting a branch address in the PSW address field. There are two types of branch instructions, namely:

• Conditional branch
• Unconditional branch

A conditional branch performs the branching operation only if certain conditions are satisfied. If the conditions are not satisfied, branching does not take place and the instruction at the succeeding storage location is executed. The instructions BRANCH ON CONDITION, BRANCH ON COUNT, BRANCH ON INDEX HIGH, and BRANCH ON INDEX LOW OR EQUAL are of this type (Table 3-18). In executing these instructions, the following steps are observed:

Table 3-18 Branch Instructions

INSTRUCTION	MNEMONIC	FORMAT
BRANCH ON CONDITION	BCR	RR
BRANCH ON CONDITION	BC	RX
BRANCH AND LINK	BALR	RR
BRANCH AND LINK	BAL	RX
BRANCH ON COUNT	BCTR	RR
BRANCH ON COUNT	BCT	RX
BRANCH ON INDEX HIGH	BXH	RS
BRANCH ON INDEX LOW OR EQUAL	BXLE	RS

- The branch address is generated first. If the instruction is in the RR format, R2 contains the branch address. If R2 is zero, no branch is taken. If the instruction is in the RX format, the branch address is obtained by adding {B2}, {X2} and D2 if X2 is not zero. If X2 is zero, then the address is obtained by adding {B2} to D2.
- An operation such as incrementing {R1} is performed for BRANCH ON COUNT.
- The occurrence of the specified condition is verified, and if the condition has occurred, the branch address is placed in the PSW address field and the branch is taken.

An unconditional branch instruction generates the branch address, places the branch address in the PSW address field, and the instruction at the branch address is executed next. The instruction BRANCH AND LINK is of this type.

The BRANCH ON CONDITION instruction is in both RR and RX formats. The R1 field (bits 8–11) does not denote a register but a 4-bit mask M1. The branch address is generated from the second operand using the rules described earlier. The mask bit positions specify one or more condition code settings that cause branching. In other words, the mask field is viewed as 4-bit unsigned binary integer and specific values correspond to condition code settings, as shown in Table 3-19.

Thus, if the M1 field contains 8, a branch is taken if condition code is zero. If a branch is to be taken when a condition code has a value that is one of a set of values, the value of M1 should be the sum of the appropriate values shown in Table 3-19. Thus, when the value for M1 is 13, it means that a branch is taken if the condition code is 0 or 1 or 3. A value of 15 for M1 indicates that an unconditional branch is to be taken.

The BRANCH ON COUNT instructions cause a branch to be taken if {R1} - 1 is not equal to zero. The steps associated with this instruction are the following:

Table 3-19 Four-Bit Mask

VALUE OF M1	CONDITION CODE	MASK BIT ON
8	0	8
4	1	9
2	2	10
1	3	11

• The branch address is generated.
• {R1} is decremented by one.
• The branch is taken if {R1} is not equal to zero.
The BRANCH ON COUNT instructions are often used in looping.

The BRANCH ON INDEX HIGH (and BRANCH ON INDEX LOW OR EQUAL) instructions cause a branch to be taken when {R1} + {R3} is greater than (less or equal to) {R3} or {R3 + 1}, depending on whether R3 is odd or even.
The steps associated with BRANCH ON INDEX HIGH instructions are the following:

• The branch address is generated.
• {R1} is incremented by {R3} (i.e., {R1} = {R1} + {R3}).
• If R3 is even, the branch is taken if {R1} > {R3 + 1}.
• If R3 is odd, the branch is taken if {R1} > {R3}.

These instructions are useful in indexing in connection with arrays or tables.
The BRANCH AND LINK instructions store the rightmost word of the PSW in R1 and then branch to the address (which is {R2} or {X2} + {B2} + D2). The rightmost word of the PSW stored in R1 contains the following "link" information:

• Instruction length code
• Condition code
• Program mask
• Instruction address (of the next serial instruction)

These instructions are used in connection with subroutine calls. The main program places the address of the subroutine in R2 (assuming that the RR format is used) and executes the BRANCH AND LINK instruction. The subroutine saves the link information. After execution, it returns to the calling program by unconditionally branching to the instruction address contained in the link information.

3.5.9 Miscellaneous Instructions

In this section we discuss various instructions that perform functions that are useful and, in some cases, essential from a programmers point of view.

The SUPERVISORY CALL instruction (SVC) is used for requesting the supervisor to perform a service, such as an I/O operation. The supervisor is run in a privileged state; thus it can issue privileged instructions, such as a START I/O. The instruction is in the RR format, but the eight bits used for the R1 and R2 fields are interpreted as an unsigned binary integer ranging from 0 to 255. This number is used by the supervisor to execute the appropriate supervisory routine. This instruction causes an SVC interruption, which causes control to be passed to the supervisor.

The LOAD ADDRESS instruction loads a register with an address specified as part of the instruction. It is in the RX format. Register R1 is loaded with an address obtained as {X2} + {B2} + D2. The first eight bits of R1 are set to zero. X2 or B2 cannot have the value zero.

The TRANSLATE instruction can translate a character string from one encoded representation to another. A practical use is in converting a character string from EBCDIC to ASCII, or vice versa. Assume that it is desired to translate from EBCDIC to ASCII. An array of 256 bytes (corresponding to the 256 EBCDIC codes) is defined. The ith byte in this array contains the ASCII code for the ith EBCDIC representation; i.e., the EBCDIC representation that has the binary value i. The TRANSLATE instruction is in the SS format. The L field contains the length of the character string to be translated; its address is given as {B1} + D1. The abovementioned array is located at {B2} + D2.

3.5.10 Privileged Instructions

The instructions under this group are the following:

- I/O instructions
- Instructions for setting and inserting a storage key
- Instructions for loading the entire PSW (LOAD PSW), or fields of the PSW (e.g., program mask, system mask)
- An interlocking instruction (TEST AND SET)
- Instructions for reading or writing direct signals (READ DIRECT, WRITE DIRECT).

The I/O instructions have been described under the I/O architecture. The instructions for setting and inserting storage keys have been described under storage architecture. The instructions that load or modify the PSW are the following:

- LOAD PSW
- SET PROGRAM MASK
- SET SYSTEM MASK.

The LOAD PSW instruction is in the SI format. The I2 field (the immediate data field) is ignored. The PSW is loaded with the contents of the doubleword specified by {B1} + D1. The SET PROGRAM MASK is in the RR format. Bits 2–7 of register R1 replace the condition code and the program mask of the PSW. The R2 field is ignored. The SET SYSTEM MASK is in the SI format. The immediate data field is ignored and the byte at location {B1} + D1 replaces the system mask field.

The TEST AND SET instruction is in the SI format and performs two operations:

- The byte at location {B1} + D1 is tested to see if its leftmost bit is zero or one, and the condition code is set to "0" or "1" accordingly.
- The byte is set to all ones. The byte is not allowed to be accessed until both operations are complete.

This instruction is used for testing common storage areas used by more than one program, in a multiprogramming environment.

3.6 PRINCIPLES OF PROGRAM EXECUTION

The 360 Principles of Operation [1] and related publications such as Mealy [4] assume that an operating system is an integral part of the architecture. The following quotation, taken from [4], is worthy of attention:

"In the notion of an 'extended machine,' a computing system is viewed as being composed of a number of layers, like an onion. Few programmers deal with the innermost layer, which is that provided by the hardware itself. A FORTRAN programmer, for instance, deals with an outer layer defined by the FORTRAN language. To a large extent, he acts as though he were dealing with hardware that accepted and executed FORTRAN statements directly. The SYSTEM/360 instruction set represents two inner layers, one when operating in the supervisor state, another when operating in the problem state.

The supervisor state is employed by OS/360 for the supervisor portion of the control program. Because all other programs operate in the problem state and must rely upon unprivileged instructions, they use system macroinstructions for invoking the supervisor. These macroinstructions gain the attention of the supervisor by means of SVC, the supervisor-call instruction.

All OS/360 programs with the exception of the supervisor operate in the problem state. In fact, one of the fundamental design tenets is that these programs (compilers, sorts, or the like) are, to all intents and purposes, problem programs and must be treated as such by the supervisor. Precisely the same set of facilities is offered to system and problem programs. At any point in time, the system consists of its given supervisor plus all programs that are available in on-line storage. Inasmuch as an installation may introduce new compilers, payroll programs, etc., the extended machine may grow."

The 360 architecture lays down certain rules in regard to the instructions and data that comprise a program. These rules are summarized:

- Instructions should be those contained in the instruction set. An operation exception occurs when the CPU decodes an instruction not in the instruction set.
- Instructions are one, two, or three halfwords in length. The op code is so designed that its first two bits indicate the length of the instruction (e.g., 00, 01, and 10 indicate lengths of 1, 2, and 3 halfwords).
- Addresses are specified using 24 bits. The maximum addressable storage location is 16,777,215. Arithmetic used in address generation (e.g., addition of contents of base or index registers to the displacement) treats addresses as unsigned 24-bit binary integers. If the arithmetic results in overflow, the resultant 24 bits denote the address, i.e., a "wraparound" takes place.
- Instructions are normally executed in a conceptual sequence, based on the ascending sequence in which they appear in storage. Thus, it is possible to modify an instruction in storage by means of the immediately preceding instruction. This sequential execution may not be followed after the execution of a branch instruction. An SVC instruction and all interruptions also change the instruction sequence and cause the machine to branch to appropriate routines.

• Improper specification of data (as in the case of decimals) results in a data specification error and causes a program interruption. The appropriate interruption-handling routine performs the necessary action, such as terminating the program or notifying the programmer.

The 360 was intended to run batch programs concurrently. Main storage was partitioned among these programs. The programs were swapped in and out of storage based on various utilization criteria.

3.7 LIMITATIONS OF THE 360 ARCHITECTURE

Perhaps the severest critics of the 360 architecture are various groups within IBM, especially the group of researchers in the 801 project who have been pioneers in reduced instruction set computer (RISC) architecture. The comments in this paragraph have been influenced by the illuminating analysis of Radin [5] and Hopkins [6]. The work of Myers [7] also throws light on the many shortcomings of the 360 and 370 machines.

The 360 architecture can be characterized along the following lines:

1. It is a register-oriented architecture.
2. It is a complex instruction set computer (CISC) architecture.
3. Its instruction set is meant for an assembly language programmer.
4. Its commercial and scientific instruction sets are not integrated.
5. It is a uniprocessor architecture.
6. It is a real storage architecture.

Each of the foregoing characterizations carries with it a set of drawbacks, which will be elaborated upon by us. The limitations of items 5 and 6 are described in detail in the next two chapters. Here we shall discuss only items 1–4.

By a register-oriented architecture is meant an architecture that attaches undue importance to and specifies extensive usage of registers in the instruction set. The motivation for emphasizing the use of registers is that from a price/performance point of view registers provide optimization of instruction execution. Unfortunately, the use of registers cause a number of problems. First of all, the binary operations are implemented in such a way that the first argument is destroyed. Thus, the instruction ADD R1, R2 replaces the contents of R1 with the sum of the contents of R1 and R2. The motivation is to avoid a fetch and also to save the space needed for specifying a third operand, as in ADD R1, R2, R3, where R3 contains the sum of R1 and R2. The consequence of the destruction of the first operand is that it has to be saved prior to execution (in the case of multiplication, two registers have to be saved).

The second drawback with the use of registers in the 360 is the arbitrariness of specifications. We have seen a number of instances where arguments are not specified using a set of general rules but on an ad hoc basis. The following is a partial list of such instructions:

- The MULTIPLY instruction does not specify the first operand directly. The instruction MR 4, 8 multiplies the contents of register 5 with those of register 8 and places the 64-bit product in registers 4 and 5.
- A field in RR instruction normally refers to a register number. In the case of the BRANCH ON CONDITION (BCR) instruction, which is in RR format, the R1 field is a data value (i.e., the value of the condition code). In the case of the SUPERVISORY CALL (SVC) instruction, both R1 and R2 fields are data values.
- In shift instructions, the second operand, namely, D2(B2), is used to indicate the number of bits to be shifted. Normally, D2(B2) specifies an address given as {B2} + D2 and the second operand is located at this address. In the case of the shift instructions, the lower order six bits of {B2} + D2 indicate the number of bits to be shifted.
- The LOAD ADDRESS instruction is in the RX format. Normally, the second operation is located at {X2} + {B2} + D2. However, in the LOAD ADDRESS instruction, the second operand is {X2} + {B2} + D2 itself.

A third drawback has to do with the use of registers in subroutines. The BRANCH AND LINK instructions require that the link information (the address of the next instruction if the branch has not been taken) be stored in a register. This means, in languages that use procedure calls heavily (such as "C"), registers have to be dedicated to storing link information or have to be copied to storage and loaded subsequently. Of the 16 registers that are available, one or two are needed for addressability, one is needed for link information, and this leaves 13 to 14 for use. Fixed-point arithmetic, logical operations, and data movement operations require the use of registers (they are mostly in RR and RX formats). Thus, there is contention for the use of registers that can be resolved only by moving their contents into and back from main storage, which requires overhead.

A complex instruction set computer (CISC) provides instructions for performing complex functions, usually to benefit an assembly language programmer. A complex instruction set computer provides instructions that are implementable in terms of simpler instructions provided in the architecture. The rationale for specifying a complex instruction in the architecture is the following:

• The programmer does not have to code the set of instructions that correspond to the complex instruction. Hence, there is saving in space.
• The complex instruction is implemented in microcode or in hardware. In either case, the execution is faster than it would be if the set of instructions corresponding to the complex instruction was executed.

The price that has to be paid for implementing complex instructions is in the increased storage requirements for microcode and also in the logic complexity of the machine. Complex instructions may impede the performance of primitives on account of the logical circuit overhead needed for instruction decoding [5]. These instructions reside in high-speed control storage even though they may be rarely used, whereas many sections of code that are frequently used, such as the dispatcher and interrupt handlers, reside in main storage (or in the cache) [5], [6].

The 360 instruction set is meant for use by an assembly language programmer. According to the 360 architects, "When we did the 360, we had to assume that a significant fraction of the programming was going to be in assembly language. Today you might begin by dispensing with a rational human-engineered interface at the assembly language instruction level [8]." The fact of the matter is that a significant fraction of programming in today's world is done in higher-level languages. A study of commonly used instructions as found in several representative job mixes was done by the 801 project [16]. The ten most frequently used instructions and their frequency are shown below:

1. BRANCH ON CONDITION	(BC)	20.16%
2. LOAD	(L)	15.49%
3. TEST UNDER MASK	(TM)	6.06%

4. STORE	(ST)	5.88%
5. LOAD	(LR)	4.70%
6. LOAD ADDRESS	(LA)	4.06%
7. LOAD AND TEST REGISTER	(LTR)	3.78%
8. BRANCH ON CONDITION	(BCR)	2.69%
9. MOVE CHARACTER	(MVC)	2.10%
10. LOAD HALFWORD	(LH)	1.88%

These instructions add up to two-thirds of all instructions executed. These results raise fundamental questions about the use of the instruction set by high-level language compilers, such as the following:

• What instructions should an instruction set provide?
• How should the instructions be defined or specified?

The study quoted above [6] was done in the context of the design of a RISC computer, and the recommendations are for reducing the size of instruction set. For example, there are a number of binary instructions that have one operand in a register and the other in storage. These instructions consist of two basic functions, namely, fetching an operand from storage and performing an arithmetical or logical operation on two operands. Should these basic functions be combined to form new instructions, considering that the frequency of usage is less than 6.5 percent [6]?

The other issue has to do with the so-called "semantic gap," — the semantical difference between assembly language and high-level language constructs. Myers [7] gives a number of examples of a mismatch between an assembly language instruction and the corresponding high-level language construct. One example is that of the BRANCH AND LINK instruction, which is supposed to help in making procedure calls. As pointed out by Myers, this instruction does very little in providing that kind of support in procedure invocation in high-level languages.

The 360 does not integrate decimal, binary, and floating-point instructions in its instruction set. There are separate arithmetic instructions for each type (e.g., binary, decimal, floating point) and for each subtype within a type (e.g., halfword, fullword , etc. under binary arithmetic). Thus, there are 15 instructions each for addition and subtraction, 11 instructions for multiplication, and 7 for division. Contrast this with the approach taken in the instruction set of the System 38, where an instruction is composed of a generic part and a type. Thus, decimal addition is performed by the generic ADD instruction, with type set to "decimal."

Many more comments in this vein are offered in Chapter 15 of this book.

REFERENCES

1. IBM System/360 Principles of Operation, Order No. GA 22-6821.
2. IBM System/370 Principles of Operation, Order No. GA 22-7000.
3. IBM System/370 XA Principles of Operation, Publication No. SA 22-7085.
4. Mealy, G.H.: "The Functional Structure of OS/360," *IBM Systems Journal*, vol. 5, no. 1, 1966.
5. Radin, G.: "The 801 Minicomputer," *IBM Journal of Research and Development*, vol. 27, no. 3, May 1983.
6. Hopkins, M.E.: "A Perspective on the 801/Reduced Instruction Set Computer," *IBM Systems Journal*, vol. 26, no. 1, 1987.
7. Myers, G.: *Advances in Computer Architecture,* John Wiley & Sons, 1982.
8. Gifford, D. and A. Spector: "Case Study: IBM's System/360-370 Architecture," *Communications of the ACM*, vol. 30, no. 4, 1987. (This is a transcript of an interview with Richard Case and Andris Padegs.)

ADDITIONAL READING

The following articles by the architects of the System 360 give an overview of the architecture:

Amdahl, G.M., G.A. Blaauw, and F.P. Brooks: "Architecture of the IBM System/360," *IBM Journal of Research and Development*, vol. 8, no. 2, April 1964.

Amdahl, G.M., et al.: "The Structure of the System 360," *IBM Systems Journal*, vol. 3, no. 2, 1964.

For more recent views on the 360 and 370 architectures, see the following:

Evans, B.O.: "System/360: A Retrospective View," *Annals of the History of Computing*, vol. 8, no. 2, April 1986.

4

370 Architecture

The 370 architecture is evolutionary in the sense that it was based on IBM's experience with the 360 architecture for about a decade. This experience showed that the storage architecture of the 360 had to be drastically changed in order to function in an on-line multi-programming environment. The 370 architecture introduced the concept of virtual storage, and this resulted in changes to the overall 360 architecture. Another concept introduced in the 370 architecture was that of multiprocessing, under which the conceptual machine is composed of one or more central processing units running under a single operating system and sharing a common memory. Such sharing necessitates the mapping of memory using different sequential numbering schemes for each CPU, instructions for communication among CPUs and instructions that cause interlocking of words and doublewords. All of these are provided in the 370 architecture.

4.1 MOTIVATION FOR THE 370 ARCHITECTURE

The 370 architecture is viewed by its architects as an extension of the 360 architecture, necessitated by technological growth as well as by the demands made by operating system concepts (Case and Padegs [4]). Technological growth made it possible to have cheaper and faster main storage, but the 24-bit addressing scheme used in the 360 architecture made it impossible to go beyond the limit of 16 MB for memory. The 370 architecture, however, did not change the 24-bit addressing scheme, mainly because "the operating systems and compiler-produced application programs had used the extra bits in address words for control purposes, and hence required extensive modifications." [4] It was not until the advent of the 370/XA architecture that the 24-bit addressing was changed to 31-bit addressing. The evolution in multiprogramming operating systems concepts needed virtual storage for their implementation. This was provided by the 370 architecture and is probably the most significant distinction between the 360 and 370 architectures.

One may regard the 370 architecture as an interim architecture between the 360 and the 370/XA. The 370/XA is truly more of a revision of the 360 architecture in the sense that not only was the addressing extended to 31 bits but also the concepts of true multiprocessing and of an I/O processor separate from CPUs were incorporated in that architecture.

4.2 EXTENSIONS MADE TO THE 360 ARCHITECTURE THAT RESULTED IN THE 370 ARCHITECTURE

The extensions to the 360 architecture that resulted in the 370 architecture are broken down under CPU, storage and I/O.

CPU

The 370 CPU retains the essential features of the 360 CPU such as the sixteen 32-bit general registers, the Program Status Word (PSW), the instruction set, and the methodology for handling interruptions. The 370 architecture is compatible with the 360 architecture in the sense that a program written for a 360 computer produces the same result when run on a 370 computer. This compatibility is achieved by providing two modes of operation, namely, the 360 mode and the 370 mode.

New instructions have been added for serialization (e.g., COMPARE AND SWAP) and also for compatibility with PL/1 and other languages (e.g., COMPARE LOGICAL LONG, MOVE LONG). The PSW format has been changed. Additional registers called control registers have been introduced, primarily for use by the operating system and also for implementing the virtual storage concept. A new class of interruption (RESTART) has been introduced. Extensive features have been introduced for debugging (PROGRAM EVENT RECORDING) and for monitoring (MONITOR CALL). A new instruction (SIGNAL PROCESSOR) has been provided for multiprocessing.

Storage

There are three main 370 architectural concepts pertaining to storage: main storage, real storage, and virtual storage.

The 370 uses the same main storage organization as the 360. Thus, the lowest addressable unit of data is a byte. Bytes are grouped into halfwords, fullwords, and doublewords. Binary, decimal and character data are represented using the same conventions described under the 360 architecture.

The view of main storage as seen by each CPU is called real storage. Each CPU uses a different addressing scheme for accessing main storage. The address used by a CPU internally in referring to a byte location in main storage is called a real address. In order to access main storage, the real address has to be converted to a main storage address (called an absolute address).

Virtual storage is used by programs instead of real storage and the translation of a virtual to a real address is accomplished by hardware. This is called the Dynamic Address Translation (DAT) capability. As a consequence, it has been necessary to divide main storage into page frames (2K or 4K bytes in size). For the sake of efficiency, it is necessary to keep translated addresses and to know whether or not a page frame is being used by a program. Hence, facilities have been incorporated for translation look-aside buffering (TLB) and for noting changes in the status of page frames.

I/O

The I/O structure is essentially the same as the 360 machine, but some changes have been made. The 370 introduces a block multiplexer channel that is like the selector channel in the sense that it can be used for transfer of blocks of data to disk or tape. However, unlike the selector channel, the block multiplexer channel does not have to remain connected to a device for the entire duration of an operation. Disk drives that have rotational position-sensing capability can disconnect from the channel during the SEEK operation. A new instruction called START I/O FAST RELEASE (SIOF) has been introduced to be used in conjunction with the block multiplexer channel.

The concept of virtual storage, also, has been extended to data transfer between main storage and device via a channel. The Dynamic Address Translation (DAT) facility is not used for this purpose. Instead, the channel-indirect-data-addressing (CIDA) facility is provided to assist the operating system in translating virtual storage addresses in channel programs to main storage locations.

4.3 COMPUTER ORGANIZATION

The organization of the System 370 conceptual machine is shown in Figure 4-1. It is similar to the 360 machine, except that multiple CPUs are allowed. The components of the System 370 are the following:

- CPU(s)
- Storage
- Channel(s)
- Control Unit(s)
- Device(s)

In the case of a single CPU machine (a uniprocessor), the interaction between the above components is similar to the 360 machine.

In the case of a machine with multiple CPUs (a multiprocessor), the CPUs share main storage in the sense that each CPU can access any location in main storage. Each CPU has its own set of channels (called the channel set of the CPU), and an I/O operation initiated by

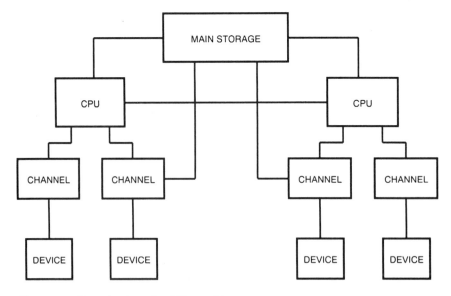

Figure 4-1 Organization of a 370 machine.

a CPU can be implemented only by a channel attached to that CPU. Also, an I/O interruption has to be handled by the CPU that initiated the I/O operation. These restrictions were subsequently removed in the 370/XA architecture.

4.4   CPU ARCHITECTURE

As in the case of the 360, the CPU fetches an instruction from main storage, decodes the instruction, fetches (if necessary) operands of the instruction from main storage, and executes the instruction. In the 360, an instruction was viewed as atomic in the sense that it is executed in its entirety without interruption. This is no longer the case, and the instructions MOVE LONG and COMPARE LONG whose operands are long character strings are interruptible at various points.

In the 360, instructions occupy contiguous locations in main storage. This is no longer true because of the introduction of virtual storage. Virtual storage is organized as one or more address spaces. An address space is a fictitious sequence of bytes numbered 0, 1, 2, ... N. This sequence of virtual addresses is used by a program. The PSW contains the address of the next sequential instruction in the address space of the program currently being executed (see Figure 4-2). This next sequential instruction is executed after the current instruction, except when the current instruction is a branch instruction or an interruption takes place. The branch instructions are similar to those specified in the 360 architecture. Interruption handling is conceptually similar to the 360 interruption handling, but there are differences at a detail level.

As in the 360, the 370 architecture distinguishes between two classes of programs, namely, the supervisor program and the problem program. Only the supervisor program can execute privileged instructions or use the control registers. The problem program can request the services of the supervisor program via the SVC instruction.

4.4.1   General Registers

As in the case of the 360, there are 16 general registers. Each register is a fullword in size. These registers are used as base and index registers in instructions and for the execution of binary, arithmetic, and logical operations, as in the case of the 360.

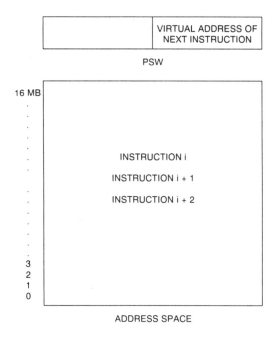

Figure 4-2 Program execution sequence.

4.4.2 Control Registers

Sixteen control registers are provided for internal use by the CPU (in address translation) as well as by the operating system. A control register has the same size as the general register. Separate instructions (LOAD CONTROL, STORE CONTROL) are provided for loading and storing these registers.

4.4.3 Dynamic Address Translation (DAT)

The CPU translates a virtual address into a real address before fetching an instruction or an operand from main storage. The translation is accomplished by a table look-up at two levels, as described later. Translation tables used for this purpose are kept in main storage. A translation look-aside buffer (TLB) that keeps the results of most recent translations is also part of the CPU. The TLB is a set of registers that enable the CPU to bypass main storage references to the translation tables 99 percent of the time [4], thus improving performance. The instruction PURGE TLB can be used to clear entries in the TLB.

The architecture provides the capability to suppress DAT, i.e., to use real addresses instead of virtual addresses. A bit in the PSW can be used to indicate that the DAT capability should be suppressed.

4.4.4   Program Status Word (PSW)

The PSW has two different formats depending on whether the basic control (BC) mode or extended control mode (EC) is used. The BC mode is used for providing IBM 360 compatibility. In this mode, the PSW has the 360 format. The EC mode is the native mode for the 370 architecture. Figure 4-3 shows the format of the PSW in the EC mode. The PSW contains the following information:

- Address of next instruction
- Mask bits for masking interruptions
- PSW key
- CPU states (problem, supervisor, stopped, operating)
- DAT on/off bit
- Condition code.

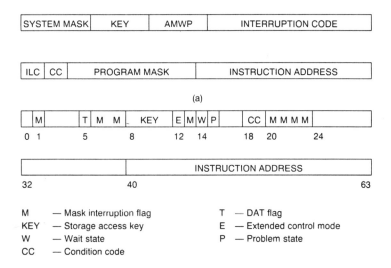

Figure 4-3 PSW format.

Address of the Next Instruction

As in the 360 architecture, the PSW contains the address of the next instruction to be executed. In the case of sequential execution, the PSW updates this instruction address by adding the instruction length to the current address. For example, if I is the virtual address of the current instruction, which has a length of K bytes, then the contents of the instruction address field of the PSW is I + K. In the case of a branch instruction, a branch address replaces the instruction address field of the PSW if a branch is taken by the program; if the branch is not taken, normal sequential instruction execution is performed and the PSW contains the address of the next instruction.

Interruption Action

The interruption action is similar to that specified in the 360 architecture. An interruption temporarily suspends the currently executing program, and the CPU starts executing a new program to process the interruption (i.e., interruption handler). The 370 architecture specifies the following PSW-related functions when an interruption is accepted by the CPU (assuming that the CPU is enabled to accept the interruption):

1. Save the current PSW by storing its contents in a pre-assigned real storage location.
2. Load the PSW with the contents of a pre-assigned real storage location.

The PSW that is loaded contains the address of the interruption handler. The status of an interrupted program is saved by storing the PSW and general registers.

Masking Bits

Masking bits can disable interruptions from certain sources. For instance, if bit 6 is off, the CPU is disabled for all I/O interruptions; when bit 6 is on, interruptions are allowed from those channels whose corresponding masking bits are in Control Register 2.

Storage Protection

The PSW key is used in conjunction with storage protection. Main storage is protected from unauthorized use; for a storage access to be successful, the PSW key should match a storage key, as in the 360 architecture.

States of the CPU

The CPU is put in a wait state if bit 14 of the PSW is set to one. Usually the CPU is put in a wait state by the operating system dispatcher when the queue of tasks is empty, meaning there is no work to be performed by the CPU. This can happen because application or system programs that are being executed are waiting for the completion of I/O operations, and as soon as an interruption occurs, the CPU is put back into the running state by setting bit 14 of the PSW to zero. In the wait state there is no instruction execution, but an interruption is processed in the usual manner and the processor changes its state from wait to running after an interruption.

When the CPU is in the running state, it can be either in the problem state or supervisor state (bit 15 of the PSW is set to one or zero). In the problem state the CPU executes only a subset of its instructions, but in the supervisor state it can execute all instructions.

Condition Code

As in the 360, the execution of certain instructions can cause a condition code to be set. The condition code field is two bits long and values 0–3 are used for specifying conditions, as in the 360 architecture. The branch on condition instructions can be used to branch to a new instruction based on the setting of the condition code.

4.4.5 Interruptions

Interruptions are grouped into six classes, namely I/O, external, program, supervisor call, machine check and restart. On interruption, the hardware stores the old PSW and loads a new PSW (see Figure 4-4). For each class, there are two locations in real storage, which correspond to the old and new PSWs.

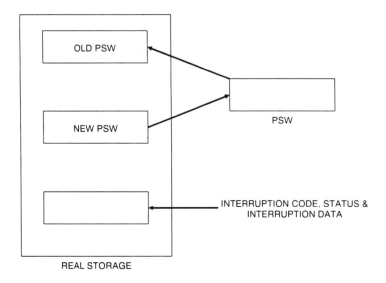

Figure 4-4 Hardware interruption action.

Table 4-1 Classes of Interruptions

CLASS	SOURCE OF INTERRUPTION	EVENT CAUSING INTERRUPTION
I/O	CHANNEL	COMPLETION OF I/O OPERATION, I/O EVENTS, I/O ERRORS
EXTERNAL	TIMER EXTERNAL SIGNAL	TIMER EXPIRATION SIGNAL SENSING
SVC	PROGRAM	SVC INSTRUCTION
PROGRAM	PROGRAM	EXCEPTION
MACHINE CHECK	HARDWARE	HARDWARE ERROR
RESTART	RESTART KEY	PRESSING RESTART KEY

We shall discuss next the various classes of interruptions and the specific actions performed in each case. Table 4-1 shows the source of the interruption and the events causing the interruption for each of the six classes.

I/O Interruption

The source of an I/O interruption is a channel. During the course of an I/O operation a channel may interrupt the CPU several times. A detailed discussion of I/O interruption is given later in this chapter.

External Interruption

The sources of external interruption can be grouped into four classes: clocks, timers, another CPU, and sources connected to signal lines. In each of these case, the old PSW is stored at location 24, a new PSW is loaded from location 88, and the source of the interruption is stored in locations 134 and 135.

CLOCKS. The 370 architecture provides for a time-of-day (TOD) clock and a clock comparator. The TOD clock is sharable by CPUs in a multiprocessing environment, but each CPU has its own clock comparator. The TOD clock's resolution varies from model to model, depending on the cycle time of the CPU. Its function is to provide a standard reference time for use by programs. It is usually set to a standard time origin, namely, January 1, 1900, 00:00 A.M. Greenwich mean time (GMT). The clock is essentially a binary counter having 64 bits and a cycle of approximately 143 years.

The clock comparator is used to preset a time value that is compared against the TOD clock time. When the latter exceeds the former, an external interruption is generated. The clock comparator is a binary counter similar to the TOD clock, and its resolution varies according to the model. The clock comparator can be used for setting time thresholds that trigger the execution of specified programs.

TIMERS. The 370 architecture provides for two types of timers — a CPU timer and an interval timer. The CPU timer is a binary counter having the same format as the TOD clock. Its functions are

1. To measure the elapsed CPU time.
2. To generate an interrupt at the end of a specified CPU elapsed time interval.

The uses of the CPU timer are to measure CPU execution intervals for accounting and other purposes, to indicate the end of a specified time interval on the CPU.

An interval timer provides the same functions as the CPU timer, except that its resolution is coarser.

SIGNALS FROM ANOTHER CPU. In a multiprocessing environment, signals generated by one CPU to another CPU cause the latter to be interrupted. The section on multiprocessing gives additional details on this topic.

EXTERNAL SIGNALS. The architecture provides for a direct control feature that comprises an external signal facility and a read-write-direct facility. The purpose of this feature is to provide single byte data transfer capabilities independent of those provided by channels.

Supervisor Call (SVC) Interruption

As in the 360, the supervisor call (SVC) is the only means whereby a program can invoke the services of the operating system for performing an I/O operation, obtaining virtual storage, passing control to another program, and several other such functions. The SVC instruction specifies a numerical identification code. Eight bits are provided for this parameter, which means that 256 SVC functions are allowed.

The execution of the SVC instruction causes an interruption and the hardware stores the old PSW in location 32, loads a new PSW from location 96, and stores in locations 138 and 139 the interruption code. The new PSW contains the address of the operating system routine for SVC handling. The SVC handling routine performs the functions required by the requesting program by invoking other operating system routines, and after completion of such functions, returns control to the program that issued the SVC.

Program Interruption

A program interruption is caused by an error or abnormal condition arising from the execution of an instruction in a program. It is the function of the interruption handler to determine whether or not the error or condition is resolvable and to take appropriate action.

The hardware places the old PSW in location 40, loads the new PSW from location 104 and stores an interruption code that identifies the cause of the interruption in locations 142 and 143.

We refer to the events that cause a program interruption in the 360 architecture as described in Chapter 3. These are applicable to the 370 architecture also. In addition, the following events unique to the 370 architecture will cause a program interruption.

PAGE TRANSLATION EXCEPTION. During dynamic address translation the address of a real page frame corresponding to a virtual page is obtained from the Page Table. If the Page Table shows that there is no real page frame entry corresponding to the virtual page, a page translation exception (also known as page fault) is recognized by hardware. This condition triggers a program interruption. The program interruption handler passes control to appropriate operating system modules that assign a page frame to the page and perform a page-in operation.

SEGMENT TRANSLATION EXCEPTION. During dynamic address translation, the segment table is referred to in the process of converting a virtual address to a real address. If a segment portion of the virtual address is not in the segment table, an exception is recognized by hardware. This condition causes an interruption.

TRANSLATION SPECIFICATION EXCEPTION. A translation specification is recognized when the data in control register 1, Segment Table or Page Table does not contain data in the format specified by the architecture. For example, bits 13 and 14 of a Page Table entry should be zero and if there is not the case, a translation specification exception is recognized. This evolution causes an interruption.

Machine Check Interruption

As in the 360, a machine check interruption is caused by failure of a hardware component, which may be a channel, CPU or storage. The 370 architecture provides a more elaborate anlysis of machine checks.

The interruption stores the old PSW in location 48, copies the new PSW from location 112, saves registers and stores an 8-byte machine check interruption or code (MCIC) in locations 232–239. In certain cases, logout information is stored in specified storage locations.

A hardware error is called exigent when it is nonrecoverable; it is called repressible when recoverable. Error detection is provided by the addition of redundant check bits (parity bits) in program data, by having redundant circuits and by timeouts for I/O instruction and I/O interruption. Many processors (e.g., 3033) have main storage units that contain error checking and correction (ECC) hardware that detect and rectify single-bit errors. (In the case of multiple-bit errors, only detection capability is provided.) Also, some processors (e.g., 3033) have "instruction retry" capability, under which an instruction is re-executed if there is an error. In order to do this, it is necessary to save the state of a machine at checkpoints. These checkpoints can be taken at the beginning of an instruction. The MCIC has bit settings to indicate the source or type of hardware error. Some of these codes are described below.

INSTRUCTION PROCESSING DAMAGE. This is an exigent machine check condition and indicates that the CPU must discontinue its operation. It can have various causes such as malfunction in dynamic address translation, an unretryable processor error, etc.

STORAGE ERRORS. Storage errors can be due to errors in storage keys or errors in main storage. Some of the storage errors are repressible (e.g., the 3033 can self-correct a single-bit processor storage error by means of its error-checking and correction capabilities). Other errors are exigent (e.g., a multiple-bit error in processor storage in the 3033).

SYSTEM RECOVERY. This subclass of errors is repressible and indicates that malfunctions have been detected and corrected (e.g., a single-bit storage error mentioned above or a similar malfunction that is correctable).

DEGRADATION. The definition of degradation is model-dependent. For instance, in the case of the 3033, an error that results in the deletion of a row in the cache or an error that causes a deletion of one-half of the TLB is viewed as degradation, and is treated as a repressible error.

Restart Interruption

The restart interruption occurs as a result of the manual activation of the restart key or by another CPU in a multiprocessing environment issuing a restart order.

The restart interruption causes the current PSW to be stored at location 8 and copies a new PSW from location 0. The new PSW contains the address of the appropriate interruption handler routine that performs necessary functions.

Point of Interruption

The CPU is normally allowed to complete the execution of an instruction before it accepts an interruption, but in the case of two instructions that involve movement of long data strings (namely COMPARE LOGICAL LONG and MOVE LONG), an interruption is permitted when the instruction is in a stage of partial completion. With the exception of the two previously mentioned instructions, all other instructions are non-interruptible. The term "unit of operation" is used to describe a non-interruptible quantum of work done by the processor in instruction execution. The two interruptible instructions consist of multiple units of operation, and the CPU accepts interruptions in between units of operations. All other instructions are executed as one unit of operation.

Enabling and Disabling

Certain interruption classes can be masked by setting mask bits in the PSW and control registers. When a mask bit is one, the CPU is enabled for a class of interruption; i.e., the interruption is accepted by the CPU, and the hardware performs all functions associated with the handling of the interruption. When the mask bit is zero, the interruption is kept pending until the mask bit is set to one except in the case of certain machine check interruptions, which are either ignored or cause the CPU to enter the check-stop state. The CPU is said to be in a disabled state when the mask bit is zero, and the interruption is said to be pending if it is handled after enablement.

The CPU can be disabled for external, I/O and machine check interruptions. It cannot be disabled for SVC and restart interruptions; in regard to program interruptions, certain subclasses can be disabled by setting mask bits (e.g., overflows in fixed-point and decimal arithmetic operations).

Priority of Interruptions

During the execution of a unit of operation (an instruction or a part of an interruptible instruction) several interruption conditions can take place. For example, an instruction may cause SVC and machine check interruptions; also, an I/O or external interruption may be waiting to be accepted after the execution of the instruction. The architecture specifies a priority in which multiple interruptions are presented to the processor.

An exigent machine check interruption is assigned the highest priority. Owing to the nature of this interruption, the acceptance of subsequent interruptions depends on the severity of the hardware error. The priority of presentation of the remaining interruptions is as follows:

- SVC
- Program
- Repressible machine check
- External
- I/O
- Restart

The hardware accepts an SVC interruption first, program interruption next, and so forth. The operating system's interruption handler can change, by means of disabling, the actual order of presentation of concurrent interruption requests in certain cases.

4.4.6   Serialization, Synchronization, and Interlock

The execution of a single instruction on a uniprocessor consists of a series of discrete steps (e.g., instruction fetching, decoding, operand fetching, instruction execution). In a multiprogramming or multiprocessing environment, conflicts can arise because of overlapped accesses to storage during instruction execution by the various CPUs.

"In a multiprocessing system, the results of all communication between CPUs through main storage are based on the actual storage accesses. When these accesses are observed by another processor, they may differ from the expected operation in the following ways:

1. A single instruction may make a number of distinct accesses to main storage and accesses associated with single instructions may be interleaved by CPUs.
2. The accesses due to a single instruction and due to any two instructions are not necessarily performed in the specified order.
3. Accesses within a field such as for an instruction or an operand may be made piecemeal.

4. Multiple accesses may be made to a storage location for a single use of its contents.

Results become unpredictable and the conventions of a uniprocessor communications protocol become inadequate when one CPU is changing the contents of a common storage while the other is observing it, or when both CPUs are updating the contents of the location at the same time." [4]

The 370 architecture requires serialization by a CPU on interruption, or after the execution of certain instructions (e.g., all I/O instructions, COMPARE AND SWAP, LOAD PSW, etc.). A serialization consists in completing all conceptually prior accesses to storage by the CPU as observed by other users of storage such as channels or another CPU.

The architecture also specifies that certain storage accesses done by the CPU should be performed synchronously, i.e., bytes should not be accessed in a piecemeal manner, but all at once or concurrently. Examples are the fetching of entries in the segment and page tables discussed under dynamic address translation (DAT). The architecture states that all bytes in an entry should be fetched concurrently, to prevent one CPU from changing entries in the table while another CPU is using it.

Interlocking refers to the exclusive access to a byte, word or doubleword in storage to one CPU (among several CPUs) during the execution of an instruction that reads and subsequently modifies the storage location. Channels are not locked out and can read or write to the interlocked location. The instructions COMPARE AND SWAP, COMPARE AND DOUBLE SWAP, TEST AND SET cause interlocks. In COMPARE AND SWAP, a word in storage is compared to a word in register R1. If the two words are the same, a third operand from register R3 is stored into the same location in storage. One of the uses of the instruction is in implementing software locks by the operating system.

4.5 STORAGE ARCHITECTURE

The 370 architecture defines three types of storage, namely absolute storage, virtual storage and real storage. It also defines five types of addresses, namely absolute, virtual, real, logical and effective.

4.5.1 Absolute Storage

Main storage as defined in the 360 is called absolute storage. The organization of absolute storage is identical to the organization of main storage in the 360. Absolute storage is organized into bytes, halfwords, fullwords, and doublewords. The bytes are numbered as 0, 1, 2, ... An absolute address is the number associated with a byte in absolute storage and is also known as the location of a byte in absolute storage. The maximum absolute address specified in the architecture is 16 M.

4.5.2 Real Storage

Real storage is the same as absolute storage in a uniprocessor configuration. In a multiprocessor configuration, each CPU requires the first 4K locations of main storage for its exclusive usage (e.g., storing PSWs, machine check, save areas, etc.). Clearly, it is impossible to assign the first 4K block of absolute storage to the exclusive use of each CPU. The mechanism of prefixing is used to map the first 4K block of absolute storage to a different 4K block in absolute storage. Prefixing consists of using the value (bits 8–19) of a register called the prefix register to obtain the desired mapping. A real address is converted to an absolute address (a) if bits 8–19 of the real address are all zeros (i.e., it is in the first 4K block) by replacing bits 8–19 with the corresponding bits of the prefix register; or (b) if bits 8–19 of the real address are equal to bits 8–19 of the prefix register, in which case they are replaced by zeros. In all other cases, a real address is synonymous with an absolute address. See section 4.9 for more details.

4.5.3 Virtual Storage

Virtual storage is used to denote a wide range of addressing and storage management schemes. The basic ideas used in all these schemes are the following:

- Instructions and data use virtual addresses, which are numbers ranging from 0 to $2^n - 1$ where n is the number of bits available for address generation.
- A virtual address is translated into a real address and then into an absolute address before accessing absolute storage. The translation

is done by using tables that map a virtual address into a real address. This translation is usually done by hardware and is regarded as part of instruction fetching and execution.
- An address space is the set of values that can be assumed by a virtual address, i.e., it is the set of addresses ranging from 0 to 2^n - 1 where n is the number of bits available for address generation; more than one address space may be used, in which case each address space has a distinct ID that is used in translation.

A single virtual storage (SVS) scheme uses only one address space. A multiple virtual storage (MVS) scheme uses multiple address spaces, each address space having an identification number. The SVS scheme was used by IBM in an early operating system, OS1. The MVS scheme is used in the MVS operating systems, which are the standard operating systems for IBM mainframes.

The motivation for using virtual storage arose from the fact that the use of absolute addresses by programs in an on-line multiprogramming environment caused problems that resulted in response time degradation. Some of these problems are listed [4]:

- Each program was assigned absolute addresses when it was initiated. A program might be swapped out of main storage into secondary storage while it is waiting for an I/O completion, such as data entry from a terminal. Before the program could be swapped in (returned to main storage to resume execution), it was necessary to make available the same real storage locations that it used previously.
- Since a program required contiguous main storage locations, sometimes a waiting program could not be executed because it could not be fitted into available main storage. A consequence was that "holes" would be found in main storage that were individually too small for any waiting program but collectively larger than the space needed for some or all waiting programs.
- The smaller models usually have smaller installed main storages. Hence, the goal of downward compatibility was not possible unless the program was redesigned to work with a smaller main storage.

4.5.4 Dynamic Address Translation

Virtual storage is organized hierarchically into address space, segment, page, and byte, as illustrated in Figure 4-5. Within an address space, virtual storage is divided into segments. A segment is a block

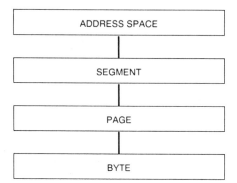

Figure 4-6 Virtual storage organization.

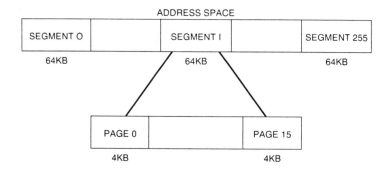

Figure 4-5 Division of address space into segments and pages.

of contiguous virtual storage; its size can be either 64 KB or 1 MB. A page is a block of contiguous virtual storage within a segment and its size can be either 2 KB or 4 KB. Figure 4-6 shows the division of an address space into segments and pages.

A virtual address consists a segment index, page index, and byte index, as shown in Figure 4-7. The idea is to uniquely identify a byte within an address space by specifying a segment number, a page number, and a byte number. An address space can be divided into 256 segments and each segment can be divided into 16 pages (using 64 KB and 4 KB for segment and page sizes). In such a case, the segment index can assume values from 0 to 255, the page index can assume values from 0 to 15, and the byte index varies from 0 to 4K - 1.

	SEGMENT INDEX	PAGE INDEX	BYTE INDEX
0	8	16	20 31

Figure 4-7 Virtual address format.

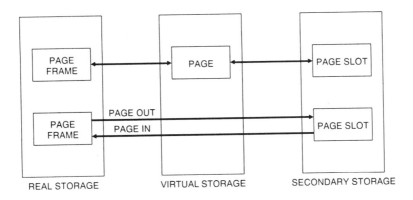

Figure 4-8 Mapping of a page.

A page in an address space can physically reside in main storage or in secondary storage. The terms "page frame" and "page slot" are used to denote the storage areas that hold a page in main storage or secondary storage. A page can be moved from a page frame to a page slot and vice versa (see Figure 4-8). The transfer of a page from a page frame to a page slot is called a page-out; the transfer of a page from a page slot to a page frame is called a page-in.

Dynamic address translation maps a virtual address in an address space to a real address. Actually, all that is necessary is to translate a page address to the address of a page frame. Thus, referring back to Figure 4-7, the segment index and the page index are mapped to a page frame address. This is assuming that the page has a page frame assigned to it. If the page has no frame assigned to it (this condition is called a page fault), the page is moved from the page slot to the page frame and then translated.

Dynamic address translation is done by hardware that references the following:

- Control Registers 0 and 1
- Segment Tables (in real storage)
- Page Tables (in real storage)

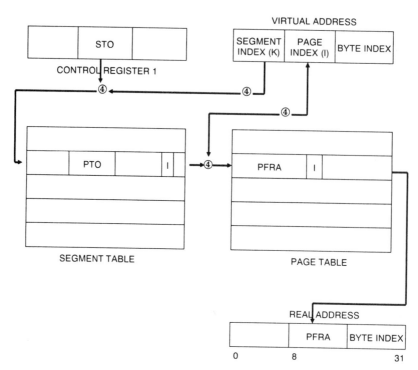

Figure 4-9 Dynamic address translation.

The architecture provides for page sizes of 2K and 4K, and segment sizes of 64K and 1M. (A page size of 4K and a segment size of 64K is used by the MVS Operating System.) The page and segment sizes are input parameters of the translation procedure and are contained in Control Register 0.

The translation procedure is schematically illustrated in Figure 4-9. In the following discussion it is assumed that 4K pages and 64K segments are used. (In the case of other page or segment sizes, a similar procedure is applicable.) The procedure translates the address of a virtual page given by the segment index and page index to a page frame address in real storage. The byte index of the virtual address is not converted but added to the page frame address.

There is a segment table for every address space. This table has 256 entries (one per segment), and each entry contains the address of a page table, a flag indicating segment validity, and the length of the page table (see Figure 4-10). The page table contains 16 entries (one per page), and each entry contains the address of a page frame and one flag bit.

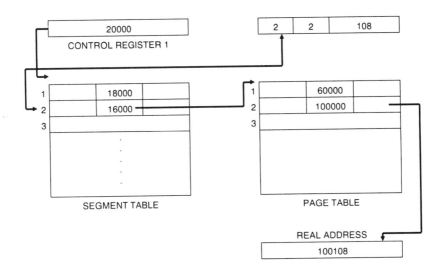

Figure 4-10 DAT example.

The segment and page tables associated with all active address spaces are always kept in real storage (i.e., they are never paged out). These tables are created by the operating system at the time of initializing an address space. The page table entries change during the course of program execution because a page may be paged out to make room for another page from the same or a different address space. The operating system has page replacement algorithms designed to optimally allocate page frames among contending address spaces. The flag bit (I) in the page table entry indicates whether the page frame address is valid or invalid. This bit is set to zero by the operating system to indicate that the page has a page frame assigned to it, as shown by the page table entry. The bit is set to one by the operating system when the page frame is taken away from the page and allocated to another, or when the page is not assigned a frame. The instruction INVALIDATE PAGE TABLE ENTRY can be used for this purpose.

The address of the segment table (known as Segment Table Origin or STO) is contained in Control Register 1, and the operating system loads the register with this information when it decides to execute programs in an address space.

Logically, the virtual-to-real address translation procedure (see Figure 4-9) works as follows:

1. The segment index is multiplied by 4 (the segment table entry size is 4 bytes) and added to the segment table address given in Control Register 1, to obtain an offset to the correct entry in the segment table.
2. The page table address (PTO) from the segment table entry is added to the page index multiplied by 2 (the page table entry size is 2 bytes) to obtain an offset to the page table entry; it is assumed that the flag bit I shows that the segment is valid and, if it is not, a program interruption (segment translation exception) occurs.
3. The offset to the page table entry obtained in step 2 is used in examining the entry in the page table; if the I bit shows that the entry is valid, the real address of the page frame (PFRA) is concatenated with the byte index to obtain the real address; if the entry is not valid, a program interruption (page translation exception) occurs.

A numerical example of dynamic address translation is shown in Figure 4-10. The segment index 2 is used to obtain the second entry in the segment table. The page table location for the second segment is 16,000 and the third entry of the page table (corresponding to page index 3) is used to obtain the address of the page frame (shown as 100,000) occupied by the virtual page. The byte index of 108 is added to this address to obtain a real address of 100,108.

Translation Look-Aside Buffer

The function of the translation look-aside buffer (TLB) is to store translated real addresses of page frames and thus minimize the frequency of dynamic address translation. In the previous section we saw that the byte index of the virtual address was the same as the byte index of the real address and that the translation procedure essentially consisted of obtaining a page frame address corresponding to the segment and page indexes. This means that if the instructions in a virtual 4K page are executed in sequence, the same page frame address can be used for all instructions within the page. The TLB is designated by the architecture to store previously translated page frame addresses and the corresponding segment and page indexes. The implementation of TLB varies among models. See Chapter 8 for a specific TLB implementation. The instruction PURGE TLB clears the TLB of all entries.

4.5.5   Logical Address and Effective Address

A logical address is an operand address. It is interpreted as a virtual address if the DAT bit in the PSW is on, and as a real address if the DAT bit is off. An effective address is an address before translation, regardless of whether it is absolute, real, or virtual.

4.5.6   Storage Protection

Storage protection is necessary because multiple address spaces execute concurrently under an operating system like MVS, and the real storage used by one address space has to be protected against violation by another address space. Also, the operating system itself needs protection of real storage areas that it uses for keeping tables, queues, and other data areas as well as the critical part of its code, called the nucleus.

The operating system needs to know whether a page frame has been used during past time periods by any of the concurrently executing address spaces, so that it can reallocate page frames according to usage among competing address spaces. This usage can be of two kinds, reference or change. When a byte within a page frame is read by a CPU or a channel, a reference indicator is set by the hardware. Likewise, when a byte within a page frame is modified by the CPU or a channel, a change indicator is set by hardware.

Storage Protection Key

Main storage is organized into 2K blocks for storage protection purposes, and for every block there is a 7-bit key having four fields, as shown in Figure 4-11.

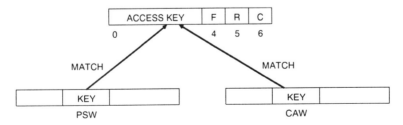

Figure 4-11 Storage key.

Bits 0–3 contain the protection key. For every request for a main storage operation involving that block, a matching key should be present in the Program Status Word (PSW) or Channel Status Word (CSW).

Bit 4 is the fetch protection bit. A zero value implies that protection is applicable only to storing data in main storage and not to fetching; a one implies that both storing and fetching are protected.

Bit 5 is the reference bit. It is set to one when a main storage location in the corresponding block is referenced either for fetching or storing.

Bit 6 is the change bit. It is set to one when a main storage location in the corresponding block is updated by a storage operation.

The reference and change bits are used by the MVS operating system in real storage management. The operating system, in order to manage real storage efficiently, needs the following information pertaining to page frames:

• The time interval for which a page frame has gone unreferenced.
• Whether or not the page frame has been modified as a result of either program activity or channel activity.

This information provides the operating system with a basis to assign page frames among multiple programs and also to page-out modified page frames before they are reassigned.

Here is how storage protection works in action:

1. The CPU uses a key in the PSW and the channel uses a key contained in the Channel Status Word (CSW) to access main storage.

2. The key for each 2K block of storage is matched against the access key used by CPU or channel. If the keys do not match, the requested storage operation does not take place. A program interruption denoting storage protection violation is generated by the hardware if the CPU is requesting the operation; a protection check is indicated in the CSW if the channel is requesting the operation.

3. Not all accesses to main storage by CPU or channel are subject to storage protection. Examples of operations where protection is not applicable are the following:
   • Swapping PSWs on interruption
   • Fetching page and segment tables during dynamic address translation
   • Updating an interval timer.

4. The storage key can be read or modified by the following privileged instructions:
   • INSERT STORAGE KEY loads the storage key into a general register.
   • RESET REFERENCE BIT sets the reference bit to zero.
   • SET STORAGE KEY replaces the storage key with that contained in a general register.

Low Address Protection

This feature is used to protect real storage locations 0–511 (which are used by the CPU in interruption handling, for example) from modification by unauthorized programs. Bit 3 of Control Register 0 is used for controlling low address protection. When this bit is set to one, low address protection is guaranteed; when it is zero there is no such guarantee.

4.6 I/O ARCHITECTURE

The 370 architecture uses the same principles of input/output operations as the 360 architecture. The steps in initiating an I/O operation and completing it are the same as those described in Chapter 3. However, extensions have been made to the 360 architecture for the reasons given below:

• A new type of channel, the block multiplexer, is available. A new instruction START I/O FAST RELEASE (SIOF) and a new interruption condition (channel available) have been introduced in connection with this channel. This channel is ideally suited for use with disks having the rotational position-sensing capability (e.g. IBM 3350).
• The concept of virtual storage is applicable to I/O operations, also, but instead of Dynamic Address Translation a Channel Indirect Data Addressing (CIDA) facility has been introduced to translate virtual addresses in channel programs to absolute addresses.
• The formats of the Channel Command Word (CCW) and the Channel Access Word (CAW) have been modified.

4.6.1   Types of Channels

The 370 architecture specifies three types of channels, namely:

• Byte multiplexer
• Selector
• Block multiplexer

The byte multiplexer channel and selector channels were described in Chapter 3. Briefly, a byte multiplexer channel is capable of performing concurrent I/O operations on several low-speed devices that are attached to it. A selector channel, on the other hand, is capable of operating with only one device at a time; however, the device can have a high data-transfer rate. The block multiplexer channel supports concurrent I/O operations with many devices that have high data-transfer rates.

Block Multiplexer Channel

The block multiplexer channel is used for connecting high-speed devices. Like the selector channel, it has a high data-transfer rate but, unlike the selector channel, it performs multiple I/O operations concurrently. The device disconnects from the channel while the device is performing a control operation (e.g., positioning the read/write head). The channel is free to execute another channel program pertaining to a different device connected to it. During data transfer, the device stays connected to the channel until data transfer is complete. The channel is dedicated to the device for the duration of data transfer, and does not interleave bytes from several devices like a byte multiplexer channel.

The block multiplexer channel is ideally suited for use with direct access storage devices (DASD) that have rotational position sensing (see Chapter 13 for a definition of rotational position sensing). The channel is disconnected from the device during the rotational delay necessary before an addressed sector appears under the read/write head. During this time it can service another device. When the addressed sector on the first device is approaching, it reconnects with the channel and a data transfer takes place; if the channel is busy with the second device, the first device tries to reconnect after another rotation.

The characteristics of the block multiplexer channel are summarized:

1. The channel can "multiplex" I/O operations (perform overlapping I/O operations).
2. The channel is not connected to a device for the entire duration of an I/O operation.
3. The channel is suited for attaching DASD, high-speed tapes, and communications controller to the mainframe.
4. The channel performs data transfer operation to one device at a time (data transfer is not multiplexed); however, control operations (e.g., performing a seek) to other devices can be overlapped with data transfer.

Subchannels

Logically, a channel is divided into subchannels. A subchannel is the memory within a channel for recording addresses, byte count, and status and control information associated with each I/O operation that the channel is executing at any given time. Thus, a selector channel has only one subchannel because it executes only one I/O operation at any given time. Both byte multiplexers and block multiplexers can have several subchannels because they execute several I/I operations concurrently.

A subchannel can be shared by several devices or used exclusively by a single device. When shared by several devices, only one device is logically connected to the subchannel for the duration of an I/O operation. The physical mapping of a subchannel is the Unit Control Word (UCW). For instance, in the case of a byte multiplexer channel, a table of 256 UCWs is stored within the channel, corresponding to the maximum of 256 device addresses. Each UCW contains the address, count, and status and control information pertaining to an I/O operation. Figure 4-12 shows the relationship between subchannels, UCWs, and devices.

The sharing of a subchannel by various devices is made possible by assigning UCWs to devices during system installation. Each UCW is designated as shared or nonshared. In the case of a shared UCW, contiguous addresses are assigned to the devices that are shared by the UCW. If the UCW is not shared, only one device is assigned to it, and this device has a unique UCW.

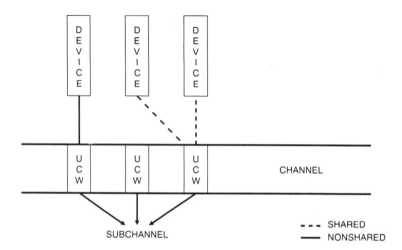

Figure 4-12 Device/subchannel mapping.

4.6.2 I/O Instructions

The 360 had four I/O instructions, namely START I/O, TEST I/O, HALT I/O, and TEST CHANNEL. The 370 uses these instructions and has five additional ones. The I/O instructions use the S format, instead of the SI format used in the 360 architecture. A definition of the S format can be found later in this chapter.

The additional instructions are START I/O FAST RELEASE, CLEAR I/O, CLEAR CHANNEL, HALT DEVICE, and STORE CHANNEL ID. Each instruction format contains the operation code, the channel address, and the device address (which includes the control unit address) as shown in Figure 4-13a.

Start I/O (SIO)

This instruction is used for initiating an input/output operation. During execution of this instruction, the channel reads the contents of the Channel Access Word (CAW) at location 72 of main storage. The program that issues the SIO instruction, normally the I/O Supervisor of the operating system, should load location 72 with the correct CAW. The format of the CAW is shown in Figure 4-13b. The CAW contains two fields used by the channel, namely, a storage protection key and the address of the first Channel Command Word (CCW) of the channel program. The storage protection key is

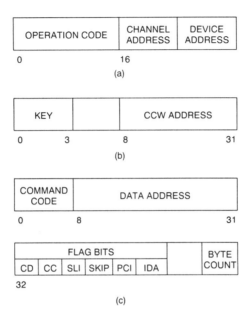

Figure 4-13 (a) I/O instruction format. (b) CAW format. (c) CCW format.

matched with the storage key for a 2K storage block when reference is made to a main storage location during the I/O operation.

The format of the CCW is shown in Figure 4-13c. The CCW contains a command code, the address of the first byte of data to be transferred, six flags, and the number of bytes to be transferred (byte count). The command codes are the same as in the case of the 360.

The flags in the CCW indicate whether any one of the following features are present: data chaining (DC), command chaining (CC), suppress length indication (SLI), skip (SKIP), program controlled interruption (PCI), and indirect data addressing. These were discussed in Chapter 3, except for indirect data addressing, which is described later in this chapter.

The I/O operation is initiated if subchannel and device are available and the channel is either available or in the interruption-pending state and no device errors have been detected. Assuming that channel, subchannel, and device are available, the CPU is released for performing its next instruction after the device is selected.

The condition code in the PSW shows whether or not the I/O operation has been initiated. An I/O operation is not initiated if the channel or subchannel is not available, or if there is an error associated with the device. In the case of error, status bits are stored in the Channel Status Word (CSW).

Start I/O Fast Release (SIOF)

This instruction is similar to the START I/O instruction in the sense that it initiates an input/output operation, but it differs from the SIO instruction in the following respects:

1. It is meant for use with block multiplexer channel.
2. It initiates an I/O operation regardless of whether or not the device is available, providing that (a) the subchannel is available and (b) the channel is either available or in the interruption-pending state and device errors have not been detected.

The advantage that the SIOF has over SIO lies in the fact that SIOF initiates the I/O operation before device selection, and it frees the CPU earlier than the SIO instruction. If the device or control unit is busy, an I/O interruption is subsequently generated by the channel.

Test Channel (TCH)

This instruction tests whether or not the channel is operational and sets a condition code.

Test I/O (TIO)

This instruction is used to check the status of a channel, subchannel, and device. The status is indicated by the condition code in the PSW.

Store Channel ID (STID)

This instruction is executed when information pertinent to the addressed channel such as channel type (selector, byte multiplexer, block multiplexer), channel model number, and the maximum I/O extended logout length that can be stored by the channel during an I/O interruption is required.

Halt I/O (HIO)

This instruction terminates the current I/O operation at the device level, subchannel level, or channel level, depending on the address.

Halt Device (HDV)

This instruction terminates the current I/O operation of the addressed I/O device. This instruction is used with block multiplexer channels to halt the I/O operation pertaining to a specific device, without interfering with other I/O operations in progress.

Clear I/O (CLRIO)

This instruction serves the same purpose as the TEST I/O instruction, and is used instead of the Test I/O in the case of block multiplexer channels.

Clear Channel

This instruction resets the I/O interface connected to the channel, if the channel is not busy doing an I/O operation. A condition code is set to indicate whether or not the reset was performed, and if not, whether the channel was busy or not operational.

4.6.3   Channel Indirect Data Addressing (CIDA)

This facility is used to transfer data to and from noncontiguous page frames (see Figure 4-14).

When the IDA flag in the CCW is on, the data address in the CCW is no longer a main storage location but a pointer to a main storage location. Specifically, the data address field contains the location of the first Indirect Data Address Word (IDAW) to be used for data transfer. Additional IDAWs are in successive locations in storage. The first IDAW contains the address of a main storage location and data is transferred to or from that location until a 2K byte block boundary is reached. Then the next IDAW is used. It contains the starting address of another 2K block of main storage, and the process is repeated.

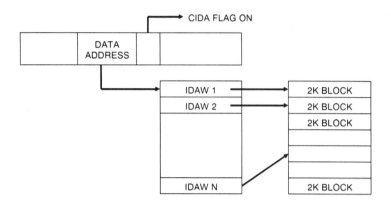

Figure 4-14 Channel indirect data addressing (CIDA).

The reason for using CIDA is that contiguous page frames in main storage may not be available for data transfer under a virtual storage operating system. For example, assume 8K bytes of data are to be transferred to main storage from a disk. Before issuing the START I/O instruction, the I/O Supervisor of the operating system page-fixes the buffer for the data transfer (i.e., two not necessarily contiguous 4K pages are allocated in main storage for this operation). CIDA is a convenient technique for indicating that noncontiguous page frames are used in data transfer. The same result can be achieved using data chaining; the difference is that only one CCW is used in CIDA, whereas multiple CCWs are used in the case of data chaining.

4.6.4 I/O Interruption

The action taken on I/O interruption is illustrated schematically in Figures 4-15 and 4-16. The hardware stores the old PSW in real storage locations 56–63, loads the new PSW from locations 120–127, and stores the following additional information:

- Channel Status Word in locations 64–71
- Channel and Device Address in locations 186–187
- Limited channel logout information (in case of error) in locations 176–175, and extended logout information in locations whose starting address is given in locations 172–175.

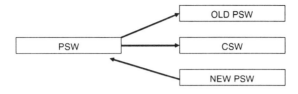

Figure 4-15 Interruption hardware action.

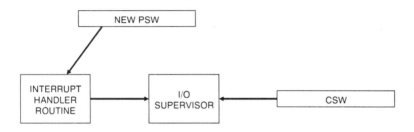

Figure 4-16 Interruption software action.

The new PSW contains the address of an interruption handler routine that is executed after the interruption. The details of handling the interruption depends on the operating system but, in general, the following actions take place:
• Error-handling operations are performed if an error in the I/O operation is indicated.
• If there are no errors, the program that initiated the I/O operation is notified of the completion of the I/O operation.

Channel Status Word (CSW)

The format of the CSW is shown in Figure 4-17. The CSW is a doubleword and is stored at real address location 64. It is available for use until the next I/O interruption occurs or the next I/O instruction causes a change in its contents.

The key field contains a 4-bit storage protection key. The L flag (bit 5) indicates that a pending logout condition exists. The CC code (bits 6 and 7) indicate whether or not a deferred condition code for START I/O FAST RELEASE is present. The CCW address field gives an address that is 8 bytes greater than the address of the last CCW

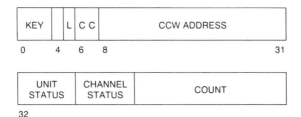

Figure 4-17 CSW format.

used. Bits 32–47 identify the status, and each one of the 16 bits is used to flag conditions, such as channel end, device end, etc. These were described in Chapter 3.

Channel Logout Facility

The channel logout facility is used for diagnostic or error recovery purposes in case of abnormal termination of an I/O operation due to channel malfunctioning. There are two sections to the logout, a limited channel logout and an extended channel logout. The limited channel logout provides information that is independent of the actual channel model used. The extended channel logout contains information that is dependent on the actual channel model that is in use. The I/O Communications Area (IOCA) a 32-byte table in real address locations 160–191 contains limited channel logout information (4 bytes) and, if applicable, a pointer to the extended logout information area. The information in the channel logout identifies the storage control unit, the most likely source of error (e.g., CPU, channel, control unit, storage), the type of termination, and so forth.

4.6.5   Phases in Execution of an I/O Operation

Following is a summary of the events that take place during the execution of a complete I/O operation. There are three instruction components in the execution of an I/O operation: an I/O instruction, channel commands, and device orders (as in the case of the 360). The I/O instruction is executed by the CPU, the channel command is decoded by the channel, and orders are passed on to control unit and device for execution.

In what follows we shall consider the execution of a START I/O instruction using a byte multiplexer channel and the follow-through of the instruction to the point of the I/O interruption.

Initial Selection Phase

The CPU initiates this phase with the START I/O instruction, which contains channel and device addresses. The channel fetches the CAW from a fixed location in main storage. The channel sends the address of the device to all control units attached to the channel. A control unit that recognizes the address responds by sending the address in return. The channel now sends a command (obtained from the CCW, which in turn is pointed to by the CAW) to the device, and the device returns a status byte to indicate whether or not it can execute the command.

The Start I/O operation is complete at this stage, and the PSW and CSW contain condition codes.

Data Transfer Phase

The channel transfers data between device and main storage under read or write commands. An I/O operation may involve transfer to several noncontiguous storage areas. In this case multiple CCWs coupled by data chaining are used to effect the data transfer. When multiple commands are necessary to effect an I/O operation, command chaining is used. Channel indirect addressing is used to support virtual storage architecture.

Data transfer takes place one byte at a time, and the CPU may perform other functions while transfer is in progress.

Conclusion Phase

The normal conclusion of an I/O operation is indicated by the channel end and device end conditions. These conditions are indicated by the Channel Status Word (CSW), which is stored at a fixed location in main storage.

Interruption Phase

Unless the CPU is disabled, the termination of an I/O operation causes an interrupt action to take place, which causes the old PSW to be saved and a new PSW to be loaded.

4.7   INSTRUCTION SET

The instruction set of the 370 is derived from that of the 360 by adding approximately 40 instructions (see Table 4-2). Of these, only 6 instructions are of interest to the application programmers. The remaining 34 instructions are primarily for floating-point arithmetic (7) or for operating system functions (27).

Two noteworthy instructions that have been introduced are for movement and comparison of long character strings (MOVE LONG and COMPARE LOGICAL LONG). They are of use in optimizing character string manipulation in PL/1. They provide for operand lengths of 16 MB, as compared to the 360 MOVE CHARACTER and COMPARE instructions, which permitted lengths of up to 256 bytes.

Instructions to insert, store, or compare selected bytes (e.g., the first and third bytes) from a word by using four bits as a mask are also available (INSERT CHARACTERS UNDER MASK, STORE CHARACTERS UNDER MASK, COMPARE LOGICAL CHARACTERS UNDER MASK).

Two other instructions that need special mention are COMPARE AND SWAP (CS) and COMPARE AND DOUBLE SWAP (CDS). These are intended for use by the operating system in a multiprocessing environment to serialize access to common storage areas. They are described under multiprocessing. These instructions have been designed to be used by software locks in the operating system.

4.7.1   General Remarks Pertaining to Instructions

As in the case of the 360, an instruction can be two, four, or six bytes in length and has to be on an integral boundary. An instruction is divided into several fields. The first field is the operation code. The other fields can refer directly to any of the following:

• The number of a register (general, control, or floating point)
• A real or virtual address
• A data item ("immediate operand")
• A mask (a string of bits)
• A number (e.g., to indicate shifting of bits)

Separate instructions are provided for loading, storing or manipulating the various objects (or entities) mentioned in the 370 architecture, such as:

Table 4-2 New Instructions for the 370

INSTRUCTION	MNEMONIC	TYPE	
ADD NORMALIZED (extended)	AXR	RR	UNPRIV
CLEAR I/O	CLRIO	S	PRIV
COMPARE AND SWAP	CS	RS	UNPRIV
COMPARE DOUBLE AND SWAP	CDS	RS	UNPRIV
COMPARE LOGICAL CHARACTERS UNDER MASK	CLM	RS	UNPRIV
COMPARE LOGICAL LONG	CLCL	RR	UNPRIV
HALT DEVICE	HDV	S	PRIV
INSERT CHARACTERS UNDER MASK	ICM	RS	UNPRIV
INSERT PSW KEY	IPK	S	PRIV
LOAD CONTROL	LCTL	RS	PRIV
LOAD REAL ADDRESS	LRA	RX	PRIV
LOAD ROUNDED (extended to long)	LRDR	RR	UNPRIV
LOAD ROUNDED (long to short)	LRER	RR	UNPRIV
MONITOR CALL	MC	SI	UNPRIV
MOVE LONG	MVCL	RR	UNPRIV
MULTIPLY (extended)	MXR	RR	UNPRIV
MULTIPLY (long to extended)	MXDR	RR	UNPRIV
MULTIPLY (long to extended)	MXD	RX	UNPRIV
PURGE TLB	PTLB	S	PRIV
RESET REFERENCE BIT	RRB	S	PRIV
SET CLOCK	SCK	S	PRIV
SET CLOCK COMPARATOR	SCKC	S	PRIV
SET CPU TIMER	SPT	S	PRIV
SET PREFIX	SPX	S	PRIV
SET PSW KEY FROM ADDRESS	SPKA	S	PRIV
SHIFT AND ROUND DECIMAL	SRP	SS	UNPRIV
SIGNAL PROCESSOR	SIGP	RS	PRIV
START I/O FAST RELEASE	SIOF	S	PRIV
STORE CHANNEL ID	STIDC	S	PRIV
STORE CHARACTERS UNDER MASK	STCM	RS	UNPRIV
STORE CLOCK	STCK	S	UNPRIV
STORE CLOCK COMPARATOR	STCKC	S	PRIV
STORE CONTROL	STCTL	RS	PRIV
STORE CPU ADDRESS	STAP	S	PRIV
STORE CPU ID	STIDP	S	PRIV
STORE CPU TIMER	STPT	S	PRIV
STORE PREFIX	STPX	S	PRIV
STORE THEN AND SYSTEM MASK	STNSM	SI	PRIV
STORE THEN OR SYSTEM MASK	STOSM	SI	PRIV
SUBTRACT NORMALIZED (extended)	SXR	RR	UNPRIV

- CHANNEL SET (connect, disconnect)
- PSW (load)
- CLOCK (set, store)
- CLOCK COMPARATOR (set, store)
- CONTROL REGISTER (load, store)

- PAGE TABLE (invalidate entry)
- TLB (purge)
- STORAGE KEY (insert, set, reset reference bit)
- CPU (signal)

In the foregoing, the operations performed on the object are enclosed within parentheses.

A few instructions require serialization. Examples of instructions that require serialization have been described in earlier.

4.7.2   Instruction Formats

The formats RR, RX, RS, SI, and SS used in the 360 architecture were kept. In addition, three new formats using an extended op code field (extended from 1 byte to 2 bytes) were introduced. The 1-byte op code field permitted a maximum of 256 instructions. With 2 bytes, the size of the instruction set can reach a maximum of 64K. The formats S, RRE, and SSE use the 16-bit op code field (see Figure 4-18). The RRE and SSE formats are used by privileged instructions. The S format has only one operand and is used generally to perform an action on an object (e.g., LOAD PSW, SET CLOCK, STORE CLOCK). The I/O instructions also use the S format instead of the SI format used in the 360 architecture.

4.7.3   Instruction Classification

The 370 Principles of Operation uses the following classification of instructions:

- General instructions
- Decimal instructions
- Floating-point instructions
- Control instructions
- I/O instructions

This classification roughly conforms to register usage in the sense that floating-point registers are used in floating-point instructions, control registers are used in control instructions, and general registers are used by general instructions. The decimal instructions use the SS format and the I/O instructions use the S format.

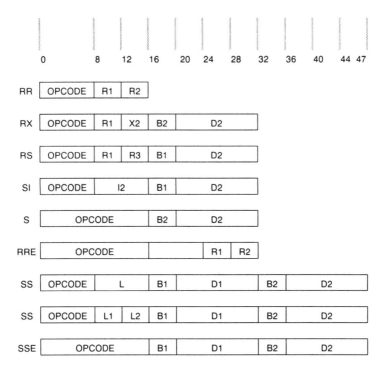

Figure 4-18 Instruction formats.

The 360 classification of instructions into problem and privileged classes is valid for the 370 also. The control instructions and I/O instructions are privileged instructions and can be executed only in the supervisory state. The general, decimal, and floating-point instructions can be executed in the problem state or supervisor state. A new class called semiprivileged instructions have been introduced in connection with the dual address spaces and is discussed later.

In describing instructions, we shall use the same classification tree described earlier in connection with the 360 architecture (see Figure 3-21).

Arithmetic Instructions

The instructions described in the 360 architecture are all valid for the 370 also. They are performed in the same manner (except that addresses are interpreted to be logical addresses). In the case of

floating-point instructions, the 360 provided for short and long formats. A new format called extended format provides the capability
for storing floating-point numbers in four words and thus offering a
high degree of precision. Instructions using this capability for addition, subtraction, and multiplication are available. These instructions
are not described here; the interested reader is referred to the 370
Principles of Operation [2].

Logical Instructions

The AND, OR, and EXCLUSIVE OR instructions are the same as in
the case of the 360. No new instructions have been added.
    The following logical comparison instructions have been added:

- COMPARE AND SWAP (CS)
- COMPARE DOUBLE AND SWAP (DS)
- COMPARE LOGICAL LONG
- COMPARE LOGICAL CHARACTERS UNDER MASK

    In the case of COMPARE AND SWAP, the first operand is com-
pared with the second operand. The condition code is set to 0 on
equal comparison, and the third operand is stored at the second
operand location. The condition code is set to 1 on unequal comparison, and the second operand is loaded into the first operand location. The instruction is in the RS format. All operands are fullwords.
The COMPARE DOUBLE AND SWAP instruction works the same
way, except that all operands are doublewords and the first and
third operands occupy pairs of even/odd registers. The second
operand is a doubleword in storage.
    The COMPARE LOGICAL LONG instruction is in the RR format.
Both R1 and R2 must be even and denote an even/odd pair of
registers (R1, R1 + 1) and (R2, R2 + 1). Bits 8–31 of R1 and R2
specify the address of the first and second operands, respectively.
Bits 8–31 of R1 + 1 and R2 + 1 specify the length of the first and
second operands, respectively. Bits 0–7 of R2 + 1 specify a pad character, which is used to extend the shorter operand on the right until
both operands have equal length. The comparison proceeds from left
to right, byte by byte, and stops if (a) two corresponding bytes are
unequal or (b) the entire operation is complete. In the case of (a), the
addresses of the two bytes will be placed in R1 and R2. The condition
codes are set to 1, 2, and 3 to indicate that the two operands are
equal, the first operand is low, or the first operand is high, respec-

tively. Note that this instruction is interruptible after a byte comparison. The use of this instruction, as mentioned before, is for comparing long character strings, as in PL/1.

The COMPARE LOGICAL CHARACTERS UNDER MASK is in RS format, but instead of R3, a mask M3 having four bits is used. The mask bits that are used to select the corresponding bytes from R1 and the bytes thus extracted are concatenated to form the first operand. For example, if M3 = "1001," the first and fourth byte of R1 form a two-byte operand, which is compared with a corresponding two-byte field starting at the location of second operand. The condition code settings are the same as in COMPARE LOGICAL LONG. This instruction is useful in comparing varying character strings that are 1–4 bytes in length, using a register for the first operand. One use mentioned in [4] for this instruction is to test 24-bit addresses.

Data Movement Instructions

All the instructions specified in the 360 architecture apply to the 370, also. The following additional instructions are also provided:

- INSERT CHARACTERS UNDER MASK (ICM)
- STORE CHARACTERS UNDER MASK (STCM)
- MOVE LONG (MVCL).

The first two instructions load (or store) selected bytes specified by a mask, as in the case of COMPARE LOGICAL CHARACTERS UNDER MASK. In the case of ICM, byte positions in R1 indicated by a one in the mask field M3 are filled left to right from contiguous bytes in storage, starting at the second operand location. In the case of STCM, bytes from R1 in positions indicated by a one in M3 are moved in left-to-right sequence to contiguous storage locations, starting at the second operand location.

The MOVE LONG instruction is used for moving long character strings; 24 bits are specified for the length of each operand (up to 16 MB). The operands can be overlapping. This instruction works in a manner similar to the COMPARE LOGICAL LONG INSTRUCTION. The two pairs of registers R1, R1 + 1 and R2, R2 + 1 specify the address and length of the first and second operand, respectively. The first byte of R2 + 1 contains a pad character, which is used to fill the rightmost byte positions in the first operand if the first operand is larger than the second operand. The uses for this instruction are as follows [4]:

- By setting the pad character and the second operand length to zero, storage in excess of 256 bytes can be initialized to zero; this method is faster than repeatedly using the MOVE instruction. Many compilers initialize all locations to zero, and this instruction is useful in such a context.
- Long character strings can be moved by this instruction and the object code (e.g., in PL/1) becomes more compact in size.

Branch Instructions

The branch instructions specified in the 360 architecture apply to the 370 architecture also, even though the PSW format has changed. We shall briefly review the branch instructions by function.

SUBROUTINE CALLS. The BRANCH AND LINK instruction, as in the case of the 360, saves in register R1 the following "link" information:

- Instruction length code
- Condition code
- Program mask
- Next instruction address

These fields correspond to the right half of the PSW in the BC mode, whether BC or EC mode is used. The next instruction address can be used by the subroutine to return to the calling program.

CONDITIONAL BRANCHES. The BRANCH ON CONDITION, BRANCH ON COUNT, BRANCH ON INDEX HIGH and BRANCH ON INDEX LOW OR EQUAL instructions described in the 360 architecture apply to the 370 architecture also. The instruction address in the PSW is replaced by the branch address when the condition is satisfied. The interpretations of these instructions are similar to those specified for the 360.

UNCONDITIONAL BRANCH. The BRANCH ON CONDITION can be used for unconditional branching by specifying the value of 15 in the mask field M1, as in the case of the 360.

Shift Instructions

The shift instructions specified in the 360 architecture apply to the 370 also.

Control Instructions

The control instructions, as mentioned before, are not available to the application programmer. They can be executed only in a privileged or semiprivileged mode. In Figure 4-19 we group control instructions by objects that they refer to, such as clocks, timers, PSW, TLB, CPU, etc.

The first group of control instructions in Figure 4-19 deals with clocks, timers, and comparators. The SET CLOCK instruction sets the TOD clock to a value given in location D2(B2). The SET CPU TIMER and SET CLOCK COMPARATOR instructions perform a similar function. The STORE CPU TIMER and STORE CLOCK COMPARATOR instructions store the current value of the CPU timer or clock comparator in the location indicated by D2(B2). Note that STORE CLOCK is not a privileged instruction but is available as a general instruction.

The instructions that deal with the PSW consist of (a) a LOAD instruction that copies the contents of the doubleword located at D2(B2) into the PSW and (b) instructions that modify or store certain fields of the PSW, as listed:

- The SET SYSTEM MASK replaces the first byte of the PSW with the contents of the byte located at D2(B2).
- The STORE THEN AND SYSTEM MASK stores the first byte of the PSW in the byte location specified by D1(B1) and replaces the first byte of the PSW by the logical AND of itself with I2.
- The STORE THEN OR SYSTEM MASK works the same way as STNSM except that a logical OR is used instead of AND.
- The SET PSW KEY FROM ADDRESS replaces bits 8–11 of the PSW (i.e., the PSW key) from bits 24–27 of the D2 field (note that B2 and D2 are not used for generating addresses).
- The INSERT PSW KEY places bits 8–11 of the PSW (i.e., the PSW key) in bit positions 24–27 of general register 2 and also resets bits 28–31 of that register to zeros.

The LOAD CONTROL instruction loads control registers in sequence from storage and works in the same manner as the LOAD

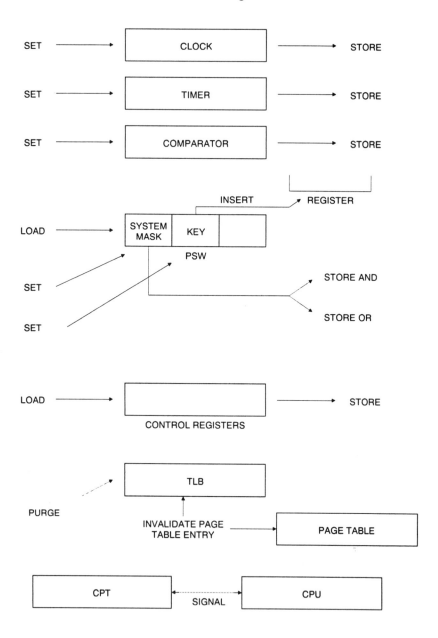

Figure 4-19 Control instructions and objects.

MULTIPLE instruction. The STORE CONTROL stores control registers in sequence and works in the same manner as the STORE MULTIPLE instruction. Note that arithmetic or logical operations cannot be performed using control registers.

The PURGE TLB instruction clears the TLB (of the CPU that issues the instruction) of entries.

The INVALIDATE PAGE TABLE ENTRY makes invalid the page table entry specified by R1 and R2. The register R1 contains the page table origin, and register R2 contains the page index. This instruction also clears applicable entries from the TLB of the CPU that executes the instruction. It also signals all other CPUs to clear applicable entries from their TLBs.

The SIGNAL PROCESSOR instruction is used for communication between CPUs. It is described in later.

4.8 DUAL ADDRESS SPACES (DAS) AND INTER-ADDRESS SPACE INSTRUCTIONS

It is often necessary for a program in one address space to refer to data in another address space or to cause execution of a program in another address space. For example, IBM's database management and data communication system, IMS DB/DC, uses multiple address spaces (called regions); one control region contains database management and data communication management routines coordinating the activities of several message-processing regions that contain application programs. These message-processing regions have to communicate with the control region, and the 370 architecture provides instructions for this purpose.

Moving Data Between Address Spaces

DAS provides the capability for moving data between two address spaces (called primary and secondary) by means of the instructions MOVE TO PRIMARY and MOVE TO SECONDARY. Each instruction specifies two operands, a virtual address in the primary address space and a virtual address in the secondary address space. The virtual address in the primary address space is translated by DAT using the segment table origin (PSTO) in control register 1, in the normal manner. The virtual storage address in the secondary address space is translated by DAS as follows (see Figure 4-20):

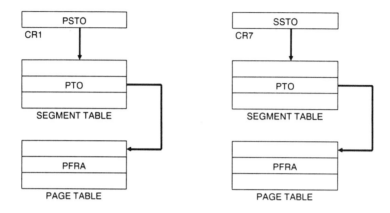

Figure 4-20 Concurrent translation of two address spaces.

- Bit 5 of control register 0 is set to 1 to indicate that the secondary address space is accessed.
- Control register 7 contains the address of the segment table for the secondary address space (SSTO).
- The same procedure used in primary address translation is used for secondary address translation also, except that control register 7 is used instead of control register 1.
- The translation of the primary and secondary addresses is performed concurrently by the DAT hardware.

Linking Programs in Different Address Spaces

DAS also provides the capability for a program executing in one address space to link with a subroutine in another address space. An instruction called PROGRAM CALL allows the switching of a program from one address space to another. The instruction PROGRAM TRANSFER returns control to the calling program.

The PROGRAM CALL instruction uses a 20-bit number that consists of two fields, a linkage index (LX) and an entry index (EX). Control register 5 contains the address of a linkage table, and LX points to a specific entry in the linkage table. The linkage table entry contains the address of an entry table, and EX points to a specific entry table entry (ETE). The ETE specifies an address space number

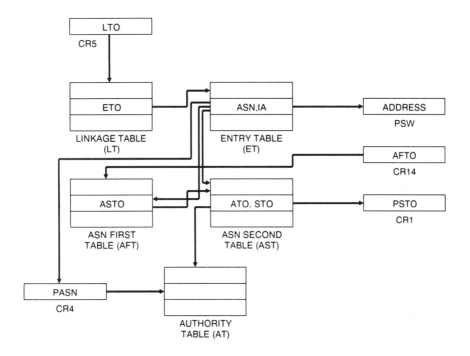

Figure 4-21 Simplified logic of program call.

(ASN) of the address space to be switched to and also an address in that address space, which is copied to the PSW (see Figure 4-21).

An address space is assigned a 16-bit number (ASN). This number consists of two fields, a first table index (AFX) and a second table index (ASX). Control register 14 contains the address of the ASN first table (AFT). AFX points to a specific entry in the AFT. The AFT entry contains the address of the second table (AST). ASX points to a specific entry in the AST. The AST entry in turn contains the address of an authority table (AT) and the origin of the segment table (STO) for the address space. A look-up of the authority table is performed using an authorization index (pointer) in control register 4. The origin of the segment table is placed in control register 1, and address-space switching is accomplished.

Thus, PROGRAM CALL is implemented using a complicated series of table look-ups using the linkage table, ASN first and second tables, and the authority table. The estimated improvement in using this method of implementation over software is of the order of eight to one.

4.9 MULTIPROCESSING

The 370 architecture provides for restricted forms of multiprocessing. Each CPU in a multiprocessing environment has its own set of channels (called the "channel set"). Sharing of channels among CPUs is not allowed. However, main storage is shared and each CPU has access to all locations of main storage. This is accomplished by prefixing.

The CPUs are controlled by a single copy of the operating system, in the sense that units of work are assigned to each CPU by the operating system. Each unit of work is executed by a CPU independently of other CPUs.

The characteristics of multiprocessing specified in the 370 architecture are given below:

• Two CPUs share main storage, each CPU having its own real storage, which is mapped into main storage by prefixing.
• The CPUs do not share channels; when each CPU has its own set of channels (the CPU's channel set), the computer system is called a tightly coupled multiprocessing system.
• One CPU can have a channel set and the other CPU no channel set (i.e., it does not perform I/O operations), in which case the computer system is called an attached processing system.
• In a tightly coupled multiprocessing system, channel sets can be switched and the functions of a failing CPU can be taken over by the remaining CPU, thus providing increased system reliability and availability.
• The CPUs communicate with each other using an instruction called SIGNAL PROCESSOR, which is described later on. When one CPU fails it can send an emergency signal by executing the SIGNAL PROCESSOR instruction and this causes an external interruption on the other CPU.

Prefixing

The architecture allocates, in the case of a single CPU, the first 4K byte locations in main storage known as Prefixed Storage Area (PSA) for storing data that is used by CPU for control and operational purposes.

• Interruption codes
• CAW

- CSW
- Old PSWs
- New PSWs

In the case of multiprocessing, both CPUs cannot use the first 4K byte locations in main storage for this purpose because one CPU may destroy the data necessary for operation of the other CPU. A different 4K location is therefore assigned to each CPU. Also a distinction is made between the addresses used by a CPU and absolute addresses. The address used by the CPU is called the real address. To each CPU it would appear that the first 4K byte locations of main storage are available to it as PSA. The real addresses are translated by hardware into different absolute storage addresses, as explained next.

Each CPU is assigned a new register called the Prefix Value Register (PVR). The PVR contains a 12-bit address portion (corresponding to the locations 0–4095), which is matched against bits 8–19 of the 24-bit address generated by the CPU. The translation of real address to absolute address proceeds as follows:

1. If bits 8–19 of the address generated by the CPU are all zero (the address is within the range 0–4095), they are replaced with the contents of the PVR; this is known as forward prefixing.
2. If bits 8–19 of the address generated by the CPU are not all zeros (the address is greater than 4095) and do not match the address portion of the PVR, no change is made to the address.
3. If bits 8–19 of the address generated by the CPU are not all zeros and are equal to the contents of the PVR, they are set to zeros; this is known as reverse prefixing.

In other words, if R is the real address used by the CPU and P is the binary number obtained by appending 12 zeros to the 12-bit address portion contained in the PVR, then R is converted to an absolute address A using the following algorithm:

1. If R is less than 4K, A = P + R.
2. If R is greater than or equal to 4K but less than P, A = R.
3. If R is greater than or equal to P but less than P + 4K, A = R - P.
4. If R is greater than or equal to P + 4K, A = R.

Note that the setting of actual values in the PVR for each CPU is done at installation time. The architecture also provides privileged instructions for loading and storing the contents of the PVR, so that the PVR can be changed dynamically.

An example of prefixing is illustrated schematically in Figure 4-22. There are two CPUs, which we shall denote by 0 and 1. Each CPU has a real address range of 0 to 8 MB. The prefix values for CPU 0 and CPU 1 are 200K and 100K, respectively. Figure 4-22 shows the actual mapping of real storage for each CPU into absolute storage. For CPU 0, a real address in the 0 to 4K range is mapped into absolute locations 200K to 204K; likewise, a real address in the range 200K to 204K is mapped into an absolute address range of 0 to 4K. The real address and absolute address are the same in the ranges between 4K and 200K and between 204K and 8 MB.

Prefixing, as described above, is performed after dynamic address translation. The sequence of conversions from virtual to absolute addresses takes place as follows:

1. The virtual address is converted to a real address by means of dynamic address translation.
2. The real address is converted to an absolute address by means of prefixing.

Signaling Between CPUs

A new instruction called Signal Processor instruction (SIGP) is used for inter-CPU communication. The CPU that generates a SIGP is called the sender, and the CPU that receives the SIGP is called the

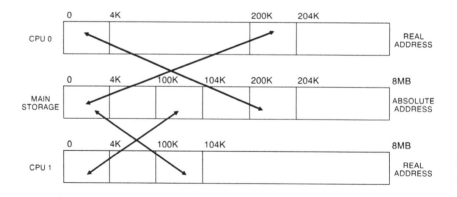

Figure 4-22 Real-to-absolute address mapping.

receiver. The following list shows some of the orders that are issued by the sender via the SIGP instruction:

1. SENSE — The receiver sends its status to the sender.
2. START — The receiver enters the operating state if it is in the stop state.
3. STOP — The receiver enters the stop state if it is in the operating state.
4. STOP and STORE STATUS — The receiver enters the stop state and the status is saved in absolute storage locations 216–512.
5. INITIAL MICROPROGRAM LOAD (IML) — The receiver does an initial program reset and performs IML.
6. RESET — The receiver performs a reset.
7. RESTART — The receiver begins program execution by fetching a new PSW and storing the old PSW.
8. EXTERNAL CALL — An external interruption is sent by one CPU to another as a request to provide services (known as "shoulder tapping").
9. EMERGENCY SIGNAL — An external interruption is presented to the receiver.

The section on 3033 implementation describes hardware aspects of signaling implementation and the reader is referred to it for details.

4.10 REVIEW OF THE 370 ARCHITECTURE

The 370 architecture can be characterized along the following lines:

1. It is a virtual storage architecture.
2. It is a CISC architecture.
3. It is an operating system driven architecture.
4. It is a dual-processor architecture.

Each of these characterizations have associated drawbacks and penalties, which are discussed in the following paragraphs.

There is no doubt that virtual storage is necessary to provide efficient storage management in a multiprogramming environment. Its effect on the architecture, however, has been to introduce many layers of complexity. Consider, for example, new concepts that have been introduced, such as address space, DAT, DAS, program call, TLB, etc. Many of these concepts are linked to operating system concepts, especially those introduced by MVS. Also, consider tables such as Page Table, Segment Table, Linkage Table, Entry Table, ASN First Table, ASN Second Table, etc., and the dedicated control registers for accessing these tables needed by virtual storage. These require overhead in the form of storage and logic needed for implementing table search in hardware. Also, certain associated instructions like INVALIDATE PAGE TABLE ENTRY require synchronization with other processors. For example, INVALIDATE PAGE TABLE ENTRY clears TLBs attached to every CPU of the specified page table entry. All this points as to the need for a redefinition of virtual storage in a mutliprocessing environment and the choice of an instruction set, registers, and other objects.

The 370 architecture has provided additional instructions for use with high-level language compilers. Most notable of these are the MOVE LONG (MVCL) and COMPARE LONG (CLCL), which are supposed to help PL/1 compiler writers. These instructions are typical of CISC architectures and have been the target of much criticism. The need for MVCL has been questioned because the typical character move consists of about 7 bytes [5]. The need for CLCL can be questioned because it is not directly related to string operations used by high-level languages [6].

The 370 architecture also raises the issue of the interface between the operating system and the microcode. An instruction such as PROGRAM CALL was implemented previously as part of the operating system layer. Now it is part of the microcode and resides in control storage. The question arises as to why the dispatcher or the interruption handler (both of which are more frequently used than PROGRAM CALL) should not also be implemented in microcode.

The 370 is a dual processor architecture and not a true multiprocessing architecture. The 370/XA removes the limitations in this area, as described in the next chapter.

REFERENCES

1. IBM System/360 Principles of Operation, Order No. GA 22-6821.
2. IBM System/370 Principles of Operation, Order No. GA 22-7000.
3. IBM System/370 XA Principles of Operation, Publication No. SA 22-7085.
4. Case, R.P., and A. Padegs: "Architecture of the IBM System/370," *Communications of the ACM*, vol. 21, no. 1, January 1978.

5. Hopkins, M.E.: "A Perspective on the 801/Reduced Instruction Set Computer," *IBM Systems Journal*, vol. 26, no. 1, 1987.
6. Myers G.: *Advances in Computer Architecture,* John Wiley & Sons, 1982.

ADDITIONAL READING

The following is recommended as a useful tutorial on the 370 architecture:

Prasad, N.: *Architecture and Implementation of Large Scale IBM Systems,* QED, 1981.

5

370/XA Architecture

The 370 extended architecture (XA) evolved from IBM's experience
with the 370 architecture [1], [2], [3]. This experience indicated that
changes had to be made to the 370 architecture to function effective-
ly in a large-scale on-line multiprogramming environment. The changes can be classified as (a) extensions and (b) new concepts. These
extensions and new concepts will be discussed in this chapter.

5.1 MOTIVATIONS FOR THE 370/XA ARCHITECTURE

The following considerations are given as motivations for the 370/XA
architecture by the 370/XA architects (Padegs [4] and Cormier [5]):

- Extension of real storage
- Extension of virtual storage
- Streamlining multiprocessing operations
- Improvement of I/O performance and better operating efficiency on
  I/O operations

These topics are discussed briefly next.

Extension of Main Storage

One of the key requirements facing the 370/XA architects was to
extend the size of main storage. The System 370/168 machine had

already realized the maximum available limit of 16 MB of main storage. Hence, the architecture had to be extended to allow the installation of storage beyond the 16-MB limit.

Extension of Virtual Storage

The requirements for virtual storage in large installations using on-line systems such as IMS or CICS were growing at a phenomenal rate. This growth was caused by the virtual storage needs for the MVS operating system, CICS, or IMS, and the application programs themselves. Many installations decided to introduce more and more on-line systems or to consolidate and centralize existing systems. The result was a chronic shortage of virtual storage with dire consequences in on-line response times.

Streamlining Multiprocessing Operations

It was recognized that multiprocessing operations could be made more efficient by transforming the bulk of the I/O operations (including some of the I/O interruption handling) to a dedicated I/O processor. Also, the facilities for communication between CPUs had to be extended.

Improvement of I/O Performance

The 370 I/O architecture was found to be inadequate in large installations, for the following reasons:

- It was geared to a uniprocessor environment. In a multiprocessing environment, each CPU was assigned a dedicated channel set. Each CPU had to work with its own channel set. If a device was connected only to a single CPU via a channel, that specific CPU had to be running all programs that required data transfer from the device.
- The channel operation was inefficient in a shared environment where multiple devices were connected to multiple CPUs via multiple channels. First of all, the physical channel that was used for initiation of the I/O operation had to be used for continuation of the operation. This caused delays especially when devices could not reconnect because the original channel was busy.

• The I/O module of the operating system performed many functions, and this resulted in CPU overhead. These functions included handling control-unit-busy or device-busy indications as well as handling interruptions arising from device end and control unit end conditions.
• The number of devices that could be supported was limited to 4K.

All of these drawbacks were eliminated in the 370/XA architecture.

5.2 EXTENSIONS MADE TO THE 370 ARCHITECTURE THAT RESULTED IN THE 370XA ARCHITECTURE

The extensions made to the 370 architecture are listed:

• 31-bit addressing is used instead of the 24-bit addressing used in 370.
• Multiprocessing has been streamlined.
• The I/O architecture has been replaced by a new one.

In the following paragraphs, the impact of these changes on CPU, storage, and I/O is described.

CPU

The 370/XA CPU retains the essential features of the 370 CPU. There are no changes in fundamental concepts regarding instruction execution or the handling of interruptions. The general, control, and floating-point registers used in the 370 have the same functions and formats in the 370/XA architecture. The format of the PSW has been changed to incorporate 31-bit addressing. The unprivileged instruction set for the 370 has been kept and two new branch instructions and an extended-precision divide instruction have been added. The 370 set of I/O instructions have been replaced by a new set.

Storage

The 370/XA uses the same principles for storage organization as the 370. The lowest addressable unit in storage is a byte. Bytes are grouped into halfwords, words and doublewords. The virtual storage concepts used in the 370s are similar to those used in the 370. Thus, the concepts of address spaces, dynamic address translation, logical and effective addresses, dual address spaces, etc., are used in the 370/XA also.

The effect of changing 24-bit addressing in the 370 to 31-bit addressing in the 370/XA is to increase real storage and virtual storage from 16 MB to 2048 MB (i.e., by a factor of 128).

I/O

The I/O architecture of the 370/XA is different from that of the 370 in the following respects:

• An I/O processor called the channel subsystem performs many functions previously performed by the CPU (i.e., by the operating system).
• Devices up to 64K are supported, instead of the 4K supported by the 370.
• Every device has an associated subchannel and there is a one-to-one correspondence between device and subchannel.
• Some control blocks have been changed.
• The interruption sequence has been changed in the sense that fewer interruptions are handled by the CPU (the operating system).
• The I/O instructions have been changed to conform to the new architecture. The channel address does not appear in the I/O instructions. The instructions address a device directly. Instead of START I/O, HALT I/O, etc., we have START SUBCHANNEL, HALT SUBCHANNEL, etc.

The overall effect has been to clean up the I/O architecture and to remove the limitations of channel-oriented architectural problems.

5.3   COMPUTER ORGANIZATION

The conceptual machine of the 370/XA architecture is shown in Figure 5-1. Its main components are the following:

• CPU(s)
• Main storage
• Channel subsystem
• Control unit(s)
• Device(s)

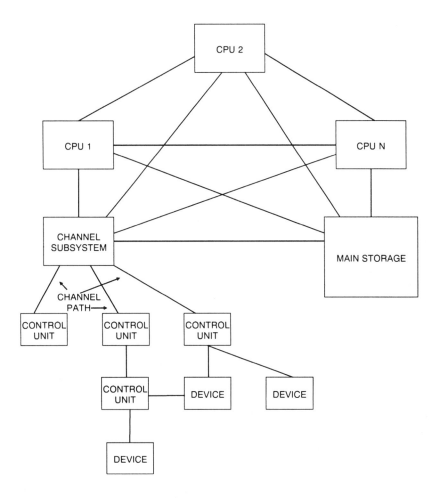

Figure 5-1 Organization of the 370/XA machine.

Multiple CPUs and the channel subsystem share main storage. The CPUs share the channel subsystem in the sense that any CPU can issue an I/O instruction to the channel subsystem. Devices are connected via control units to multiple channel paths, which are managed by the channel subsystem. A channel path is physically the same as a 370 channel. The differences between the 370/XA and 370 views of a channel are the following:

• Channels are no longer owned by a single CPU but are connected to the channel subsystem.

- Channels no longer own control units or devices but are used only as paths for transferring data.

The configuration in Figure 5-1 fits in with the definition of asymmetric multiprocessing in Chapter 2, if the channel subsystem is viewed as a processor performing a dedicated function. If we disregard the channel subsystem, the configuration is reduced to that of symmetric multiprocessing.

5.4 CPU ARCHITECTURE

The 370/XA architecture supports two instruction sets, the 370 instruction set and the 370/XA instruction set. Two modes of operation are provided, the 370 mode and the 370/XA mode. The mode is indicated by setting a bit in the PSW.

The 370/XA uses the same number of general registers, control registers, and floating-point registers as the 370 architecture. All registers are 32 bits in size, as before. The PSW format is slightly different in the 370/XA architecture and has the 31-bit addressing capability. Main storage is the same as in the 370 architecture, except that 31-bit addressing is provided. There are minor changes in virtual storage organization; these are discussed later in this chapter. Channels are no longer regarded as objects by the instruction set; their place is taken by the channel subsystem. The interval timer is dropped in the 370/XA architecture, but the TOD clock is kept and the old instructions apply.

The unprivileged and semiprivileged instructions used by the 370 have not been changed. Four new unprivileged instructions have been added. These are described in the section on instruction set. The I/O instructions are new and are described in the section on I/O architecture.

5.4.1 General Registers

As in the case of the 360 and 370, there are 16 general registers. Each register can hold a full word. The general registers are used as base and index registers in address generation and also as accumulators to store results of binary and logical operations.

5.4.2 Control Registers

As in the case of the 370, there are 16 control registers. Each register can hold a full word. They are used for dynamic address translation, dual address-spaces instructions, and other functions described in Chapter 4. They are not available for use by the problem (application) programmer.

5.4.3 Program Status Word (PSW)

The 370/XA PSW is quite similar to the 370 PSW. In Figure 5-2, the 370/XA PSW is shown side by side with the 370 PSW. The changes are in the following fields:

- The instruction address is 32 bits long (bits 33–64) instead of 24 bits.
- The A-bit (bit 32) controls the mode of operation; if it is on, 31-bit addressing is specified; and if it is off, 24-bit addressing is in effect.
- Bit positions 0, 2–4, 17, and 24–31 are unassigned and must contain zeros (a specification exception is recognized otherwise).
- Bit position 12, which was used to specify BC or EC mode of operation in the 370, is set to 1 in the 370/XA architecture.

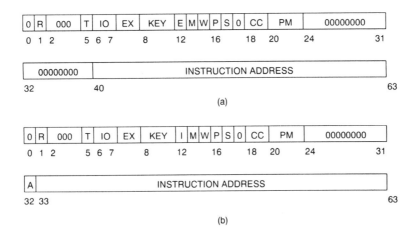

Figure 5-2 Format of the 370/XA PSW. (a) 370 PSW. (b) 370/XA PSW.

These changes are primarily due to the change in addressing, from 24 to 31 bits.

5.4.4   States of the CPU

The states of the CPU are the same as those described in Chapter 4 for the 370 architecture. Bit positions in the PSW specify various states, such as problem, supervisor, wait, operational, etc.

5.4.5   Interruptions

The interruption structure is similar to that described in the 370 architecture. On an interruption, the hardware stores the current PSW in main storage in an old PSW location and loads the PSW with the contents of the new PSW location in main storage. Additional information (an interruption code) identifying the cause of the interruption is also stored in predefined storage locations.

Interruptions are divided into six classes, namely:

• Input/output
• External
• Supervisor call
• Program
• Machine check
• Restart

Mask bits in the PSW can be used to disable external, I/O, machine check, and certain program interruptions. In such a case, the interruption is regarded as pending.

Program Interruption

As in the 370, a program interruption causes the old PSW to be stored at location 40 and a new PSW to be fetched from location 104. An interruption code is placed in locations 142 and 143.

The cause of a program interruption is an exception. An exception is a violation of a rule or the occurrence of an abnormal situation or condition. The following is a partial list of exceptions:

- Decimal divide (divisor is zero, or quotient exceeds the specified size)
- Decimal overflow
- Floating-point exponent overflow
- Floating-point exponent underflow
- Floating-point overflow
- Fixed point divide (divisor is zero, or quotient is greater than the maximum 32-bit signed binary integer)
- Addressing exception (an address outside the available main storage is specified)
- Data exception (invalid decimal sign or digit codes and violations of rules for decimal operations)
- Operation exception (invalid operation code)
- Operand exception (invalid operand in I/O instructions)
- Specification exception (incorrect values in PSW fields, integral boundary violation, invalid use of registers such as odd instead of even, etc.)
- Page translation (there is no real page frame entry corresponding to the virtual page).

Other exceptions were described in Chapter 3 and 4. The 370/XA Principles of Operation [3] lists a number of exceptions, with detailed rules regarding their handling.

Supervisor Call (SVC) Interruption

As in the 360 and 370 architectures, the SVC instruction is used to invoke the services of the supervisor (i.e., the operating system). The SVC instruction contains a code (0–255) that is used to indicate the specific service required by the operating system. The hardware stores the old PSW in locations with starting address 32 and fetches a new PSW from location 96. The interruption code is stored in locations 138 and 139. This is similar to the way SVC interruptions are handled in the 370.

External Interruption

An external interruption is an interruption used for interacting with another CPU, the TOD clock, or the clock comparator. The old PSW is stored in storage location 24, and the new PSW is fetched from location 88. The interruption code is stored in locations 134 and 135. This is how the 370 handles external interruptions, also.

The interval timer has been dropped form the 370/XA architecture and hence the descriptions that deal with handling interruptions from that source are no longer applicable.

Machine Check Interruption

The machine check interruption is a means of notifying a CPU of malfunction of equipment. In some cases, the interruption is of a "floating" kind, i.e., any CPU can be notified. The interruption causes the old PSW to be stored in location 48 and fetches the new PSW from location 112. The interruption code is stored in locations 232–239.

The 370/XA Principles of Operation describes various types of malfunction conditions. Hardware errors are classified as exigent (non-recoverable) or repressible (recoverable), as in the case of the 370.

I/O Interruption

The source of an I/O interruption is a device or the channel subsystem. An I/O interruption condition can be presented to any CPU in a multiprocessing environment (such interruptions are called "floating interruptions"). I/O interruptions are grouped into eight subclasses (numbered 0–7). Mask bits are provided in control register 6 for disabling interruptions from a device belonging to a subclass.

An I/O interruption causes the old PSW to be stored at location 56 and a new PSW to be fetched from location 120. An 8-byte interruption code is stored in locations 184–191. The interruption code is described later.

The major differences from the 370 architecture are noted:

• Channels do not interrupt the CPU.
• I/O interruptions are of the floating kind, as described above.

Restart Interruption

The restart interruption is initiated by means of the restart key or by specifying the restart order in a SIGNAL PROCESSOR instruction. The old PSW is stored at location 8, and a new PSW (specifying the starting address of the program to be executed) is fetched from real location 0. The interruption code is not stored.

5.5 STORAGE ARCHITECTURE

The 370/XA architecture uses the same basic concepts for storage architecture as the 370. The lowest addressable unit is a byte. The bits in a byte are numbered from 0 to 7, from left to right. A group of consecutive bytes is addressed by the leftmost byte of the group. A halfword, fullword, and doubleword denote groups of two, four, and eight bytes on integral boundaries (an integral boundary has an address that is a multiple of the length of the corresponding group of bytes). An instruction should be on a two-byte integral boundary. Operands need not be on an integral boundary.

Three types of storage, absolute, real, and virtual, are defined, as in the case of the 370. Their definitions are similar to the 370 definitions. The addresses used in the 370/XA are of the following types:

- Absolute address
- Real address
- Virtual address (qualified as primary and secondary)
- Logical address
- Effective address.

Their definitions are similar to those used in the 370 architecture. Generally speaking, programs use a virtual address that is translated into a real address by DAT, and the real address is converted into an absolute address (main storage location) by prefixing. When dual address spaces are used by an instruction (e.g., MOVE TO PRIMARY, MOVE TO SECONDARY), the first virtual address space is called the primary address space and the second is called the secondary address space. Generally, a logical address is the address actually used by an instruction (it is the real address, primary address, or secondary address depending on the mode setting of the PSW). The term effective address is used to denote the address before translation.

5.5.1 Absolute Storage

Absolute storage is synonymous with main storage. It is a collection of bytes numbered 0, 1, ... n, where the maximum limit of n is $2^{31} - 1$ or $2^G - 1$ bytes. Absolute storage is organized in 4K-byte blocks. Note the following differences from the 370 architecture:

- The limit for n was 16 MB in the 370 architecture.
- A storage block could be 2K or 4K bytes in size in the 370 architecture.

5.5.2   Real Storage

Real storage and not absolute storage is used by the CPUs in a multiprocessing environment. Each CPU needs the first 4K byte of storage for its internal use (such as storing PSWs, logout areas, save areas, etc.). Prefixing provides the capability to assign the first 4K bytes used by a CPU to some other 4K-byte storage block in absolute storage.

In the 370/XA architecture, the prefix for each CPU is a 19-bit value (as opposed to 8 bits in the 370 architecture) contained in a prefix register. A real address is transformed into an absolute address as follows:

- If bits 1–19 of the real address are all zeros, they are replaced by the prefix to obtain the absolute address.
- If bits 1–19 of the real address are equal to the prefix, they are replaced by zeros to obtain the absolute address.
- In all other cases, the absolute address is equal to the real address.

Thus, prefixing shifts around the first 4K-byte block to another block in absolute storage for each CPU.

5.5.3   Virtual Storage

Virtual storage consists of up to 64K address spaces, each address space being 2G bytes in size. An address space is a collection of byte addresses numbered 0, ... n where n is 2G minus 1. These byte addresses are called virtual addresses.

As in the case of the 370 architecture, an address space is divided into segments and segments are divided into pages (see Figure 5-3). The size of a segment is 1 MB and that of a page is 4 KB. Note that the 370 gave options of 1 MB and 64 KB for the size of segments and 4 KB and 2 KB for pages. The 370/XA architecture specifies only one size for segments and for pages.

A virtual address consists of three fields, an 11-bit segment index (SX), an 8-bit page index (PX), and a 12-bit byte index (BX) (see

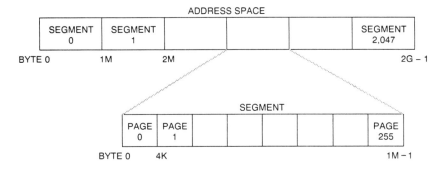

Figure 5-3 370/XA address space organization.

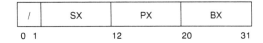

Figure 5-4 370/XA virtual address.

Figure 5-4). In the 370 architecture, the field lengths were 4 bits for SX, 8 bits for PX, and 12 bits for BX (assuming 1 MB segments and 4K pages are used).

Paging operations are similar to those described under the 370 architecture. A page resides in a page slot in secondary storage, or a page frame in main storage. The assignment of pages to page frames is done by means of two tables, the segment table and the page table. The segment table entries are in segment number sequence. Each entry contains the following fields (see Figure 5-5):

- The address of the page table for that segment denoted as Page Table Origin (PTO)
- A flag bit (I) to indicate whether or not the entry in the table is valid
- The length of the page table (PTL) in units of 64 bytes

The segment table begins on a 4K boundary. Each entry is 4 bytes long. The page table begins on a 64-byte boundary and each entry is 4 bytes in length. These factors make it possible to store only non-zero portions of addresses and thus obtain economy in storage.

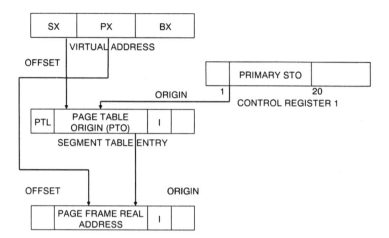

Figure 5-5 DAT 2 level table look up.

5.5.4   Dynamic Address Translation (DAT)

This is similar to the procedure described in the 370 architecture. A virtual address is translated to a real address by a look-up of the segment table and the page table. Control register 1 contains the length, in units of 64 bytes, and the address of the segment table, the Segment Table Origin (STO) for the address space whose virtual addresses are to be translated. The operating system is expected to load control register 1 with the required information.

The translation consists of the following steps:

• The segment index (SX) of the virtual address is multiplied by 4 and added to the segment table origin (STO) to obtain the segment table entry for that segment.
• The page index (PX) of the virtual address is multiplied by 2 and added to the page table origin (PTO) to access the page table entry for that page.
• The page table entry contains the address of the page frame assigned to the page.

A translation look-aside buffer (TLB) is used to store recently used translation data. The TLB entries pertain to segments as well as pages. The segment entries contain STO, SX, PTO, and a few other fields. The page entries contain PTO, PX, PFRA, and other fields.

The TLB is accessed before the segment and page tables. If the address is in the TLB, there is no need to access the segment and page tables. The use of the TLB cuts down main storage access from three to one. Without a TLB, dynamic address translation would be unacceptable from a performance point of view.

5.5.5 Storage Protection

The principles of storage protection are similar to those specified in the 370 architecture. Main storage is organized into 4K-byte blocks. Each block has a 7-bit key associated with it (see Figure 5-6). This key has the following fields:

- Bits 0–3 are called the access control bits (ACC). They are matched with the 4-bit access key contained in the PSW or in the operation request block (ORB) of the channel subsystem. Matching is said to occur when the access key is equal to zero or when it is equal to the value in the ACC field.
- The fetch protection bit (F) indicates whether or not fetching should be protected also. Storing is always protected, but fetch protection is optional. A one in this bit position indicates that fetching should be monitored also.
- The reference bit (R) is set to 1 when the storage block is accessed. This information is needed by the real storage management routines of the operating system, to allocate page frames optimally.
- The change bit (C) indicates whether any change has been made in that storage block. This information also is needed by storage management routines of the operating system. A changed page frame has to be paged out before it can be assigned to a new page. An unchanged frame can be assigned to a new page without a page-out.

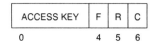

Figure 5-6 Storage key.

5.6 I/O ARCHITECTURE

The 370/XA I/O architecture is quite different from the 370 I/O architecture and introduces radically new concepts. The I/O instructions available for the 370 have been replaced by a new set of instructions and the interruption structure also has been completely changed. The 370/XA I/O architecture is schematically illustrated in Figure 5-7. One or more CPUs issue I/O instructions pertaining to a specific device to a channel subsystem that decodes the I/O instruction and selects a path to the device. The device decodes the commands for the I/O operation and performs the I/O operation. It can reconnect to any path to which it is attached, rather than the path that initiated the I/O operation. The channel subsystem interrupts any available CPU on completion of the I/O operation.

The 370 I/O architectural principles, on the other hand, are completely different, as explained below:

- Each CPU owns a set of channels, i.e., a set of channels is dedicated to a CPU.
- A channel can be addressed only by the CPU to which it is connected.
- An I/O instruction specifies a channel address and a device address (which includes the control unit address).
- On completion of an I/O operation, a channel can interrupt only that CPU to which it is connected.

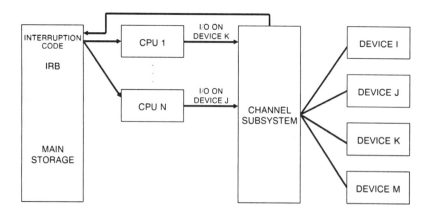

Figure 5-7 370/XA I/O architecture.

- When the operating system attempts an I/O operation, it is necessary to specify the path (i.e., the channel address and control unit address) as part of the SIO or SIOF operation; if the path is busy, the operating system selects another path and retries the I/O operation.
- When a device disconnects from a channel during an I/O operation, it must reconnect to the same channel when it is ready to resume the I/O operation; if the channel is busy, the device must wait until the channel is free.

The 370/XA I/O architecture is based on a set of rules for optimization of CPU time in I/O processing, reduction of delays, operational ease, and maximization of data transfer rates. These were developed from many years of observation of the 360 and 370 I/O architectures in practical environments.

Symmetry in I/O Processing

Any CPU should be able to perform an I/O operation on any device in the computer system. In the 370, a device could be accessed by a CPU only if a channel connected to the CPU was attached to the device. In the 370/XA, any CPU can access any device in the system.

Specification at Device Level

An I/O instruction should specify only a device number and not the physical I/O path. In the 370, the address of the channel, control unit, and device are specified as part of the I/O operation. In practical situations, there may be multiple paths that can be used for I/O operations on a device. Specifications of a particular path in an I/O instruction is giving preferential treatment to a path, which is not warranted.

Dynamic Reconnection

The IBM 3380 disk drive is an example of a device that has dynamic reconnection capability; i.e., it can connect to a channel other than the one that initiated the I/O operation when it is ready to go ahead with data transfer. A block multiplexer channel in the 370 works with a disk drive that has rotational position-sensing capability in the following manner. The channel disconnects from the device after it has issued a search ID equal command prior to the read command. The device attempts to reconnect with the channel when the addressed sector is approaching the read/write head. If the channel is not ready, it attempts to reconnect at the end of the next revolution. With the dynamic reconnection capability, the disk can reconnect to any available channel that has been defined as a path. Thus, delays in I/O completion are minimized.

Avoidance of CPU Overhead

The CPU (the operating system) is responsible for channel path management under the 370 architecture. Channel path management consists of testing the availability of channel paths associated with the device. This involved substantial overhead for the CPU. In the 370/XA architecture, the channel subsystem is responsible for channel path management.

Also, under the 370 architecture, the CPU was interrupted at the end of various phases of execution of the I/O operation. Under the 370/XA architecture, the channel subsystem handles most of the intermediate interruptions, and a CPU is interrupted at the end of the I/O operation.

The 370/XA architecture thus eliminates the bottlenecks present in the 370 architecture. It also offers a conceptually cleaner way of handling of input/output operations.

5.6.1 The Channel Subsystem

The channel subsystem, in a physical sense, is an I/O processor that interacts with multiple CPUs (for implementation details, see Chapters 9 and 10). From an architectural point of view, the channel subsystem logically consists of a set of subchannels. Each subchannel has a unique number and is in one-to-one correspondence with a device (see Figure 5-8). There can be up to 64K subchannels in a channel subsystem.

The functions of the channel subsystem are the following:

- Accept I/O instructions from any CPU.
- Decode the instruction and find a path (from one of possibly several available paths) to the device.
- Interrupt any CPU when the operation is complete.

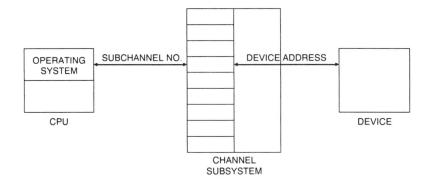

Figure 5-8 Subchannel/device correspondence.

The word "subchannel" is used in the 370/XA architecture in a different sense than it is used in the 370 architecture. Each channel in the 370 has a set of subchannels (which may be shared). Communication between a device and channel uses a subchannel and takes place over a physical path provided by the channel. If the device is connected to more than one channel, an I/O using the second channel requires a different subchannel. In the 370/XA architecture, subchannels are no longer a property of the channel, with each channel owning its own set of subchannels. Instead, a subchannel and a device are logically tied together and the device appears to the operating system as a subchannel (see Figure 5-8).

The subchannel contains information such as the address of the current Channel Command Word (CCW), channel-path identifier, device number, and other relevant data. It also contains status indicators pertaining to the device. A subchannel is connected to a device by up to 8 paths. A path physically consists of a channel connected to a device via a control unit. A device can be connected to one or more control units. A control unit can be connected to one or more devices. A channel can be connected to one or more control units. A control unit can be connected to one or more channels.

Every device has at least one path connecting it to a subchannel. The details of the connection between a subchannel and a device is stored by the channel subsystem during system installation.

A CPU initiates an I/O operation by means of a START SUBCHANNEL instruction. The address of the desired subchannel is provided by the CPU. Each device, as mentioned before, has one and only one subchannel address. The subchannel address therefore uniquely identifies the device. Path selection is done by the channel subsystem. The channel subsystem selects a path and initiates the I/O operation. If the path is busy or unavailable, it tries another path.

Channel Path

The channel path physically is a channel, as described in the 370 architecture (Chapter 4). It is called a channel path in the 370/XA architecture because its function has been relegated to that of providing a path for initiating an I/O operation and for data transfer. The channel is no longer addressed by the CPU. The channel subsystem communicates with channels, but this is done in a manner completely transparent to the CPU. The words "channel" and "channel path" will be used interchangeably by us, with the understanding that the channel is viewed as a passive vehicle for data transfer.

The channel subsystem communicates with a device by using one or more channel paths. These channel paths are connected to control units, which in turn are connected to devices. Each channel path is given an 8-bit identifier (CHPID). There can be up to 256 channel paths in a computer configuration.

I/O Device Designations

A device is designated by three numbers. It is referred to by a sub-channel number in interactions between a CPU and the channel subsystem during I/O operations. The channel subsystem interacts with the device using a device address. When communication between a system operator and the control program regarding an I/O device is necessary, a device number is used. Thus, there are three designations pertaining to an I/O device.

5.6.2   I/O Instructions

The I/O instructions are grouped under two functions, basic I/O functions and other functions. The basic I/O functions are those that cause the channel subsystem to perform specific I/O related actions. The major instructions in the basic group are the following:

- START SUBCHANNEL
- RESUME SUBCHANNEL
- HALT SUBCHANNEL.

The major instructions in the second group are the following:

- STORE SUBCHANNEL
- MODIFY SUBCHANNEL
- TEST SUBCHANNEL
- SET CHANNEL MONITOR.

All I/O instructions use the S format and contain an op code and an address in the B2(D2) format. They also use general register 1 (and sometimes general register 2) as an implied operand. The subchannel address, for example, is placed in general register 1. During the execution of some of the I/O instructions, the condition code in the PSW is set. Normally, a condition code of 0 indicates that the instruction execution was successful. The other codes (1–3) indicate varying degrees of ineffective instruction execution.

The START SUBCHANNEL instruction is used for starting an I/O operation. It replaces the START I/O instruction in the 370 architecture. The HALT SUBCHANNEL (HSCH) instruction is used to terminate a currently ongoing I/O operation at a subchannel. The HALT SUBCHANNEL instruction causes a halt signal to be issued to the device associated with the subchannel. The RESUME SUB-CHANNEL (RSCH) instruction is used to resume the execution of a suspended channel program. A channel program can be suspended at any stage of the I/O operation. This instruction functions in a manner similar to the START SUBCHANNEL instruction.

It is possible to modify the functional capabilities of a subchannel by the CPU. For example, a path can be disabled or the entire subchannel can be deactivated. This is done by the MODIFY SUB-CHANNEL instruction. The STORE SUBCHANNEL instruction provides the capability of storing the information pertaining to a subchannel for use by the operating system.

The TEST SUBCHANNEL instruction causes device status to be stored in the Interruption Request Block (IRB), which is described later under I/O Interruptions. The SET CHANNEL MONITOR activates or deactivates the monitoring capabilities of the channel subsystem.

5.6.3 Initiation of an I/O Operation

The START SUBCHANNEL instruction (SSCH) initiates an I/O operation for a device. The subchannel number is contained in general register 1 (see Figure 5-9). The B2 and D2 fields are used to

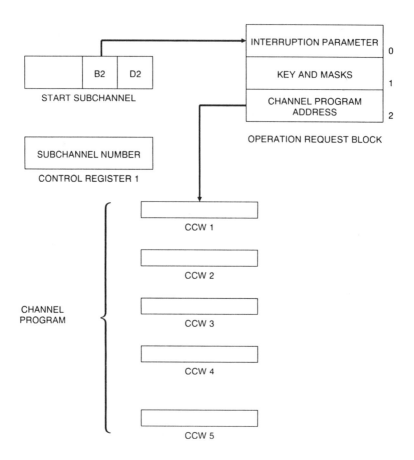

Figure 5-9 Initiation of I/O operation.

specify the address of an Operation Request Block (ORB), whose parameters are used by the Channel Subsystem.

The ORB contains several fields, but we shall restrict our discussion to the following ones:

• The first word of the ORB is called an interruption parameter. This word is returned on interruption by the channel subsystem, as part of the interruption code.
• The second word contains the storage key to be used for gaining access to the area of main storage that will be affected by data transfer. The second word also contains an 8 bit logical path mask (LPM). This mask is used to disable one or more of the eight paths that can be used for connecting the device to the subchannel.

• The third word contains the starting address of the channel program (the first Channel Command Word) used in the I/O operation.

5.6.4 Channel Programs

As in the 360 and 370 architectures, the detailed specification of an input/output operation involving device orders (e.g., rewind, seek) and data transfer (e.g., read) is done by means of a channel program. A channel program is composed of channel command words (CCWs). A CCW contains a command code, an address for transfer of data, the number of bytes that are to be transferred, and various chaining flags. Each CCW is executed individually. A command chaining flag in the CCW indicates whether or not the next CCW is to be executed. If the flag is on, the CCW at the next contiguous location is executed. Branching and looping in a channel program are provided indirectly by means of a transfer in channel command, which branches to a CCW shown in the data address field of the current CCW.

Conceptually, the 370/XA channel programs are similar to the 370 channel programs. However, there are some minor differences in regard to the format of the CCW.

A CCW can be in one of two formats:

• The 370 CCW format, called Format-0
• The 370/XA format, called Format-1.

The two formats are similar except for the data address field, which is 31 bits long in Format-1 and 24 bits long in Format-0 (see Figure 5-10).

The commands are identical to the 360 and 370 commands and are listed below for reference:

• Write (MMMM MM01)
• Read (MMMM MM10)
• Read Backward (MMMM 1100)
• Control (MMMM MM11)
• Sense (MMMM 0100)
• Sense ID (1110 0100)
• Transfer in Channel (XXXX 1000).

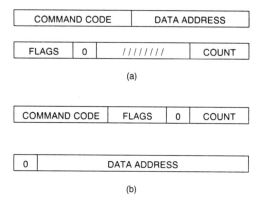

Figure 5-10 CCW formats.

An M indicates a modifier bit. The modifier bits specify to the device how the command is to be executed in terms of device orders. An X indicates a bit that is ignored for a Format-0 CCW but must be 0 in a Format-1 CCW.

The flags indicate various functions to be performed in the course of the I/O operation such as:

• Command chaining
• Data chaining
• Skipping
• Program controlled interruption
• Indirect data addressing.

The first four functions are present in the 360 and 370 architectures, and the last is present in the 370 architecture. We shall briefly review these functions.

Command chaining is used for sequential execution of the CCWs that comprise a channel program. Every CCW except the last one in the channel program has a command chaining flag. When the flag is on, the next sequential CCW is fetched, decoded, and executed by the channel subsystem after the execution of the current CCW (the device-end signal is received from the device).

Data chaining causes a new CCW to be executed as in command chaining. The new CCW continues the operation initiated by the previous CCW. The data address and count can be different in the new CCW.

Skipping indicates that no data transfer to the designated data address takes place, but the operation of the devices continues and the byte count will be updated. Skipping, when combined with data chaining, enables the channel program to place selected portions of a block of data on a device in contiguous or noncontiguous portions of main storage.

The program-controlled interruption (PCI) flag in a CCW is used for indicating that the subchannel should cause an interruption. The point of interruption varies depending on the CCW. For example, if the CCW is the first CCW in the channel program, the interruption occurs after execution of the CCW. For a CCW that has become the current CCW as a result of command chaining, the interruption occurs before the execution of the CCW. PCI provides the capability of notification to a CPU the intermediate status of complex I/O operations.

Indirect data addressing (IDA) is the counterpart of dynamic address translation (DAT), applied to the channel subsystem. It allows a channel program to use virtual data addresses. When the IDA flag is on, the data address in the CCW is interpreted as a pointer to a list of indirect data address words (IDAWs). Each IDAW contains the address of a 2K-byte block in absolute storage. These addresses are used for data transfer, in successive 2K-byte blocks.

There is a capability in the 370/XA (which is not present in the 370 architecture) for channel program suspension. A new flag field is introduced; its function is to indicate whether or not the channel program is to be suspended. This function provides the ability to stop a channel program temporarily and resume it later with the RESUME SUBCHANNEL instruction.

Storing and Modification of Subchannel Information

A CPU can ask the channel subsystem to store information pertaining to a subchannel, via the STORE SUBCHANNEL instruction. It can also modify the information in the channel subsystem pertaining to a subchannel by using the MODIFY SUBCHANNEL instruction.

These instructions use a control block called the Subchannel Information Block (SCHIB). The address of SCHIB is used as one of the operands of both STORE SUBCHANNEL and MODIFY SUBCHANNEL instructions. Another operand, of course, is the subchannel number.

An overview of SCHIB is given next. Not every field in the SCHIB is modifiable. The fields that are modifiable are those pertaining to channel path management, channel measurement, and interruption parameters.

Subchannel Information Block (SCHIB)

The SCHIB (see Figure 5-11a) contains three major fields, namely:

- Path-Management-Control Word (PMCW)
- Subchannel-Status Word (SCSW)
- Model-Dependent Area.

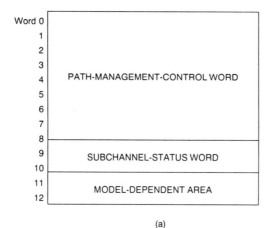

Figure 5-11 (a) Subchannel information block (SCHIB). (b) Path management control word.

The format of the PMCW is given in Figure 5-11b. The PMCW contains the following information:

- The device number of the device associated with the subchannel (as mentioned before, device numbers and subchannel numbers are in one-to-one correspondence).
- The ID numbers (up to 8) of channel paths that connect the control units attached to the device to the Channel Subsystem (denoted as CHPID-0 to CHPID-7).
- A multipath mode bit (D) to indicate that the device has the dynamic reconnection feature and can operate in the multipath mode during an I/O operation.
- Bits for indicating whether or not timing and monitoring facilities are enabled or available, such as Measurement Mode Enable (MM), Device Connect Time Measurement Enable, Timing Facility (T), Measurement Block Index (MBI).
- Bits or fields used in conjunction with channel path management, such as:
  - Logical Path Mask (LPM), which is eight bits in length and indicates whether or not a channel path is logically available.
  - Path Available Mask (PAM), which is eight bits in length, with each bit indicating whether or not the corresponding channel path is physically available for accessing the device.
  - Path Operational Mask (POM), which is eight bits in length and indicates whether or not the device was operational on the corresponding path during the last time the device was selected on that path.
  - Path Installed Mask (PIM), which is eight bits in length indicates whether or not paths are installed.
  - Path Not Operational Mask (PNOM) indicates whether these paths are operational paths.

The Subchannel Status Word (SCSW) is described in the next section.

5.6.5 I/O Interruption

An I/O interruption is the means of notification of any one of the CPUs in the computer system by the channel subsystem that a well-defined stage has been completed in an I/O operation or an event has occurred that needs the attention of a CPU.

An interruption causes the following hardware action:

- The current PSW is stored as the old PSW in location 56.
- An 8-byte interruption code, which identifies the subchannel causing the interruption and the interruption parameter (from the ORB), is placed in locations 184–191.
- A new PSW located in location 120 is loaded, and by this means control is given to the operating system to process the interruption.

Normally, several interruptions take place during an I/O operation; the conditions when these occur are listed below:

- Execution of the start function is completed by the device (called a "primary interruption condition" in the 370/XA architecture).
- Termination of an I/O operation by the device has taken place because of an alert condition (called a "secondary interruption condition" in the 370/XA architecture).
- An event of interest to the operating system in the sense that its occurrence has been requested by the operating system for notification has taken place (called an "intermediate interruption condition" in the 370/XA architecture).
- An unusual condition has taken place (called an "alert interruption condition").

The flow of events during an interruption is schematically illustrated in Figure 5-12. The device or channel subsystem can initiate an interruption. The channel subsystem is responsible in either case of performing the actual interruption. A new PSW is loaded into a CPU; this should contain the address of an interruption handling routine.

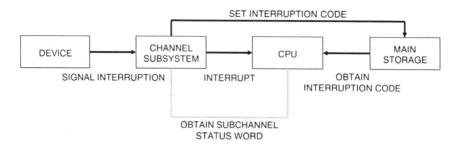

Figure 5-12 Note: Solid line indicates hardware action. Broken line indicates software action.

The details regarding the specific nature of the interruption is provided on execution of a TEST SUBCHANNEL instruction. This instruction copies the Subchannel Status Word (SCSW), which is part of the Interruption Response Block (IRB) provided by the channel subsystem in a specified location in storage.

The IRB contains three major words, namely a Subchannel Status Word (SCSW), an Extended Status Word, and an Extended Control Word (see Figure 5-13). Of these the significant information from the point of view of this discussion is in the SCSW. The other two are model dependent and are similar in concept to the channel logout and extended channel logout words used in the 370.

The SCSW contains the following fields that capture the status of various I/O related elements, as listed below.

The device status field (D status) contains the status of the device and is generated by the device. The status for the device can be any of the following:

- Device end
- Busy
- Channel end
- Control unit end
- Unit check
- Unit exception
- Attention
- Status modifier.

Each of the above conditions is indicated by a specific bit in the D status field. They have the same interpretation as in the 360 and 370 architectures.

SUBCHANNEL STATUS WORD
EXTENDED STATUS WORD
EXTENDED STATUS WORD

(a)

STORAGE KEY		AC	SC	
CCW ADDRESS				
D STATUS	S STATUS			

(b)

Figure 5-13 (a) Interruption request block. (b) Subchannel status word.

The subchannel status field (S status) identifies the conditions at the subchannel level that cause the interruption, such as PCI, protection check, etc.

The status control field (SC) is used to identify the interruption condition. The occurrence of the following conditions is indicated by this field:

- Primary interruption
- Alert interruption
- Secondary interruption
- Intermediate interruption.

A bit is designated for each of the above conditions. An additional bit (called the Status-Pending bit) is set to one when the interruption condition is generated.

The activity control field (AC field) indicates the progress of a basic I/O function being performed by the subchannel. The progress is designated by setting a specific bit to one for each of the following events:

- I/O operation is currently being done at the device level.
- Channel program is suspended.
- Any one of the following basic I/O instructions are "pending" (awaiting execution) at the subchannel:

    — START SUBCHANNEL
    — HALT SUBCHANNEL
    — RESUME SUBCHANNEL.

To sum up, the channel subsystem interrupts any processor enabled for the interruption. The interruption code provides the subchannel number necessary for identification of the source of the interruption. The subchannel is in the status pending state (it has interruption information ready). A TEST SUBCHANNEL instruction stores the contents of the Interruption Request Block (IRB) at an address specified by the instruction. The IRB contains the Subchannel Status Word (SCSW), which gives details regarding the interruption. The subchannel is cleared of its pending status at the end of the execution of TEST SUBCHANNEL.

5.7 INSTRUCTION SET

The 370/XA architecture specifies the same instruction set as the 370, except as noted below (see Table 5-1):

- The I/O instruction set of the 370 is replaced by a new set, as mentioned previously.
- Four new instructions have been added to the unprivileged instruction set.
- Two new instructions have been added to the privileged instruction set.

The new unprivileged instructions are the following:

- BRANCH AND SAVE AND SET MODE
- BRANCH AND SET MODE
- DIVIDE (extended precision)
- INSERT PROGRAM MASK.

The privileged instructions are the following:

- TRACE
- START INTERPRETIVE EXECUTION.

Table 5-1 New Instructions for 370/XA

INSTRUCTION	MNEMONIC	FORMAT	CLASSIFICATION
BRANCH AND SAVE AND SET MODE	BASSAM	RR	BRANCH
BRANCH AND SET MODE	BSM	RR	BRANCH
DIVIDE (EXTENDED)	DXR	RRE	FLOATING POINT
INSERT PROGRAM MASK	IPM	RRE	DATA MOVEMENT
TRACE	TRACE	RS	CONTROL
START INTERPRETIVE EXECUTION	SIE	S	CONTROL
CLEAR SUBCHANNEL	CSCH	S	I/O
HALT SUBCHANNEL	HSCH	S	I/O
MODIFY SUBCHANNEL	MSCH	S	I/O
RESET CHANNEL PATH	RCHP	S	I/O
RESUME SUBCHANNEL	RSCH	S	I/O
SET ADDRESS LIMIT	SAL	S	I/O
SET CHANNEL MONITOR	SCHM	S	I/O
START SUBCHANNEL	SSCH	S	I/O
STORE CHANNEL PATH STATUS	STCPS	S	I/O
STORE CHANNEL REPORT WORD	STCRW	S	I/O
STORE SUBCHANNEL	STSCH	S	I/O
TEST PENDING INTERRUPTION	TPI	S	I/O
TEST SUBCHANNEL	TSCH		

5.7.1 General Remarks Pertaining to Instructions

The 370/XA instructions use the same formats as the 370 instructions. Thus, an instruction is two, four, or six bytes in length and is located on a halfword integral boundary. An instruction should have one of the following eight formats:

- Register and register (RR)
- Register and register extended (RRE)
- Register and indexed (RX)
- Register and storage (RS)
- Storage and immediate (SI)
- Storage (of an implied operand) (S)
- Storage and storage (SS)
- Storage and storage extended (SSE).

These formats have the same interpretation and usage as in the case of the 370, except that 31-bit addresses are used instead of 24 bit addresses. Thus, the base address (contents of the base register B) and index (contents of the register X) are treated as 32-bit binary integers. The displacement field D is a 12-bit number, as in the case of the 370. In address generation, the base address, index, and displacement are added as 32-bit binary numbers, and overflow is ignored. Bit 0 of the generated address is always set to zero.

An instruction is normally non-interruptible; i.e., the execution of an instruction is an entire operation. However, certain time-consuming instructions (e.g., COMPARE LOGICAL LONG, MOVE LONG) can be interrupted as in the 370. These instructions are viewed as consisting of units of operation and interruptions are permitted between units of operation.

The execution of an instruction can end in completion, nullification, suppression, or termination. Completion denotes successful execution. Suppression is equivalent to a no-operation instruction, and the PSW shows the next instruction address. Nullification is similar to suppression except that the PSW shows the address of the current instruction. Termination denotes unsuccessful execution with unpredictable changes in registers or storage areas or other fields that are likely to be changed by the instruction.

5.7.2   Instruction Classification

As in the case of the 370, instructions are classified as general, decimal, floating point, control, and I/O. The general instructions include binary arithmetic, load, store, and logical instructions. The general, decimal, and floating-point instructions are unprivileged (problem) instructions. The control instructions are either privileged or semiprivileged. The privileged operations can be executed only in the supervisor state. The semiprivileged instructions can be executed in the problem state by authorized users.

Arithmetic Instructions

The number representation used in the 360 and 370 architectures are valid for the 370/XA architecture, also. Binary integers can be halfwords (16 bits) or fullwords (32 bits). They can be signed or unsigned. Negative binary integers are stored in two's complement notation by inverting each bit of the positive binary integer and adding one. Decimal integers can be in the packed or zoned format. In the packed format, the number of decimal digits can vary from 1 to 31. In the zoned format, the number of decimal digits can vary from 1 to 16. Floating-point numbers have short, long, and extended formats.

The 370 arithmetic instruction repertoire is kept in the 370/XA architecture. A new instruction for extended floating-point division has been added.

Logical Instructions

The AND, OR, and EXCLUSIVE OR instructions are the same as in the case of the 360. No new instructions have been added.

The 370 comparison instructions are used in the 370/XA architecture, also. No new instructions have been added.

The shift instructions specified in the 360 and 370 architectures apply to the 370/XA architecture, also.

Data Movement Instructions

The 370 instructions under this category have been kept. A new instruction, INSERT PROGRAM MASK, has been added. This instruction moves the condition code and program mask from the PSW into bit positions 2–3 and 4–7 of the general register specified in the R1 field. The instruction is in the RRE format. It specifies only one operand, namely, a general register R1 in bit positions 24–28. The reason for introducing this instruction was to provide the data required by the new branch instruction BASSM.

Branch Instructions

The branch instructions specified in the 370 architecture apply to the 370/XA architecture also. Two new instructions BRANCH AND SET MODE (BSM) and BRANCH AND SAVE AND SET MODE (BASSM) have been added. These instructions are used for switching addressing modes from 31-bit to 24-bit after branching, to provide compatibility for 370 programs that are called by 370/XA programs.

SUBROUTINE CALLS. The BRANCH AND LINK instruction of the 360 and 370 architectures has been kept for the sake of compatibility. The link information varies depending on the addressing mode. When 24-bit addressing mode is used, the link information consists of the instruction length code, the condition code, program mask, and the next instruction address, exactly as in the case of the 370. When 31-bit addressing mode is used, the link information is the right half of the 370/XA PSW (namely, addressing mode and next instruction address).

The BRANCH AND SAVE instruction saves the right half (bits 32–63) of the PSW in the register specified in the R1 field before branching to the address specified by the second operand. Note that the addressing mode (1 in the case of 31-bit addressing) indicated by bit 32 is saved also. Thus, BRANCH AND SAVE and BRANCH AND LINK are identical when 31-bit addressing is used. BRANCH AND SAVE is recommended in the Principles of Operations for the 370/XA instead of BRANCH AND LINK because of the latter's slower performance.

The BRANCH AND SET MODE instruction (BSM) is in RR format. It copies bit 32 of the PSW (the address mode bit) in bit position 0 of the register specified in the R1 field. The remaining bits are unchanged. When the R1 field indicates 0, the register is not changed at all. The register specified by the R2 field indicates the new address mode and branch address. If the R2 field is not 0, branching takes place. If the R2 field is 0, no branching takes place. This instruction, with an R1 field of 0 is intended to be the standard instruction for sue by subroutines to return to the calling program.

The BRANCH AND SAVE AND SET MODE (BASSM) functions like BRANCH AND SAVE. It is intended for use when calling a subprogram that operates in a different addressing mode. It is in the RR format. The right half of the PSW is saved in the register designated by R1. The contents of the register specified by the R2 field specify the new addressing mode and branch address. When the value of R2 is 0, no branching takes place.

CONDITIONAL BRANCH. The instructions specified in the 360 and 370 architectures are applicable for the 370/XA also. The branch address is taken to be 31 bits or 24 bits, depending on the addressing mode.

UNCONDITIONAL BRANCH. The BRANCH ON CONDITION can be used for unconditional branching, as in the case of the 360 and 370.

Control Instructions

Most of the control instructions specified in the 370 architecture apply to the 370/XA architecture also. A new instruction TRACE has been added. This instruction is useful in tracing the internal workings of a program. The contents of the TOD clock, general registers, branch addresses and primary and secondary address space information can be obtained from the TRACE entries. Each trace entry is stored in a location specified in control register 12.

As in the case of the 370, the control instructions are used to set, store or manipulate various objects that are not accessible to the problem programmer. The objects to which these instructions apply are the following:

• TOD CLOCK (set, store)
• COMPARATOR (set, store)
• CPU TIMER (set, store)
• PSW (load, set PSW key, set and store system mask)
• CONTROL REGISTER (load, store)
• TLB (purge)
• CPU (store CPU address, store CPU ID)
• PREFIX REGISTER (set, store)

In addition, the instructions that apply to dual address spaces (e.g., MOVE TO PRIMARY, MOVE TO SECONDARY, PROGRAM CALL, PROGRAM TRANSFER), which are described for the 370, apply to the 370/XA also. These instructions are executable in the semiprivileged mode.

An instruction START INTERPRETIVE EXECUTION (SIE) has been added to the instruction set. It uses a control block in storage that specifies the state and architecture of a guest program to be executed interpretively. The machine executing the instruction is called the host machine. This instruction is used in conjunction with virtual machine (VM) operation, under which programs using different operating systems can be executed concurrently on the same machine.

5.8   DUAL ADDRESS SPACES (DAS)

The treatment and use of dual address spaces under the 370/XA architecture is similar to that in the 370 architecture. Many IBM software systems require data movement between two address spaces. For example, a database management system like DB2 uses three address spaces. In addition, it has to interact with other systems, such as TSO or CICS, which run in one or more address spaces.

In the case of instructions that use dual address spaces (DAS), the primary and secondary addresses are concurrently translated using a procedure similar to that described in the 370 architecture. Control register 7 contains the address of the segment table for the secondary address space. The address of the segment table for the primary address space is, of course, in control register 1.

The instructions MOVE TO PRIMARY and MOVE TO SECONDARY move data from a secondary to a primary address space and vice versa. They specify the address, length and storage protection key of the operands.

The instructions PROGRAM CALL and PROGRAM TRANSFER are used to link to a program in a different address space and return from it to the calling program in the original address space. Each address space is assigned a unique number (ASN). Up to 64K address spaces are supported by the architecture. The PROGRAM CALL instruction operates in several phases. The instruction contains two indexes (offsets) for looking up a linkage table and an entry table (see Chapter 4). The entry table entry (ETE) can specify the ASN of the space to be switched to. This ASN is translated using the procedure described in Chapter 4.

5.9 MULTIPROCESSING

As mentioned earlier, the 370/XA multiprocessing uses cleaner architectural concepts than the 370 multiprocessing. The I/O architecture of the 370/XA is the primary reason for this improvement. The impact of the I/O architecture can be summarized as follows:

- No CPU has exclusive access to a device via a channel.
- Any CPU can handle an I/O interruption as opposed to the CPU that initiated an I/O operation.
- An I/O processor handles the bulk of the work in initiating and controlling an I/O operation.

In Chapters 9 and 10, the implementation of multiprocessing under the 308X and 3090 are described. These computers, which use the 370/XA architecture, can have up to four or six CPUs. They run under a single copy of the operating system and share main storage. Each CPU runs a unit of work (e.g., a task) independently of other CPUs. Thus the architecture provides a single image, i.e., of a computer that executes a program in the manner of a uniprocessor, to an outside observer.

The two major issues that are discussed in the 370/XA Principles of Operations in this context are sharing of main storage and signalling between CPUs.

5.9.1 Sharing Main Storage

Main storage is shared by CPUs by using prefixing. Prefixing was discussed in Chapter 4 under multiprocessing and earlier in this chapter under storage architecture. The 370/XA architecture uses a 19-bit field in the prefix register compared to the 12-bit field in the 370 architecture. The increase in length of 7 bits is due to the corresponding increase in storage address from 24 to 31 bits.

Each CPU uses a real address, i.e., a byte sequence of $0, 1, ...2^G - 1$ for its operations. The real address is converted by the CPU, using prefixing, to an absolute address that is subsequently used for storage references.

5.9.2 CPU Signaling

An instruction, SIGNAL PROCESSOR, is provided for communication between CPUs, as in the 370 architecture. It uses the following operands:

• A CPU address
• An order code
• A parameter

Each CPU is assigned an address during system installation. The order code specifies an order to be performed by the addressed CPU. These orders are described in Chapter 4 under multiprocessing. Two additional orders, SET PREFIX and STORE STATUS AT ADDRESS, have been added. The SET PREFIX order sets a specific value in the prefix register of the designated CPU. The STORE STATUS AT ADDRESS saves the CPU status at a specified location.

5.10 LIMITATIONS OF THE 370/XA ARCHITECTURE

The limitations of the 360 and 370 architectures apply to the 370/XA architecture, also. The reader is referred to Chapters 3 and 4 in this respect. The basic problem with the 370/XA machine is one of complexity, which it inherited from the 370 architecture.

Another problem is in regard to multiprocessing. The architecture does not say how the single-image effect is to be obtained. In Chapters 9 and 10, we see that it is due to a cooperative effort on the part of the operating system and design mechanisms (e.g., cache, system controller, etc.). In our opinion, the architecture should specify the underlying conceptual model. The Principles of Operation for System 370/XA [3] does specify the conceptual machine for each CPU but not for the entire machine with multiple CPUs.

REFERENCES

1. IBM System/360 Principles of Operation, Order No. GA 22-6821.
2. IBM System/370 Principles of Operation, Order No. GA 22-7000.
3. IBM System/370 XA Principles of Operation, Publication No. SA 22-7085.

4. Padegs A.: "System/370 Extended Architecture: Design Considerations," *IBM Journal of Research and Development*, vol. 27, no. 3, May 1983.

5. Cormier R.L., et al.: "System/370 Extended Architecture: The Channel Subsystem," *IBM Journal of Research and Development*, vol. 27, no. 3, May 1983.

6

ESA/370 Architecture

The Enterprise System Architecture (ESA/370) was announced by IBM as the successor to the 370/XA architecture in February 1988. The complete architecture specifications were not available at the time of this chapter's writing. The material presented here has been gathered from information released by IBM.

The new architecture will be implemented on the high end 3090 E models and 4381 E models. It provides for both single-image and multi-image multiprocessing. It also will support a new operating system, MVS/ESA. The multi-image capability is provided by the Processor Resource/Systems Manager (PR/SM), which is a hardware feature that allows a 3090 E to run as four computers with different operating systems.

The architecture also introduces new data-addressing modes that will enable the user to view or manipulate large volumes of data without restrictions. These capabilities are listed below:

- Data spaces
- HIPER spaces
- Data windowing

A brief discussion on the new capabilities is given next.

6.1   LOGICALLY PARTITIONED (LPAR) OPERATING MODE

The Processor Resource/Systems Manager (PR/SM) feature offers three modes of operation, 370,370/XA and the LPAR mode. Under the LPAR mode, an operator can define logical partitions and allocate resources to each partition. Each partition can have dedicated or shared central processors. The same applies to devices. A device can be shared between logical partitions by using channel paths that are allocated uniquely to a logical partition. Channel paths can be dynamically reconfigured among logical partitions. Main storage and expanded storage are not shared among logical partitions but are allocated to each partition in blocks of one megabyte. Each partition can run its own operating system.

6.2   DATA SPACES, HIPER SPACES, AND DATA WINDOWING

A data space is an address space that contains only data and no executable code. This address space is two gigabytes in size, like any MVS/XA address space. The data space can be used for storing buffer pools, tables, or files. It can be accessed from other address spaces, and a variety of operations can be performed on the data.

It is possible to store the contents of an entire 3380 disk in a 2-gigabyte data space. If the virtual storage implementation device for the address space is the expanded storage (see Chapter 10) used in 3090 design, substantial improvements can be obtained in many file operations (e.g., sorting) and in database management operations (e.g., joins of relations).

A High Performance (HIPER) space is virtual storage that resides on expanded storage, with the ability to be paged out to secondary storage. Its use is for storing temporary data, including paging data sets. Data is organized in 4K blocks. The total size of a HIPER space can be 2 gigabytes. Several HIPER spaces can be concatenated together through data windows. By using data windows, an application program can view up to 16 terabytes of data, in segments of 2 gigabytes at a time.

6.3   MOTIVATIONS FOR ESA/370 ARCHITECTURE

The motivations for ESA/370 seem to be the following:

- Virtual storage is enhanced by having separate data spaces
- Data is viewed separately from programs; it is claimed that this approach will enhance system reliability, especially when multiple programs share data.
- Using PR/SM it is possible to view a computer system as several logical partitions, each partition capable of running its own operating system. This approach, it is claimed, offers flexibility in system operation.

CONCLUDING REMARKS

It is premature, at this stage, to comment on the architecture. Obviously, its data manipulation capabilities are new and interesting. However, more details are necessary before these capabilities can be evaluated.

7

Techniques Used by IBM in the Design of Mainframes

In IBM mainframes, the design of a processor is distinct from its architecture. To quote Lorin [1],

> "The output of an architectural effort is a document that imposes requirements on a design. The output of a design effort is the mapping of an architecture into a technology in order to achieve stated price/ performance goals for a model of the architecture. Thus, a program-compatible product line (various models each of which respond in the same way to a list of operation codes and addresses) can be defined at different price/performance levels."

The instruction set, number of registers, and logical organization of storage are architectural ideas. The design considerations are the number of processors, the size of the cache within each processor, the functions to be implemented using microcode as opposed to hardware, the pipelining of instructions and other such details. The key design objective is the price/ performance ratio. This objective is achieved by using improved circuit technology or by design sophistication. The IBM 3090, for example, uses design concepts from its immediate ancestor, the IBM 308X system, and also from the IBM 3033. The 3033 was a highly pipelined computer that used "intelligence" in prefetching instructions and operands. It has been recognized in the industry as a prime example of sophisticated design. The 3081, on the other hand, relied on "brute force," i.e., improvement in circuit technology as a result of better packaging and integration of circuits. It did not use pipelining to any great extent and counted on the new circuitry to give it the necessary processing speed. The 3090 uses an extension of the 308X circuit technology, but incorporates in its design the pipelining concepts present in the 3033.

In this chapter, an overview of the design concepts and their parameters used in IBM mainframes is presented. In the next several chapters specific designs are discussed.

7.1 PRICE/PERFORMANCE CRITERIA

Computers that belong to a family (conform to the same architecture) are designed with price/performance ratios in mind. This is necessary because of marketing considerations. A data processing manager, for example, can be given a spectrum of options, all based on a dollar value for processing the workload at his installation.

However, it is misleading to judge a computer entirely by price/performance ratios because of the possibility of overlooking factors that have to deal with IBM's future plans for the product and long-term hardware/software compatibility with other products.

The performance of a machine is assessed by metrics such as:

• Millions of instructions processed in a second, known by the acronym MIPS
• Millions of floating-point operations per second, known by the acronym MFLOPS
• Relative instructions per second, known by the acronym RIPS, which is useful for comparing relative speeds of two machines.

The currently marketed IBM mainframes offer speeds that vary from 1 to 100 MIPS. At the high end are the 3090 series with a MIPS rating of 100 for the model 600. At the low end is the IBM 9370, whose lower models run around 1 MIPS. The price/performance ratios of IBM mainframes over a 20-year period are shown in Table 7-1.

A designer, when asked to come up with a design for a model that must satisfy price, performance, and architectural constraints, has to make decisions in regard to the considerations described next.

The first consideration is the extent of implementation of the instruction set of the architecture using hardware as opposed to microcode. Hardware implementation results in improved through-

Table 7-1 Price/Performance Ratios

ARCHITECTURE	MODEL	DATE	MIPS	PRICE ($, M)	PRICE/MIPS
360	50	8/65	0.2	1.2	7.0
	65	11/65	0.6	3.0	5.3
370	155	6/70	0.6	1.6	2.7
	165	6/70	1.9	4.0	2.1
	158	8/72	0.9	1.4	1.6
	168	5/73	2.4	4.2	1.8
	3033	3/78	5.0	3.4	0.7
370/XA	3081 K	4/82	13.5	4.6	0.3
	3084 Q	10/83	25.7	8.0	0.3
	3090–200	11/85	28.0	5.1	0.2
	3090–400	4/87	50.0	9.5	0.2

put, but microcode implementation is cheaper and easier to change. In practice, the higher-end mainframes implement most frequently used portions of the instruction set in hardware and the rest in microcode.

The next consideration is that of choosing the circuit technology for the processor and the types of memory to be used for the various levels of memory hierarchy used in storage implementation. The speed and size of the memories and circuits that are used have an impact on the price/performance ratio.

The third consideration is that of pipelined design for performance improvement. Pipelining consists in breaking up a function into sub-functions and performing each subfunction independently of the other to some extent in order to obtain throughput improvement.

The fourth consideration is the number of processors that can be incorporated in the model. This was not a consideration until the advent of the 308X series, when it was shown successfully that in-creasing the number of processors significantly improves throughput.

To put these issues in perspective, we have compiled a set of tables (Tables 7-2 and 7-3). Data for these tables were taken from Case and Padegs [2]. The tables show the features of early 360 and 370 com-puters. Some of these features are discussed in subsequent para-graphs. From an overall point of view, several remarks can be made at this stage. First of all, the microcode usage and size fluctuate. Some machines, such as the 360/195 and 370/195 which are high-end models, do not use microcode at all. The 370 138 and 148 models use relatively large amounts of microcode. Note also the size of the microword. In the case of the later 360 and 370 machines, it is 105

Table 7-2 Design Features of 370 Models

PARAMETER	MODEL											
	22	25	30	40	44	50	65	67	75	85	91	195
Year	71	68	65	65	66	65	65	66	66	69	67	71
CPU Cycle (N Sec)	750	900	750	625	250	500	200	200	195	80	60	54
Control Storage												
— Capacity (K Word)	4	8	4	4	–	3	3	3	–	2	–	–
— Word Size (Bits)	50	16	50	52	–	85	87	87	–	105	–	–
— Type	R	R. W	R	R	–	R	R	R	–	R	–	–
— Cycle (N Sec)	750	900	750	625	–	500	200	200	–	80	–	–
Main Storage												
— Cycle (N Sec)	1500	1800	1500	2500	1000	2000	750	750	750	960	780	756
— Width (Bytes)	1	2	1	2	4	4	8	8	8	16	8	8
— Interleaving	–	–	–	–	–	–	2	2	4	4	16	16
— Size	32K	48K	64K	256K	256K	256K	1M	1M	1M	4M	6M	4M
Cache												
— Cycle	–	–	–	–	–	–	–	–	–	80	–	54
— Size	–	–	–	–	–	–	–	–	–	32K	–	32
— Line Size (Bytes)	–	–	–	–	–	–	–	–	–	64		64

Table 7-3 Design Features of 360 Models

PARAMETER	MODEL											
	115	125	135	138	145	148	155	158	165	168	195	3033
Year	74	73	72	76	71	77	71	73	71	73	73	79
CPU Cycle (N Sec)	480	480	275	275	203	180	115	115	80	80	54	58
Control Storage												
— Capacity (K Word)	28	20	24	64	16	32	6	8	2	2	–	4
— Word Size (Bits)	20	19	16	16	32	32	69	69	105	105	–	105
— Type	R. W	R. W	R. W	R. W	R. W	R. W	R	R. W	R	R	–	R. W
— Cycle (N Sec)	480	480	275	275	203	180	115	115	80	80	–	58
Main Storage												
— Cycle (N Sec)	480	480	935	880	540	405	2070	920	2000	320	756	290
— Width (Bytes)	2	2	4	4	8	8	8	16				
— Interleaving	–	–	–	–	–	–	–	–				
— Size	192K	384K	512K	1M	2M	2M	2M	6M	3M	8M	4M	4M
Cache												
— Cycle	–	–	–	–	–	–	115	115	80	80	54	58
— Size	–	–	–	–	–	–	8K	8K	16K	16K	32K	644
— Line Size (Bytes)	–	–	–	–	–	–	16	16	32	32	64	64

bits as compared to 16 or 19 in the earlier machines. The larger the microword size, the more operations can be done concurrently, resulting in performance improvement. Second, the cache (introduced in the 360/85) is present in all the larger 370 mainframes. Its size varies from 8KB in the 155 to 64 KB in the 3033. Third is the overall reduction over the years in CPU-cycle and storage-cycle times. The earlier machines show large cycle times, although there are exceptions (e.g., the 360/195). In the machines introduced after the 3033 the cycle times have been reduced even more. For example, the cycle time of the 3090 is 18 nanoseconds.

7.2   CIRCUIT TECHNOLOGY

Newer circuit technology is introduced with a variety of objectives, such as the improvement of processing speed, miniaturization of components, and operational ease.

The System 360 introduced solid logic technology (SLT), under which transistor chips were directly mounted on half-inch square ceramic modules. Each module contained one or two circuits. The technology prior to SLT had used transistors individually sealed in small cans, and SLT was hailed as a breakthrough at that time.

The next step was the introduction of integrated circuits via the monolithic system technology (MST). Under this technology, several entire circuits were built on a single chip. The number of circuits per chip (the circuit density) continued to increase. As an example, the 3033, which uses MST, had a circuit density of 40.

Another major step in circuit technology was taken by IBM with the introduction of the thermal conduction module (TCM), which is used by the 308X series. Under this technology, the ceramic modules have sites for 100 logic chips, and each logic chip has cells for over 700 circuits. Thus, the circuit density has been vastly improved as a result of TCM technology. The 3090 uses a variant of the TCM technology.

The impact of circuit technology on processor cycle time has been that of steady rather than spectacular improvement. A processor cycle is defined as the time to do an atomic unit of work by the processor. A processor initiates operations relating to instruction fetching or execution at the start of a processor cycle controlled by an internal clock. Many basic operations are completed within one cycle, while others take several cycles. The processor cycle time of the 3033 was 57 nanoseconds. In 308X, the processor cycle time was reduced to 24 nanoseconds, and in the 3090 it was further reduced to 18.5 nanoseconds. The improvement in cycle time alone should contribute to factors of 2.3 and 3.2 in performance improvement. The RIPS indexes for 3081-K and 3090-400 using 3033 as the base are 2.7 and 10, respectively (see Table 7-1). This shows that other parameters discussed in this chapter are also important in improving performance.

7.3 MICROCODE VERSUS HARDWARE

As mentioned in Chapter 2, the use of microcode has made it possible to have a wide variety of computers follow the same architecture about with differing price/performance ratios. The computers discussed in the Chapters 8–12 use a mixture of microcode and hardware in instruction execution. For example, the 3090 uses special circuitry in doing decimal arithmetic because many workloads (e.g., COBOL programs) perform extensive decimal operations. The 4381, on the other hand, implements decimal instructions in microcode. The higher models of the 9370 use hardware for frequently used instructions and microcode for implementing the rest.

The size of the microword is related to the number of concurrent operations that are done during a processor cycle. The microword used by the 3090 is over 100 bits in length. The bits are organized into fields that concurrently initiate or control many activities. Thus, it is possible to access the serial adder, parallel adder, shifter, and general registers in one cycle.

What gets implemented in microcode as opposed to hardware is an engineering decision. Traditionally, an instruction is not implemented in hardware until it has "stabilized," i.e., no changes are expected in regard to its architectural specifications. Also, the instruction should be frequently used in order to justify the hardware cost. The ultimate decision is made after taking into account a number of parameters, including time for completion of the design effort. In many situations it may not be possible to come up with the perfect mix of hardware and microcode. For example, the 3033 implemented most instructions in microcode. The 3081, on the other hand, implements fixed-point multiplication and division, all floating-point arithmetic, and conversion instructions in hardware. The 3090 series implements these instructions in microcode even though special parallel circuitry is used for decimal arithmetic.

A related issue is the implementation of commonly used operating system functions in hardware or microcode. The implementation of an operating system instruction in hardware is called an assist. Thus, the instructions INSERT STORAGE KEY, LOAD REAL ADDRESS, RESET REFERENCE BIT, SET PSW KEY FROM ADDRESS, STORE CONTROL, STORE THEN AND SYSTEM MASK, STORE THEN OR SYSTEM MASK are implemented in hardware to provide the virtual machine (VM) assist, i.e., hardware support for the VM operating system (MacKinnon [3]).

It has also been the practice [3] to use new instructions for functions performed by the operating system (e.g., LINK, RETURN). These instructions are not regarded as part of architecture and are not found in the Principles of Operations. The justification for having these instructions is that considerable efficiency can be achieved by designating instruction sequences frequently used by the operating system as new instructions, and implementing these instructions in optimized microcode.

A word should be said about the organization of the control store, where microcode resides. In the old days this was a high-speed semiconductor memory. In the 308X series, microcode is distributed between control store and main storage and is paged in just like a real program. The details are given in Chapter 9.

7.4 CACHE (HIGH-SPEED BUFFER)

A cache is a relatively small high-speed memory that is used to hold the contents of most recently referenced blocks of main storage. The name is indicative of the fact that this storage mechanism is hidden from and is transparent to the user. A cache is not addressable by programs and is physically distinct from main storage.

The logic of operation of the cache is based on the sequential nature of access of instructions and data by the processor. Several bytes from sequential main-storage locations are transferred to the cache whenever main storage is accessed. The cache is always searched for instructions and data required by the processor. A cache hit (the presence of the data in the cache) avoids the need for memory access.

A cache uses an associate storage management scheme in the sense that storage is accessed by value instead of location. The specific scheme used differs among models. Generally speaking, a directory is used for storing high-order bits of an address in main storage and a kind of content addressability is used in retrieving data from the cache (see Chapters 8 and 10).

The problem of synchronization of the contents of the cache with those of main storage becomes complicated when multiple processors are involved. The 3033 used a simple store-through design, whereby data changed in the cache is immediately changed in main storage, also. Under this concept, main storage always reflected the latest changes in the data. The price to be paid was that main storage had to be accessed to store the changes. The IBM 308X and 3090 series use a more sophisticated concept, called store-in. Under the concept, a cache line (the unit of transfer between main storage and the cache) is kept in the cache until (a) the cache locations occupied by the line are required for storing newer data or (b) the cache line is referenced by another processor. In effect, this makes each processor execute instructions out of its own cache, and the cache acts like the memory in a von Neumann machine.

7.5 PIPELINING

Pipelining is the breaking down of a serial synchronous function or process into asynchronous subfunctions or subprocesses, saving time that is spent otherwise in waiting by subprocesses for completion of other subprocesses. Pipelining can also be viewed as the transformation of a serial process into one or more parallel subprocesses. The analogy between a pipeline and an assembly line is often pointed out. The underlying idea is the same, i.e., to have centers perform functions independently as far as possible, and at some point make sure that all functions are performed before the final product rolls down the line.

The CPU architecture assigns instruction execution as the main function of the CPU. Instruction execution can be broken down into the following subfunctions:

- Instruction fetching
- Instruction decoding
- Operand fetching
- Instruction execution.

If the above subfunctions were executed sequentially for a particular instruction, the elapsed time for execution of that instruction would have to include the main storage accesses for fetching an instruction and each one of its operands. Under a pipelined operation, instructions and operands are prefetched. Typically, a pipelined processor consists of an Instruction Fetching and Decoding Unit and an Execution Unit. The Instruction Fetching and Decoding Unit prefetches instructions and stores them in instruction buffers. These are decoded, and the operands are also fetched. The decoded instructions and operands are then queued for action by the Execution Unit, which executes the instruction.

In the following chapters, we give several examples of pipelining in IBM mainframes (e.g., 3033, 3081, 3090). The details vary according to the implementation. One interesting point arises in respect to the treatment of conditional branching. A branch on condition may require that the already prefetched instructions be discarded and that new instructions be prefetched at the start from the branch address. Some mainframes keep past branching results to predict future branching behavior. The predicted branch is prefetched (see Chapter 9). Others prefetch both streams in a branching sequence. Detailed discussions are given in Chapters 8, 9 and 10.

7.6 STORAGE INTERLEAVING

Storage interleaving is a technique for partitioning main storage into independently accessible units. When interleaving is not used, only one read/write request can be processed at any time by main storage. This can cause problems when multiple processors and channels are accessing main storage simultaneously. Since only one requestor can be serviced at a time, the others have to wait their turn.

Storage interleaving provides concurrent accesses to requestors of main storage. In the 3033, for example, main storage is logically partitioned into eight logical storage elements (LSEs). Each LSE can be independently accessed by a requestor. Thus, up to eight requestors can concurrently access storage. This is called eight-way interleaving.

Physically, interleaving is accomplished by providing a separate data path to each partition. This adds to the cost of main storage. There is some question as to whether or not the same objective can be accomplished by widening the data path (the number of bytes transferred concurrently) between main storage and its requestors. The 308X, interestingly enough, uses the latter approach. For a discussion in regard to its efficiency, the reader is referred to Chapter 9.

7.7 NUMBER OF PROCESSORS

The early 360 computers were uniprocessors. Multiprocessing was originally introduced in the System 360/65. It was present in the 3033 design as "attached processing" and "tightly coupled multiprocessing," but the number of processors was restricted to two. It was not until the advent of the 308X and 3090 processors that multiprocessing as opposed to dual processing was available. The 308X uses up to four processors and the 3090 up to six processors. The 308X experience showed that there were both positive and negative aspects to multiprocessing (see Chapter 9). The positive aspect is that performance increased by a factor of 1.9 when two processors instead of one were used, and by a factor of 3.8 when four processors were used. The negative aspects are that the problems of cache synchronization under the single image operation are likely to have an adverse impact as the number of processors increased. In the 3090, many improvements to the system controller (which is the physical communication and data management link between the various processors) were made to improve its performance. But the fundamental issue, namely, the number of processors that can be present without adverse impact on performance, is not yet resolved.

7.8 REVIEW OF TECHNIQUES

We shall use a case study (the 3090 series) to review the techniques discussed in this chapter (see Chapter 10 for details).

One of the designers of the 3090 series (Tucker [4]) has made many illuminating observations about the design of large mainframes. His comments show that a reevaluation of premises is often necessary at the start of the design process. A main premise is in regard to the nature of the workload. In addition to broad classification of the workload into scientific, commercial, on-line, batch, etc., subclassifications such as TSO workload, CICS workload, etc., all of which have different characteristics, are required. Those workloads are subsequently used in performance simulation. Performance stimulation is an integral part of the design process.

"In designing the 3090, performance simulators were used to evaluate the effect of many possible enhancements. These simulators ... were detailed enough to show cycle-by-cycle performance on selected job streams containing many millions of instructions. As a result of this work, many design enhancements that were found to offer good cost/performance trade-offs were included in the central processor." [4]

The options that were considered covered a lot of ground. Examples are the handling of overlapping operations for processing branches, decimal operands, fixed point instructions, etc.

The performance improvement of the 3090/200 from its immediate predecessor, the 3081KX, is of the order of 1.7 to 1.9. The circuit technology improvements resulted in cycle-time reduction from 24 to 18.5 nanoseconds, contributing to 30 percent of the improvement of the overall throughput. Pipelining and the improvement of the system controller added another 50 percent of the throughput [4].

REFERENCES

1. Lorin, H.: "Systems Architecture in Transition — An Overview," *IBM Systems Journal*, vol. 25, nos. 3/4, 1986.
2. Case R., and A. Padegs: "Architecture of the IBM System/370," *Communications of the ACM*, vol. 21, no. 1, January 1978.
3. MacKinnon, R.A.: "The Changing Virtual Environment: Interfaces to Real Hardware, Virtual Hardware and Other Virtual Machines," *IBM Systems Journal*, vol. 18, no. 1, 1979.
4. Tucker, S.G.: "The IBM 3090 System: An Overview," *IBM Systems Journal*, vol. 25, no. 1, 1986.

8

3033 Processor Design

The 303X processors were introduced by IBM in 1978. They were the last large-scale computers that implemented the native 370 architecture. The 3033 was a very popular machine for three to four years, until it was replaced by the 3081 machine. The 3033 is included in this book because its design influenced its successors, the 308X and 3090, in two different ways. The influence on the 308X was a negative one, in the sense that the 308X steered away from the design concepts introduced in the 3033. On the 3090, the influence was positive because the 3033 design concepts were refined and put to work again. Since many references are made to the 3033 design in the two following chapters, we thought it would be a good idea to describe the 3033 machine with special emphasis on its innovative pipeline operations.

8.1 TECHNOLOGY

The circuit technology used by the 3033 was the monolithic system technology (MST) introduced in 1969. Under this technology, several entire circuits were built on a single chip. The number of circuits per chip were initially few but continued to increase. In the 3033, the circuit density was 40 circuits per chip. It was the last IBM mainframe to use this technology.

The major technological features of the 3033 are listed below:

- It has a processor cycle time of 57 nanoseconds; during a cycle, instruction fetching and execution operations are overlapped.
- It uses an 8-way interleaved main storage.
- It has a 64-KB cache that has an access time equal to the processor cycle time.
- Two CPUs can function in a tightly coupled multiprocessing mode (MP) or attached processing (AP) mode.

8.2 OVERVIEW OF MACHINE ORGANIZATION

A 3033 consists of the following components (see Figure 8-1):

- Instruction Preprocessing Function (IPPF)
- Execution Function (E-UNIT)
- Processor Storage
- Processor Storage Control Function (PSCF)
- Channel Groups and Directors
- Maintenance Retry Function.

The IPPF fetches instructions, decodes them, and passes them on to the Execution Function for execution. The PSCF contains a cache, translation look-aside buffer (TLB), and the dynamic address trans-

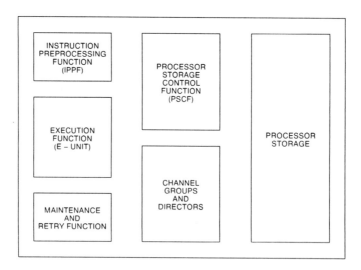

Figure 8-1 Components of the 3033 processor.

lation (DAT) capability. It also controls access to processor storage. The channel director manages channels that are grouped in channel groups.

These elements correspond roughly to the architectural components in the following manner. The CPU comprises the IPPF, Execution Unit, and PSCF. Main storage is the same as processor storage, and the channel director and groups correspond to channel sets. The Maintenance Retry Function is not mentioned in the architecture.

A stand-alone 3033 processor is called a uniprocessor. Two 3033 processors can be configured to form a tightly coupled multiprocessing configuration. A processor without channels can be attached to a uniprocessor to form an attached processing configuration.

The flow diagram in Figure 8-2 shows the main sequence of events (numbered circles) taking place in the processor. The IPPF prefetches instructions from the cache, and stores them in its buffers (Event 1). It decodes instructions one at a time, generates operand addresses, converts them to real addresses using the Translation Lookaside Buffer (TLB) and the Dynamic Address Translation (DAT) feature, and prefetches operands using the cache, and main storage (Event 2). The instructions are placed in a queue for execution (Event 3) and are executed in sequence by the Execution Unit. In the case of I/O operations, the Execution Unit issues I/O instructions to channels, and data transfer is done between channel and main storage (Events 4 and 5).

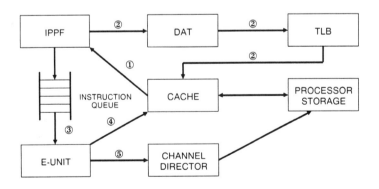

Figure 8-2 Simplified flow diagram showing 3033 operation.

8.3 INSTRUCTION PREPROCESSING FUNCTION (IPPF)

The IPPF performs a number of functions pertaining to instruction fetching and sequencing, as listed below:

- Instructions are prefetched and their op codes are decoded.
- Addresses of operands are generated and the operands are fetched.
- Instructions are passed to the Execution Unit, one at a time, for execution.
- The conceptual sequence required by the architecture is observed by means of special logic circuitry.
- Intelligence is used in processing branch instructions.

Many of these functions are performed concurrently. Also, there is overlap between instruction fetching by IPPF and execution by the Execution Unit. The IPPF contains three buffers (each buffer is four doublewords in size) for holding prefetched instructions. An instruction from one of these buffers is moved to an instruction register for decoding (see Figure 8-3). A decoded instruction is moved to a queue for subsequent execution by the Execution Unit. The queue consists of four queuing registers, each register holding a decoded instruction. IPPF has its own copy of general registers that are used for operand address generation (B1, B2, X2, etc.). A 24-bit adder that can accept up to three inputs and an address incrementor for incrementing addresses are used for the actual address calculations. There are six operand address registers for storing the generated address of operands.

One of the interesting aspects of the 3033 design is the way branching instructions are handled by the IPPF. Branching instructions are divided into two classes, namely, loop-closing branches and conditional branches. Loop-closing branches arise in connection with iteration loops. The instructions BRANCH ON INDEX LESS THAN OR EQUAL (BXLE) and BRANCH ON INDEX HIGH (BXH) increment a general register, compare the result to a limit, and branch if the limit has not been reached. These are frequently used as the last instruction in looping. In instruction processing, the outcome of these instructions is guessed as successful, and instructions are prefetched from the branch address with the hope that the loop will be executed again. The conditional branches use a BRANCH ON CONDITION, which compares the condition code to a value specified in the instruction. The IPPF prefetches two sets of instructions, namely, those that immediately follow the currently decoded branch instruction

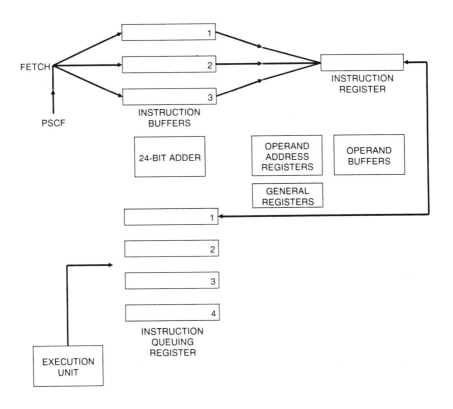

Figure 8-3 Schematic diagram for the instruction preprocessing function (IPPF).

and those located at the branch address. Thus, prefetched instructions are available whether or not the branch is taken.

8.4 EXECUTION UNIT

The Execution Unit executes the instructions that are decoded by the IPPF. It is controlled by microcode. The execution of an instruction consists of fetching and executing microwords. The microword is large (105 bits). Many instructions (approximately 50 percent of the instruction set) can be executed in one processor cycle.

Emphasis has been placed on optimizing binary and floating-point instructions. A 64-bit parallel adder is used to perform binary and floating-point arithmetic. A special high-speed multiplication unit

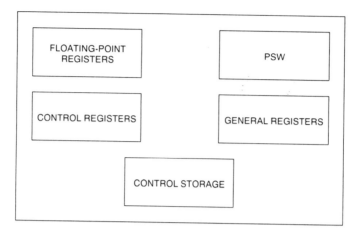

Figure 8-4 Schematic of execution unit.

speeds up binary and floating-point multiplication. The microcode for decimal arithmetic instructions has been improved over that used by earlier machines.

The Execution Unit contains general and floating-point registers, PSW, timers and control storage (see Figure 8-4). In addition to the instruction execution, it performs many related functions such as loading new PSWs after interruptions.

8.5 STORAGE ORGANIZATION

Storage is divided into eight logical storage elements (LSEs). Each LSE can be accessed independently of others to achieve eight-way storage interleaving. Contention for an LSE occurs when two requestors for storage attempt to access the same LSE. It is resolved in favor of the requestor with the higher priority; for instance, a request from a channel is given preference to a request from the IPPF.

A doubleword is the basic unit of transfer from each LSE (the data path to and from processor storage is 8 bytes wide). A doubleword can be requested from each LSE concurrently, each request separated by one processor cycle from its predecessor. Bytes in storage are numbered according to the following convention: bytes 0–7 are in LSE 0, bytes 8–15 are in LSE 1, bytes 16–23 are in LSE 2, and so forth, as shown in Figure 8-5.

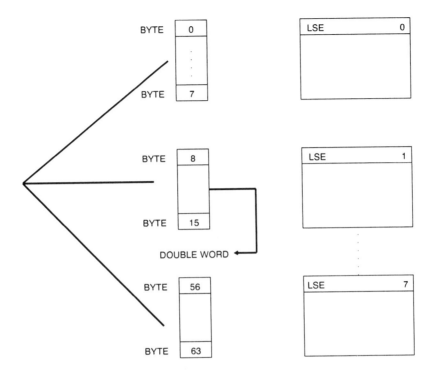

Figure 8-5 Interleaved processor storage.

A 7-bit key for each 2K byte of storage is used for storage protection, as specified in the architecture. Before an LSE is accessed, a storage protection check is made via special hardware called a storage protect array which contains the keys. Special hardware also provides for the detection and correction of one-bit errors and for the detection of all two-bit and several multibit errors.

8.6 PROCESSOR STORAGE CONTROL FUNCTION (PSCF)

Processor Storage Control Function consists of the cache, dynamic address translator, translation look-aside buffer, and the segment table origin address stack. PSCF also controls all access to processor storage.

8.6.1   Cache

The 3033 uses a 64-KB cache for storing instructions and data during program execution. The cache has the same cycle time as the processor. A doubleword can be obtained from the cache in two cycles, and a request for a doubleword can be initiated during every cycle. The Instruction Preprocessing Function Unit (IPPF) can thus access a doubleword from the cache in 114 nanoseconds as compared to 456 nanoseconds if no cache were used and the word had to be obtained from main storage.

The cache is organized as a rectangular array having 64 columns and 16 rows. Each of the 64 x 16 (= 1024) elements of the array is called a block and consists of 8 doublewords. A block is the basic unit of data in cache operation (a cache line). The cache search scheme initially searches for a block and then for the doubleword within the block. The transfer of data between cache and main storage is done eight doublewords at a time.

When the IPPF or E-unit requests a doubleword from main storage, the cache is interrogated to find out if the doubleword is in the cache. An address array having 64 columns and 16 rows is used for searching the cache, as illustrated in Figure 8-6. Each element of the address array contains a 13-bit address, a block valid bit, and a block delete bit. The procedure for checking to see whether or not a doubleword is in the cache is described below (the numbers in the procedure correspond to circled numbers in Figure 8-6):

1. The read address of the requested doubleword is given by the requestor. The column address from bits 20–25 of the real address (6 bits correspond to 64 columns) is obtained.
2. Each of the 16 elements in the column of the address array is examined to see if there is a match for bits 8–20 of the real address against the 13-bit address field.
3. If a match exists and the valid bit is one, the corresponding block in the cache is accessed and the doubleword, specified by bits 26–28 of the real address, is obtained; otherwise, a block is loaded from main storage.

A replacement array having 64 elements is associated with the cache to maintain a record of the least recently used blocks. The cache tries to keep active data in storage, and the replacement array contains, for each column of the cache, indicators of block usage.

If the requested doubleword is not in the cache, a block of eight doublewords is transferred from main storage using eight storage

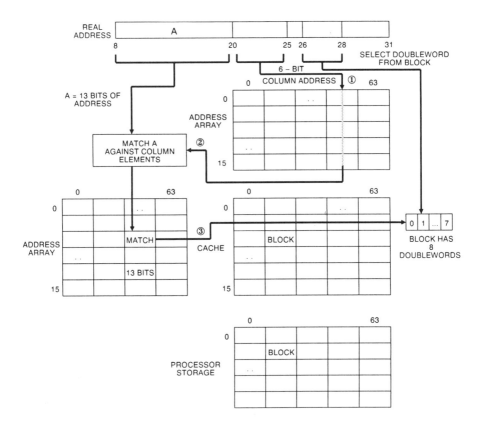

Figure 8-6 Operation of the cache.

references, one cycle apart. Processor storage is regarded as consisting of blocks for the purpose of data transfer to the cache; that is,
processor storage is regarded as having 64 columns and n rows,
where n is dependent on the available processor storage ($n = 1000$ if
processor storage is 4 MB).

Storage modification by an instruction causes both cache and
processor storage to be modified. Processor storage always contains
the latest data. This technique is called store-through.

Channels do not read from cache but directly from processor
storage. In the case of a write operation, the cache is interrogated; if
it contains the doubleword to be updated, the cache line is invalidated by setting the invalid bit in the corresponding element in
the address array.

8.6.2 Translation Look-aside Buffer (TLB)

The motivation for a TLB is that dynamic address translation takes 10–40 processor cycles, depending on whether segment and page tables are in the cache or in processor storage. TLB makes it possible to minimize requests for dynamic address translation by storing previously translated addresses. In the 3033, a TLB search is done in parallel with cache search and takes only two cycles.

Up to 128 previously translated page addresses are kept in the TLB. When a virtual address is translated to a real address, the following information is stored in the TLB entry:

- Real address (bits 8–19) of the page frame
- Virtual address (bits 8–14) of the page
- Storage protection key (SP)
- Segment table origin stack ID.

A 24-bit virtual address has a segment index, page index, and byte index as was shown in Figure 4-8. Only the segment and page indexes need be translated, since the byte index does not change under a virtual-to-real address translation. The TLB stores segment and page indexes (bits 8–19) of the real address and bits 8–14 of the virtual address of the page (a hashing scheme is employed in TLB interrogation, which is described later).

The Segment Table origin (STO) stack ID is required for storing address space information, as described later.

The TLB can be viewed as a table having 64 entries, as shown in Figure 8-7. The A and B sections are identical, and a Least Recently Used (LRU) array indicates whether A or B is in use at any given time. The inputs for TLB interrogation are the virtual address and the currently active STO Stack ID. The TLB is searched using the following algorithm:

1. Using a hashing technique on bits 9–20 of the virtual address, obtain a number k ranging from 0 to 63 corresponding to the 64 TLB entries. Check the LRU array to determine whether section A or B should be used.
2. Obtain the kth entry from section A or B, as the case may be.
3. Check if the virtual address bits 8–14 in the TLB entry match the corresponding bits of the virtual address used for searching the TLB. If the two sets of address bits match and the STO IDs are the same, the real address is formed using bits 8–19 in the TLB and concatenating it with the byte index. If the two sets of

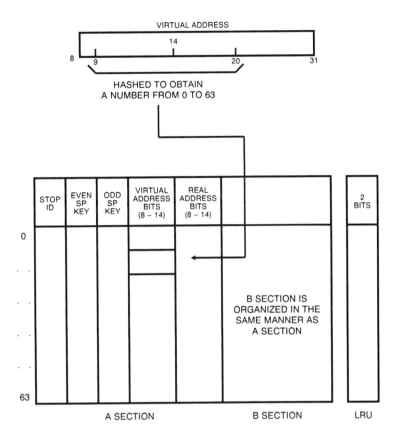

Figure 8-7 Operation of the translation look-aside buffer (TLB).

address bits do not match, or the STO IDs are not the same, the real address is not in the TLB and dynamic address translation has to be performed.

The TLB search is done in parallel with cache search and only two processor cycles are required to fetch a doubleword, assuming that the doubleword is cache-resident and its virtual address is in the TLB.

8.6.3 STO Stack

Figure 8-8 shows the information present in the STO stack. Every address space that is executing within the system is given an STO

ADDRESS SPACE ID	SEGMENT SIZE	PAGE SIZE	SEGMENT TABLE ORIGIN

Figure 8-8 Segment table origin (STO) stack.

stack ID. Before the execution of an address space, control register 1 is loaded with a segment table origin (STO) by the operating system. At this time, the hardware checks to see if the STO stack has the segment table origin; if it has, the corresponding STO stack ID is designated as being active. If there is no match, new entries for segment size, page size, and table entries are created, and the corresponding STO stack ID is designated as being active.

Thus, the function of the STO stack is to act as a repository for address space information to be used in conjunction with TLB data. The interrogation of the TLB includes the matching of the STO Stack ID in the TLB with the currently active ID to ensure that the real address pertains to the address space that is being executed.

8.7 CHANNEL GROUPS AND DIRECTORS

Channels are divided into groups of six, and each group is controlled by a director. The directors control all channel activity such as device selection and data transfer to and from storage. Each channel group (there are two such groups) consists of one byte multiplexer and five block multiplexer channels. An extended channels feature is also available for adding another group of four channels, consisting of one byte multiplexer and three block multiplexer channels, or four block multiplexer channels.

Physically, directors and channels are implemented as microcoded processors. A director shares control storage with the channels associated with it. Each director has its own arithmetic logic unit for channel and data control functions, channel buffers, storage for UCWs associated with channels, and local storage (see Figure 8-9). The block multiplexer channels within a director are controlled by a microprogram that is shared by all channels. The following channel functions are performed under microprogram control:

• CCW fetching and decoding
• Data transfer to and from processor storage
• Device selection
• I/O interruption

Specialized hardware is used for performing functions associated with control units such as data transfer to the control unit via the I/O interface. Data transfer by one channel does not significantly interfere with the operations of another channel because each channel has dedicated buffers and also the director is multiprogrammed to serve several channels concurrently.

The byte multiplexer is handled by a different microprogram within the director and performs all channel functions other than device selection. Also, this program can be interrupted by a block multiplexer channel when it needs service by the director.

A device transfers data to the channel via its control unit, one byte at a time. A two-byte interface can be installed in the first block multiplexer channel in a group; in this case, two bytes are transferred at a time between channel and control unit. A channel transfers four bytes at a time to buffers within the director, and this data is transferred to processor storage via the PSCF (see Figure 8-10). The transfer from processor storage to buffers in the director is done

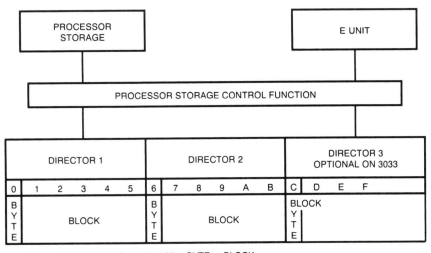

Figure 8-9 Channel implementation in the 3033.

eight bytes at a time. The maximum aggregate data rate achieved by the five block multiplexer channels within a director is 6.7 MB per second. When all three directors are used, the maximum aggregate data rate for fourteen block multiplexer channels is 18.9 MB per second.

8.8 MAINTENANCE AND RETRY FUNCTION UNIT

This unit handles interaction between a console and the processor; it also provides for instruction retry. The 3033 has the ability to retry an instruction in case of an error failure. Data that is altered by an instruction is saved beforehand, and error-handling microcode restores the E-Unit to a point where the instruction can be re-executed.

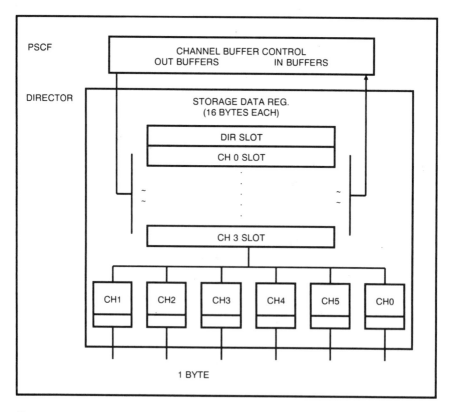

Figure 8-10 Dataflow in the director.

8.9 MULTIPROCESSING

The 3033 supports tightly coupled multiprocessing (MP) and attached processing (AP). The maximum number of allowable processors in a multiprocessing configuration is two.

8.9.1 Tightly Coupled Multiprocessing

Under tightly coupled multiprocessing two processors share main storage and run under a single operating system. Each processor has its own set of channels, which can be switched from a processor to a functioning processor by means of the instructions CHANNEL DISCONNECT, CHANNEL CONNECT. Even though the two processors do not share channels, they can share control units and devices if the control unit has channel-switching capability and if the device has string-switching capability. Channel-switching is the capability of a control unit to switch channels, and string-switching is the capability of a set of disk drives (called a string) to switch control units; these capabilities provide multiple I/O paths to a device so that more than one processor can access the device (see Chapter 13).

The components in an MP configuration are shown in Figure 8-11. The two processors are connected to each other via specialized hardware called the Multiprocessor Communications Unit (MCU). The MCU performs the following functions for both processors:

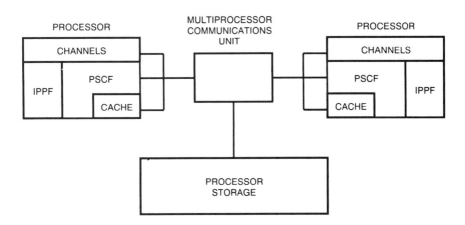

Figure 8-11 Tightly coupled multiprocessing.

- Prefixing
- Storage access
- Broadcast of storage update by either processor
- Interprocessor communication
- Configuration control.

Each of these functions is described in the following paragraphs:

Prefixing

We have seen in the chapter on architecture that each processor generates real addresses that have to be mapped to absolute addresses by means of prefixing. The first 4K locations used by each processor (called the Prefix Storage Area) is assigned to different areas in processor storage by means of offsets contained in prefix registers. Prefixing was described in Chapter 4.

Storage Access

Access to shared storage is controlled by the MCU. Each processor has to request the MCU to read or write to main storage, and this results in a slight increase in storage access time. Requests to a non-busy LSE is granted on a first-come, first-served basis. When both processors make simultaneous requests, a floating priority scheme is used whereby storage access is granted in bursts. One processor is allowed to have priority over the other processor if it can keep up a continuous request (e.g., a 64-byte fetch), but if it fails to do so, priority passes to the other processor.

Broadcast of Storage Update

When one processor updates storage, the MCU automatically broadcasts this to the second processor. If its cache contains data from the storage locations that are affected by the update, such data is automatically invalidated. Data transfers to main storage by channels are also treated in this manner. Also, when one processor modifies a storage-protect key (by means of the SET STORAGE KEY instruction), the other processor is notified of this modification and makes changes accordingly.

Interprocessor Communication

As we have seen in the chapter on 370 architecture, the SIGNAL PROCESSOR instruction enables one CPU to send signals to the other CPU. These signals can be used by one processor to start, stop, or sense the status of the other processor and to perform several other functions that have been already described.

Specialized hardware is also used in notification of malfunction alert, whereby an external interruption is generated in one processor if the other processor enters into a check-stopped state, either on account of loss of power or machine failure. This hardware is also used for synchronization of time-of-day (TOD) clock facilities.

Configuration Control

Configuration of processor storage can be done in three ways, namely:

• Each processor has its own dedicated storage (self-contained configuration).
• One processor can have exclusive use of parts of the other processor's storage (cross-configuration).
• Processor storage is shared by both processors (shared configuration).

Symmetric as well as asymmetric configurations are supported under multiprocessing. A symmetric configuration is one where there is processor symmetry, storage symmetry, and I/O symmetry. Processor symmetry means that both processors have the same features and are interchangeable. Storage symmetry means that each processor has been assigned identical amounts of main storage that is shared by both processors. I/O symmetry means that each processor has identical channel sets that share all devices by means of channel switching. A configuration that does not satisfy these criteria is called asymmetric. In practice, most MP configurations are asymmetric because a substantial operating system overhead is required in sharing devices needed for I/O symmetry.

8.9.2   Attached Processing

Attached processing is similar to tightly coupled multiprocessing, the only difference being that one processor (called the Attached Processor) does not have any channels of its own. The two processors are coupled by means of the Multiprocessing Communication Unit (MCU), which performs the function described previously.

Attached processing is an example of asymmetric multiprocessing since only one processor performs I/O operations. Note that channel set switching is possible between processors by means of CONNECT CHANNEL SET and DISCONNECT CHANNEL SET instructions.

Attached processing is used instead of multiprocessing when an extra CPU is required to meet the processing demands of a 3033 uniprocessor computer system.

8.10   REVIEW OF THE 3033

The 3033 machine was regarded highly by many commentators. Its strengths are in its pipelined operations. Its weakness is in the limited multiprocessing capability that it offered. But this is an architectural weakness and was overcome by changing the 370 architecture.

ADDITIONAL READING

A comprehensive description of the 3033 is found in the following IBM manual:

"A Guide to the IBM 3033 Processor Complex, Attached Processor Complex and Multiprocessor Complex of System/370," Order No. GC 20-1859.

The 3033 pipelining concepts are discussed in the following article:

Connors, W.D., et al: "The IBM 3033: An Inside Look," *Datamation*, vol. 25, no. 5, May 1, 1979.

The influence of the 3033 on the 3090 is discussed in the following:

Tucker, S.G.: "The IBM 3090 System: An Overview," *IBM Systems Journal*, vol. 25, no. 1, 1986.

9

308X Processor Design

The 308X series is the generic name given to a family of computers that have many design similarities. The "X" in 308X can have values of "3," "1" and "4." At the low end of the family, there is the uniprocessor machine 3083, with models E, B and J. At the next level is the dual processor (called a "dyadic" processor) machine 3081, with models D, G, and K. At the high end is the 3084 machine with four processors, with one model, Q.

The IBM 308X series is interesting because it introduced the concept of asymmetric multiprocessing among IBM mainframes. This concept is different from the early multiprocessing capability (which is really dual-processing) present in the 3033 design. As we shall see later, this concept had impact on several design aspects, such as cache, microcode storage, etc., which was carried over to its successor, the 3090 series.

The 308X machines have major differences from their immediate predecessor, the 303X series. The differences are both architecture-oriented and implementation-oriented. The 3081, for example, has two processors but, unlike the 3033 multiprogramming implementation, they cannot be separated into two uniprocessors. This concept of a "dyadic" processor is more in line with the 370/XA architectural principles. Channels are no longer owned by a processor as in the case of the 3033, 4381, etc. Instead, the External Data Controller of the 308X is truly a channel subsystem, since it interacts with both processors. The 308X processors operate in both 370 and 370/XA modes, but their architectural principles are closer to 370/XA than to the 370 architecture. From an implementation point of view, there are significant departures from the 3033, as listed:

- The 308X is not a highly pipelined machine like the 3033; its increased performance is due to faster machine-cycle time and increased data-path width in main storage operations.
- The 308X uses a "store in" concept, whereby the CPU accesses only the cache and not main storage.
- The control storage is pageable and microcode resides partly in main storage.

The various aspects of the 308X design are discussed in the following paragraphs.

9.1 TECHNOLOGY

The 308X series uses large-scale integration (LSI) technology. Very large numbers of logic circuits are necessary to implement today's complex instruction set computers. The 3081, for example, uses approximately 800,000 logic circuits. These circuits are implemented using LSI technology, and the circuit density is high. A chip, for example, can contain up to 704 logic circuits. The chips are packaged into Thermal Conduction Modules (TCMs). A TCM may contain up to 133 chips.

The impact of this technology is to minimize distance between circuits and, consequently, to reduce the processor cycle time. The 3081 processor cycle time is 25 nanoseconds, which is less than half that of the 3033.

The processor implements the 370 and 370/XA instruction sets using hardware for certain arithmetic instructions (e.g., fixed-point multiplication, division, floating-point arithmetic, conversion) and microcode for the remaining instructions. The microcode is organized in a novel manner, using static and dynamic storage concepts.

The processor uses the store-in cache management technique. It does not use storage interleaving but uses a wide data path (16 doublewords) for storage access.

The various models use from one to four processors. The low-end machines are uniprocessors. The middle-range models are dyadic processors. The machine at the high end uses four processors.

9.2   OVERVIEW OF MACHINE ORGANIZATION

The major components of the 308X processor are schematically illustrated in Figure 9-1. The words used in naming some of these components are different from those used in connection with the 3033. A 308X processor consists of the following components:

- Central processor(s)
- System controller(s)
- External data controller(s)
- Processor controller.

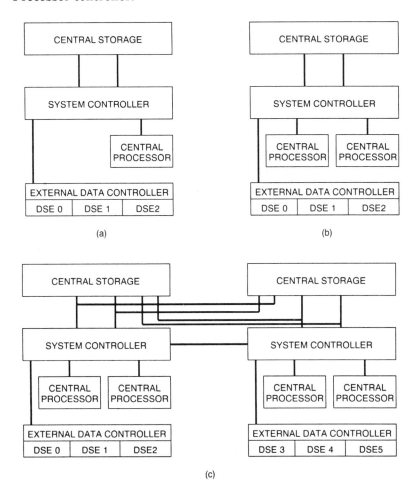

Figure 9-1 308X configurations. (a) 3083 Models 3, b, J. (b) 3081 Models D, G, K. (c) 3084 Model Q.

The central processor is the equivalent of the CPU described in the 370/XA architecture. Central storage is the same as main storage. The external data controller controls channels, manages I/O functions, and can be viewed as the channel subsystem defined in the 370/XA architecture. The system controller is not mentioned in the architecture at all. Its role is to provide storage access for central processors and channels, and to coordinate these elements in a multiprocessing environment. Likewise, the processor controller is not mentioned in the architecture; its function is to monitor and maintain the processor.

9.3 CENTRAL PROCESSOR ORGANIZATION

The central processor consists of five functional elements (see Figure 9-2) as listed below:

* Instruction Element
* Execution Element
* Variable Field Element
* Buffer Control Element (containing the cache)
* Control Store Element.

The clear division of functions between the instruction processing unit and the execution unit found in the 3033 is lacking in the 308X machines. The Instruction Element, in addition to prefetching instructions, performs execution of certain instructions also. The instruction execution function is in fact distributed among the following three elements, as indicated below:

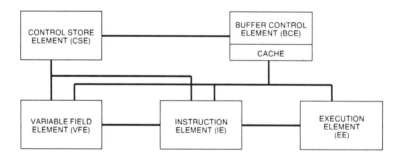

Figure 9-2 Central processor.

- Execution Element: Fixed-point multiplication and division, floating-point arithmetic, conversion
- Variable Field Element: Variable-field-length instructions of the SS format
- Instruction Element: All the remaining instructions in the instruction set

One of the design considerations in the 308X series was to divide instructions into two classes, (a) those that are executed by a hardware-controlled unit and (b) those that are executed by a microcode-controlled unit. The Execution Element is hardware controlled and, as mentioned before, is responsible for execution of all floating-point arithmetic operations, fixed-point multiplication and division, and conversion operations. These operations are stable (unlikely to change), and high execution speed is desirable in engineering applications. Hence, they have been assigned to the Execution Element. The Instruction Element and the Variable Field Element are microcode controlled and thus offer the capability of adding new instructions at a reasonable cost.

9.3.1   Instruction Element (IE)

This element prepares instructions for execution by prefetching them, decoding the operation code, generating operand addresses, and controlling the sequence of execution so that the appearance of serial execution required by the architecture is maintained.

The prefetched instructions are stored in instruction buffers. The number of buffers vary, depending on the model. The high-end models (e.g., 3084Q, 3081K) have six buffers, each a doubleword in size. The low-end model has only one doubleword buffer. When a buffer is free, new instructions are fetched from storage, one doubleword at a time.

In the high-end models, four out of the six buffers are used to store instructions in the sequence in which they appear in a program. The other two are used for storing instructions at branch addresses. The branch addresses are computed, and the instructions at these addresses are prefetched. Thus, whether a branch is taken or not, prefetched instructions are available in the instruction buffers.

The Instruction Element also executes all instructions that are not executed by the Execution Element or Variable Field Element. This means that the majority of instructions are executed by the Instruction Element. In most models, there is no overlap between instruction fetching and execution by the Instruction Element. After an instruction is fetched and decoded, it is executed and these activities take place in distinct non-overlapping phases. The Instruction Element also performs interruption handling functions.

The Instruction Element is implemented entirely in microcode. The advantage is that it is easier to incorporate architectural changes. The drawback is that instruction execution is slower than it would have been if the implementation had been in hardware.

9.3.2 Variable Field Element

This element executes all variable-field-length storage-to-storage (SS) instructions. Instruction fetching and decoding of these instructions are done by the Instruction Element. There is overlap between the operation of the Variable Field Element and the Instruction Element in performing their respective tasks. The Instruction Element performs operand fetches while the Variable Field Element is busy executing instructions.

The Variable Field Element is also implemented in microcode, as is the case with the Instruction Element.

9.3.3 Execution Element

The Execution Element executes fixed-point multiplication and division, all floating-point operations and conversion. There is no overlap between the operations of the Instruction Element and the Execution Element. After the former decodes an instruction and passes it to the latter, it waits until the execution of the instruction is complete.

The Execution Element is implemented in hardware, with the primary objective of speeding up engineering and scientific applications which use extensively floating-point and fixed-point arithmetic.

9.3.4 Cache

The cache (high-speed buffer) is used for storing instructions and data. The 308X family uses a "store in" technique for management of the data contained in the cache, as opposed to the "store through" technique used in the 303X family. Under the latter technique, main storage is updated whenever the cache is updated with the advantage that it is possible to continue machine operation even when the cache fails. The disadvantage in such a case is that there may be a large number of writes to main storage. Under the store-in technique, the data in the cache is written to main storage when changed data in the cache is regarded as inactive, and is replaced by active data. I/O operations bypass the cache and data is transferred directly between main storage and channels. Thus, the primary function of the cache is to be a repository of instructions and data needed by the central processor, with read or write operations performed on main storage only when necessary.

The size of the cache varies from model to model. The 3083 models E, B and J have 16K, 32K, and 64K-byte caches respectively. Each central processor of the 3081 models D, G, and K has a 32K cache and the 3084 model Q has a 64K cache.

The cache is contained in the buffer control element (BCE), which controls access to central storage. The BCE also performs several other functions, such as dynamic address translation and providing data required by the instruction, variable-field and execution elements.

The access to cache is managed by the System Controller. Cache operations are described later in this chapter.

9.3.5 Control Store Element

The Control Store Element (CSE) manages microcode. One of the design features of the 308X series is the splitting of the microcode into frequently used and infrequently used modules. The frequently used microcode is kept in a "static" area (8K microwords in size) in the CSE. The less frequently used modules are kept in central storage in a specially earmarked area called the Hardware System Area (HSA). This microcode is paged into a "dynamic" area (1K microword in size) in the CSE on a demand basis. The point to note here is that, unlike the 3033, the 308X stores a portion of its microcode in main storage. This provides for ease of expansion of the microcode and also for a better price/performance ratio. The microcode in the dynamic area is managed using least recently used (LRU) principles.

The CSE sequences microcode execution and presents one microword on each machine cycle to the Instruction Element or Variable Field Element. The CSE uses a trace facility and tracks events that occurred in prior cycles in order to maintain instruction execution history, which is useful for diagnostics.

9.4 CENTRAL STORAGE

The central storage (main storage) design of the 308X is different in many ways from that of the 303X. To begin with, one would expect a high-performance processor to use storage interleaving. Thus, in the case of the 370/168, 4-way storage interleaving is used; and in the case of the 3033, 8-way storage interleaving is used. The 308X does not use storage interleaving. Instead, it uses a wider data path. The rationale is that it is less expensive than the interleaved storage technology.

In the 3033, it was possible to initiate a storage operation at every processor cycle from each of the eight logical storage elements (LSE). The initial access took five cycles or more to select the required LSE. After that, a doubleword could be transferred from main storage during every processor cycle. Thus, eight doublewords could be transferred in eight processor cycles plus those required for initial selection.

In the 308X, up to 16 doublewords can be transferred in successive processor cycles, with one doubleword transferred per cycle. This is, of course, after the initial selection, which takes a few cycles. Thus, 16 doublewords could be transferred in 16 processor cycles plus the cycles required for initial selection. The 308X design gets the same results as the 3033 design, without using storage interleaving but by widening the data path. From a performance point of view, the 308X design is claimed to be slightly better because 16 doublewords can be accessed using the above technique as compared to the eight doublewords accessed by the 3033.

Even though interleaving is not used, it is still possible for various users of central storage, such as multiple processors and channels, to access central storage concurrently. Central storage is divided into four basic storage elements (BSEs), each element having a separate data path (see Figure 9-3). A basic storage controller (BSC) controls access to a pair of BSEs. Thus, it is possible to have limited two-way interleaving done within two different sections of central storage, because concurrent store and fetch requests from two originators (e.g., central processors, channels) can be supported.

9.5 EXTERNAL DATA CONTROLLER (EXDC)

The EXDC is an I/O processor that is dedicated to performing all I/O functions specified by both the 370 and 370/XA architectures. These functions differ significantly, as explained in Chapters 4 and 5.

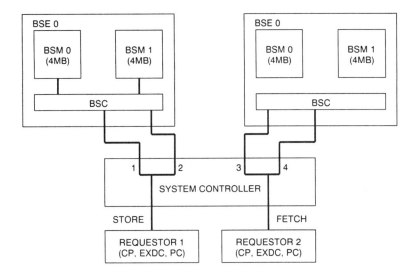

Figure 9-3 Central storage organization.

In the 370 mode of operation, the EXDC can be thought of as controlling 8, 16, or 24 channels. The channels are grouped into channel sets, and a channel set is assigned to a central processor. An SIO or SIOF instruction will specify a channel address. Channel selection is done by the CPU (the operating system).

In the 370/XA mode of operation, the EXDC functions as the channel subsystem. The operating system does not have to perform channel selection. The START SUBCHANNEL instruction directly specifies a device on which I/O is to be performed. Path selection is done by the EXDC.

The EXDC (see Figure 9-4) consists of the following logical components:

• A Channel Processing Element (CPE)
• Up to three Data Server Elements (DSEs)
• Up to eight Interface Adapter Elements (IAEs) for each DSE.

The CPE is responsible for accepting I/O instructions and for interruptions. It also manages the Data Server Elements (DSEs). It is controlled by microcode.

Each DSE has a microprocessor that controls the sequencing of instructions to the Interface Adapter Elements (IAEs). The primary

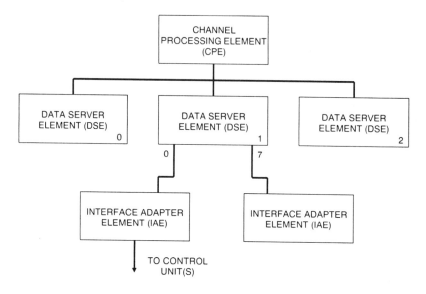

Figure 9-4 External data controller.

function of the DSE is to control the data transfer between each IAE and central storage. The microcode in the DSE causes an IAE to act as either a block or byte multiplexer channel. The DSE also provides buffering capability for the IAEs.

An IAE is functionally equivalent to a channel. It controls the data transfer to and from control units. An IAE can be configured for either byte or block multiplexing. It is implemented in hardware, and microcode is not used.

The following is a sequence of operations performed by the EXDC:

- An I/O instruction is executed by the CPU. The request reaches the EXDC via the Systems Controller. Its execution causes control blocks to be read by the CPE.
- The CPE fetches and decodes each CCW in the channel program.
- The DSE receives information from the CPE and passes it to a device via the IAE.
- The I/O operation is started at the device.
- Data transfer to central storage is done via the DSE. The data is buffered in the DSE in eight doublewords. There is only one data path to central storage and the CPE decides which of the contending DSEs get to use the path.
- At the end of the I/O operation, the DSE presents a status to the CPE. The CPE presents an interruption via the System Controller.

9.6 SYSTEM CONTROLLER (SC)

The System Controller is a new design concept geared towards the coordination and management of resources in a multiprocessing environment.

The functions of the System Controller are to control and prioritize the data flow between central processors, external data controllers (EXDCs), processor controller, and central storage, and to provide means of communication among these components.

A request for service is enqueued by the Systems Controller and assigned priority according to a fixed scheme. Requests are dequeued on a first-in-first-out (FIFO) basis. When a request is being serviced by the System Controller, the requestor can perform other functions.

The major functions of the SC are the following:

• Managing the cache
• Managing the I/O requests

In addition, it performs various miscellaneous functions.

9.6.1 Managing the Cache

The data flow in the computer is controlled by the Systems Controller. All requests for read/store operations from central storage by central processors or EXDC have to go through the Systems Controller. The Systems Controller maintains copies of directories used by caches. When a central processor does not find data in its cache, it sends a request to the System Controller. The System Controller interrogates the directory of the cache of each of the other central processors to see if the required data is present in any other cache. It also concurrently issues a request to central storage for the required data. This request is cancelled if the data is found in a cache.

Each cache line is marked as "read only" or "exclusive." Only those lines that are marked exclusive can be modified by the central processor. Instructions are marked normally as read only, whereas data is marked as exclusive. The System Controller ensures that when a cache line that is modified by one central processor is requested by another central processor, the cache line is cast out by the former and is transferred to the requesting processor. (The "cast out" process in some models, e.g., 3081D, requires that the line is initially stored in central storage and subsequently fetched to the cache of the requesting central processor.) Also, before a processor changes a cache line, the System Controller interrogates other caches to see if they contain the line, and if the line is present in any cache it is invalidated in that cache.

9.6.2 Managing I/O Request

A request involving input/output operation on a device is passed from the central processor to the EXDC via the System Controller. During the I/O operation, the requests for central storage access are managed by the System Controller. At the end of the I/O operation, the interruption is also passed to the System Controller. In the 370 mode, the central processor that initiated the I/O operation is notified. In the 370/XA mode, any central processor can be notified of the interruption.

9.6.3 Miscellaneous Functions

The TOD clock and clock comparator are located within the System Controller. The 3084 has two System Controllers and thus has two TOD clocks and two clock comparators. The TOD clocks are synchronized.

The System Controller also contains a Storage Key Array that houses storage-protect keys. All requests to main storage are checked for storage-protection violation.

9.7 PROCESSOR CONTROL

The Processor Control continually monitors the temperature, power level, and other parameters that are crucial for the smooth operation of the 308X processor. The Processor Control has a communication path to each central processor, external data controller, system controller, and central storage.

The Processor Control is, in fact, a real-time process control computer that provides functions such as the following:

• Power and thermal control and monitoring
• Error diagnosis and error handling
• Maintenance procedures for assisting the service engineer
• Communication with the service engineer using a service support console

• Initialization of the 308X processor via initial microcode load (IML).

The Processor Control is controlled by microcode, which is structured like an operating system in that it has a control program, access methods, and application modules for performing power and thermal control monitoring, error analysis, and various other functions.

9.8 MULTIPROCESSING

The 308X uses the concept of single-image multiprocessing. Under this concept, each CPU performs a unit of work independently of the other, using a single copy of the operating system. The operating system that is relevant here is the IBM Multiple Virtual Storage (MVS) System. The 308X has assists that enable MVS to run efficiently.

Each CPU runs the dispatcher module of MVS, which controls the execution of units of work. The MVS dispatcher is able to run concurrently on all CPUs. Each dispatcher scans the MVS queue of dispatchable units of work and selects the unit of work with the highest priority. To avoid two CPUs dispatching the identical unit of work, serialization among CPUs is necessary. This serialization is accomplished by the COMPARE AND SWAP instruction.

The 308X design provides synchronization among caches to ensure data integrity in a multiprocessing environment. If a central processor changes a cache line, then the same line in other caches belonging to other central processors is invalidated. Also, if a central processor requests data that is in another central processor's cache and that data has been modified, the cache line is cast out by the second processor and transferred to the first.

Another area of synchronization has to do with the translation look-aside buffer. There is a TLB associated with each central processor (CP). TLB contains entries for virtual pages that have been translated. Entries are invalidated in the TLB by the Invalidate Page Table Entry (IPTE) instruction, which invalidates page table entries also. This instruction was developed to support the MVS operating system. Prior to IPTE, there was only the PURGE TLB instruction for clearing TLB entries, and it purged all TLB entries. An entry is invalidated in the TLB when a page frame is taken away from a virtual page to which it was originally mapped (a page is stolen), or when a virtual page is relinquished (free mained), or when an address space is terminated.

Whenever an IPTE instruction is executed by a CP, other CPs are automatically notified to ensure synchronization of all TLBs. For a PURGE TLB instruction, the synchronization is done by the operating system (MVS), by using the SIGNAL instruction to instruct other CPs to execute a PURGE TLB also.

The foregoing discussion shows that there is overhead associated with multiprocessing. The problem is aggravated when a unit of work is redispatched on a new processor and instruction and data have to be loaded to the new cache. Another problem is caused by the use of common data shared by multiple units of work. For example, if four central processors are used, all four have to be synchronized whenever changes are made to the data. This synchronization requires invalidation of data in three out of four processors.

How significant is this overhead? IBM measurements show that a 3084, which operates with four processors, is 1.9 times as efficient as a 3081, which operates with two processors (note that a 3084 is made up of two 3081 processors). What happens when there are eight processors? There are no published results to indicate the estimated overhead in such a case.

9.9 REVIEW OF THE 308X

The 308X machine is a landmark machine because it is the first among the IBM mainframes to introduce true multiprocessing and the first to implement the channel subsystem architectural concept. Its design is simple and elegant. The only complaint that one can make is the bias of the designers against sophistication, as witnessed by the departure from the pipelining concepts introduced in the 303X series. The designers of the 3090 rectified this concept by making it a heavily pipelined machine.

ADDITIONAL READING

The 3081 is described in the following IBM publications:

IBM Journal of Research and Development, vol. 26, no. 1, January 1982. (The entire issue is devoted to the 3081.)

"IBM 3081 Functional Characteristics," GA 22-7076.

10

3090 Processor Design

Known as the "Sierra" series, the 3090 machines are the most powerful IBM computers built thus far. The 3090 series conforms to the 370/XA architectural principles, but some new concepts (e.g., vector processing facility, expanded storage) have been introduced in their design.

The 3090 series is very similar to the 308X machines in its internal structure. Basically a 3090 computer consists of one or more control processors, channel subsystems, and banks of central storage. A system control element (SCE) acts as a "traffic cop" in managing storage requests from other elements. Each central processor has its own cache and the store-in principle is used in cache design.

However, the 3090 machines are highly pipelined and incorporate many concepts in this area that are present in the 3033 design. Thus, the 3090 can be regarded as a highly pipelined version of the 308X series. The improvement in performance due to pipelining has been estimated at 30 to 50 percent in terms of internal throughput (Tucker [1]). The system control element (SCE) is an improved version of the system controller (SC) of the 308X. Changes also have been made to the EXDC of the 308X series, resulting in the channel subsystem of the 3090.

10.1 TECHNOLOGY

At first sight, the 3090 technology appears no different from the 308X technology. It uses the same large-scale integrated (LSI) technology found in the 308X. Thermal Conduction Modules (TCMs) contain 100 chips per module, and these are mounted on six or nine module boards. However, there is a difference inside the chip. The 3090 chips use current-switch emitter-coupled logic (ECL) circuits, which are significantly faster than the Schottky TTL logic circuits used in the 308X series. There are other improvements also, especially the many stages of logic for phase inversion required by the Schottky TTL logic circuits. The net effect of these improvements is that cycle time has been reduced by 25 percent, from 24 nanoseconds in the case of the 308X to 18.5 nanoseconds for the 3090 [1].

Since the 3090 is a highly pipelined machine, many operations are overlapped. The net result of the pipelined operations combined with the reduction in cycle time is a throughput improvement of 70 to 90 percent. A new level in storage hierarchy is introduced by means of "expanded storage," which is semiconductor memory acting as a buffer between main storage and secondary storage.

Special hardware in the form of parallel registers is provided for vector operations.

10.2 OVERVIEW OF MACHINE ORGANIZATION

The components of the 3090 Model 200 are listed below (see Figure 10-1):

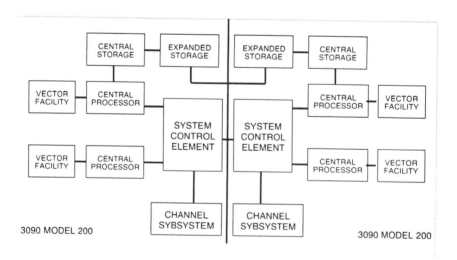

Figure 10-1 Organization of 3090 Model 400.

- Central Processor (2)
- Central Storage
- Channel Subsystem
- System Control Element
- Processor Control Element
- Expanded Storage
- Vector Facility (2).

The Model 200 is a dyadic processor, as is the 3081, and has similar characteristics. The 3090 Model 400 (see Figure 10-1) consists of two Model 200 dyadic processors interconnected to form a quadruple processor system.

The central processor performs the functions of a CPU. It is similar in design to the central processor of the 308X series. Central storage is the name for main storage, as in the case of the 308X series. The channel subsystem, as its name implies, performs the functions of its 370/XA architectural counterpart and is similar to the EXDC of the 308X series. The system control element coordinates requests from various components and is similar to the system controller in the 308X series. The processor control element monitors the processor, performs error handling and other functions, and is similar to that in the 308X series. Expanded storage is large semiconductor memory available in as a supplement to main storage. An interesting design concept of the 3090 is that of a memory hierarchy consisting of the cache at the lowest level, central storage at the next level, expanded storage at the level above, and secondary storage at the highest level.

10.3 PROCESSOR ORGANIZATION

The central processor (see Figure 10-2) consists of the following components:

- Instruction Preprocessor Element (I Element)
- Execution Element (E Element).

The I and E elements are different from their counterparts in the 308X series and are closer functionally to the instruction and execution elements of the 3033. The I Element performs instruction fetching and decoding. The E Element executes the decoded instructions. There is overlap of operations between the I and E elements.

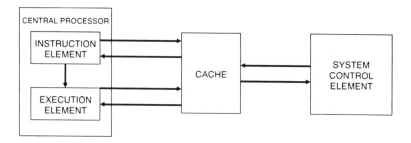

Figure 10-2 3090 central processor.

10.3.1 I Element

The function of the I Element is to prefetch instructions, decode them, generate addresses for operands, and to ensure that instructions are executed in the conceptual sequence required by the architecture.

Instructions are prefetched in doublewords by the I Element and stored in instruction buffers (see Figure 10-3). There are three instruction buffers, each four doublewords in size. An instruction is subsequently moved to an instruction register, where it is decoded and addresses are generated. The generated addresses are sent to the cache for retrieval. Note that decoding, address generation, and cache request are accomplished in one cycle.

A decoded instruction is put in a queue for execution by the E Element. This queue can have a length of up to four instructions. It serves as a speed-matching buffer between the I and E Elements in the sense that the E Element can execute other instructions in the queue in case there is a delay by the I Element in regard to an instruction in the queue. The I Element has special circuitry to ensure that the semblance of sequential instruction execution demanded by the architecture is followed even when, in reality, instructions are executed out of sequence. The following situations, for example, are detected by this special circuitry:

- A store instruction modifies an instruction that has already been prefetched (in such a case, the instruction is refetched after the store).
- A general register is used for address generation, and there is an instruction in the queue ready to modify the register.

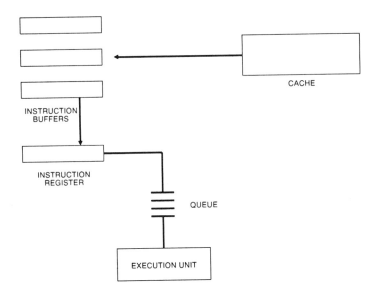

Figure 10-3 3090 instruction prefetching.

When a branch instruction is encountered, the following sequential instructions and the instructions at the branch address are prefetched. This ensures that instructions are available in the buffer for decoding, whether the branch is taken or not. Different branch instructions are treated with special attention to pipelining efficiency. The instructions BXLE and BXH increment and then compare the contents of a general register to a specified value, and branch if the value is not reached. The I Element actually executes these instructions (it has a copy of the general registers), and thus guessing is eliminated. The same procedure is applied to the BRANCH ON COUNT instructions. For the BRANCH ON CONDITION instruction, the past branching result of each branch is maintained for this purpose.

Thus, the I Element contains many sophisticated features that are not available in the Instruction Element of the 308X series.

10.3.2 E Element

The E Element has an operand buffer to hold operands required for the execution of an instruction. An instruction in the instruction queue is executed by the E Element, provided that the required operands are in the buffer. The control and floating point-registers are contained in the E Element. Both I and E Elements have copies of the general registers.

The E Element is controlled by horizontal microcode. Each microinstruction contains many fields, and consequently many microoperations can be done in parallel. For example, during a single cycle it is possible to access general registers, and to use shifters and serial and parallel adders.

The E Element has a buffer for holding operands that have been returned by the cache. When the operands are available in this buffer, an instruction from the instruction queue is executed by the E Element and removed from the queue. Simple instructions are executed in one cycle. For example, a halfword instruction takes one cycle for execution on the 3090. The 3033 executes it in two cycles.

As in the case of the I Element, many improvements of a practical nature have been made to the E Element. All fixed-point and floating-point multiplication instructions are implemented using a highly parallel adder that uses halfcycles. Multiplication by zero is recognized and treated as a special case. In the case of decimal instructions, the I Element prefetches the operands with overlap as they are executed by the E Element. Decimal multiplication and division are done by accessing the decimal multiplication and division circuits in parallel.

10.4 CENTRAL STORAGE ORGANIZATION

The organization of central storage in the 3090 is in the form of a three-way hierarchy, comprising the following elements (see Figure 10-4):

- Cache
- Central Storage
- Expanded Storage

The cache is the prime repository of data and instructions for each central processor. In the case of a cache miss, data is moved from central storage or another cache. If the data is not found in central storage (i.e., a page fault occurs), it is brought in as a 4K page from expanded storage to central storage and subsequently moved to the cache. If the data is not in expanded storage, it is transferred from secondary storage.

Figure 10-4 3090 storage hierarchy.

10.4.1 Cache

The organization, management, and principles of operation of the cache are very similar to those found in the 308X series.

The cache uses a store-in as opposed to a store-through design. The latter approach, used in the 303X series, updates main storage when the cache is updated. Thus, an instruction that modifies storage (e.g., MOVE CHARACTER) causes a write to main storage. Main storage always contains the latest copy of data used in program execution and, in the case of a cache failure, program execution would not be affected by loss of data and would continue. The store-through design was not regarded as suitable from a multiprocessing point of view because of the overhead for writes to main storage.

Under the store-in design, data that is modified is not immediately written to main storage but is kept in the cache until such time as the cache's LRU space management algorithm decides that it needs the space used by the data. Main storage does not reflect the latest changes made to the data. Each central processor executes instructions and uses data from its own cache. A cache miss causes the other caches to be interrogated. Data is fetched from main storage only if it is not available in the other caches. Also, the multiple caches are synchronized so that there is only one copy of data that is changed. The System Control Element (SCE) is responsible for cache management.

The size of the cache is 64K bytes. It can store up to 8K cache lines. A cache line is a doubleword in size. The cache is logically organized as four rows, each row containing 2K cache lines (see Figure 10-5). Associated with the cache is a directory. The directory also is organized into four rows, each row containing 2K entries. Each directory entry contains the address of the cache line in the corresponding location in the cache (the entry in row i and column j in the directory contains the address of the cache line in row i and column j of the cache, as shown in Figure 10-5).

On an access, the four directory entries and the four cache doublewords are read out concurrently. If a cache line is contained in

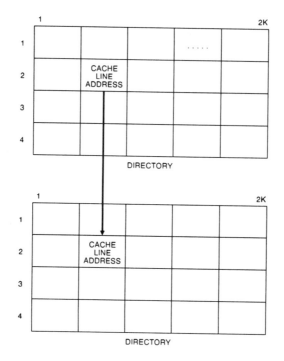

Figure 10-5 Logical organization of the 3090 cache.

the cache, its address (which is the address of the doubleword omitting lower-order bits) should be present in one of the directory entries. The specific position of the directory entry determines the position of the doubleword location in the cache that contains the cache line.

10.4.2 Expanded Storage

The expanded storage feature is a new concept in storage and is unique to the 3090 processors. It adds a third level to the two-level storage hierarchy (comprising central storage and cache) generally used by IBM mainframes.

The characteristics of expanded storage are noted below:

- Data is organized as 4K pages.
- A page is transferred to and from central storage.

- The transfer is requested by a central processor and is done synchronously, under the control of the operating system. The term "synchronous" means that the requesting processor waits for the operation to be completed and does not perform any other task during the waiting period. This is not the case with normal I/O operations, which are done "asynchronously," in the sense that the processor performs other functions during the I/O operation and is notified of completion by an interruption.
- It can hold up to 16 terabytes of data, as compared to the maximum of 2 gigabytes for central storage.

When a central processor requests data that is not available in any of the caches, four doublewords are transferred from central storage if the data is available in central storage. If the data is not available, a 4K page is transferred from expanded storage to central storage and four doublewords are then transferred to the cache. The processor does not perform any activity during this transfer. If the page is not available in expanded storage, it is paged in from secondary storage, using I/O instructions.

One way of looking at expanded storage is as a paging device with high-speed (75 microseconds per page) and synchronous data-transfer capability. It can be used to hold pages that are paged or swapped out of central storage. The design objective is to provide an extra level of storage between central and secondary storages. Thus, central storage will contain the most frequently used pages. Expanded storage will hold moderately referenced pages. The remaining pages will reside in secondary storage.

The role of expanded storage is likely to be evolutionary. Under the ESA/370 architecture, large amounts of data in expanded storage are available to the application programmer. Thus, the role of expanded storage is likely to shift from being a paging device to that of an integral storage component, equal in importance to main storage.

10.5 SYSTEM CONTROL ELEMENT (SCE)

The System Control Element (SCE) is functionally similar to the System Controller of the 308X. It coordinates and manages requests to central storage by central processors and the channel subsystem. One of the key areas of responsibility for the SCE is that of cache management and synchronization. On a storage request from a central processor, the SCE interrogates the caches owned by other central processors in the system. If the cache line is found in another cache, a transfer is made to the requesting cache without going to central storage. Also, when modification of a cache line takes place, the SCE ensures that only one copy of the cache line is kept by invalidating duplicates.

The SCE connects the central processors and channel subsystem to central storage. Each SCE services requests from two central processors, channel subsystem and other SCEs (called "remote" SCEs). An SCE has two request registers for each requestor. One register is for "store" requests and the other is for a "read" request. In one cycle, an SCE can examine up to eight requests and select a request on the basis of a fixed priority scheme.

The communication performance of the SCE has been improved significantly in the 3090. In the 308X series, address and data buses were shared, and data transmission took place only in one direction. In the 3090 these limitations have been removed. A separate bus for addresses and bidirectional data transmission have been implemented. Data transfer is accomplished by means of cross-point switches that can transfer a doubleword from any input bus to any output bus.

When a processor requests the SCE to fetch a cache line, a direct cache-to-cache transfer is initiated if the line is in another cache. The central processor is also directly connected to central storage via a "fast path," i.e., a request bus to central storage and a doubleword bus for data return. Concurrently with its request to the SCE, the central processor also initiates a request to central storage. The SCE cancels the request if the line is in another cache.

Many practical improvements also have been made in the SCE, based on the experience obtained from the System Controller of the 308X series. As an example, the MOVE LONG (MVCL) is commonly used for propagating large blocks of main storage with a pad character (such as zero). The SCE recognizes the situation and sends only a doubleword of pad bytes to main storage which replicates the entire line (of eight doublewords) with the pad bytes.

10.6 CHANNEL SUBSYSTEM

The channel subsystem performs the I/O functions specified for it in the 370/XA architecture. It is similar functionally to the EXDC of the 308X series. The channel subsystem, however, is organized differently from the EXDC. A major change is in allocating a separate microprocessor to each channel, i.e., each channel is managed by its own microprocessor. This microprocessor is controlled by horizontal microcode from a writable control store and different microcode is used for various channel type configuration parameters, such as block versus byte multiplexer, 370 mode versus 370/XA mode of operation, etc.

The components of the channel subsystem are listed below:

• I/O Processor (IOP)
• Channel (CHAN)
• Primary Data Stager (PDS)
• Secondary Data Stager (SDS)

Figure 10-6 schematically illustrates the physical structure of the channel subsystem. The I/O processor performs all I/O-related functions that do not involve channel management. These functions include the decoding of I/O instructions issued by central processors, path management functions specified in the 370/XA architecture, and initiating I/O interruptions. As mentioned in Chapter 5, in the 370 mode, the CPU that initiated the I/O operation is interrupted but in the 370/XA mode any CPU can be interrupted. The I/O processor is a

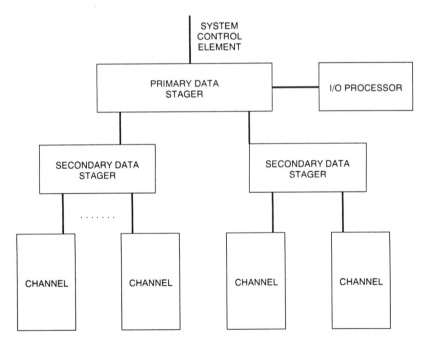

Figure 10-6 Channel subsystem.

separate computer that uses a RISC architecture. It is controlled by pageable vertical microcode.

The channels, as mentioned before, are microprocessors. They perform the same functions that were done by the 370 channels, i.e., they process chained CCWs, provide I/O interface control, and serve as a path for data transfer.

The secondary data stagers (SDSs) are essentially speed-matching buffers. Data from up to 48 channels are handled by the primary data stager (PDS), which acts as a port to central storage via the SCE.

10.7 VECTOR PROCESSING

The vector processing capability is the first of its kind in an IBM mainframe. It is of primary use in an engineering or scientific environment where thousands of equations formulated using vectors and matrices have to be solved.

The vector processing facility consists of an additional pipelined unit for performing vector operations. The 370 and 370/XA architectures provide for approximately 170 vector instructions. These instructions are the basic arithmetic and logical operations on vectors (e.g., ADD, SUBTRACT, MULTIPLY, DIVIDE, COMPARE, AND, OR, XOR) specified for different operand types and instruction formats.

The implementation consists of a set of 16 vector registers, each with 128 elements of 32 bits. Each vector register can be thought of as a slot for holding a vector of 128 elements (see Figure 10-7). The 16 vector registers can be combined to form 8 registers, each with 128 elements of 64 bits. The vector mask register contains mask bits for selecting specific elements from the registers. The vector status register is used for holding control information, such as element count. The vector activity register shows time spent in executing vector instructions. The vector operands in the registers can be input into an arithmetic logic unit (ALU) or multiplier in one machine cycle. Both the ALU and the multiplier are highly pipelined units. The time to execute a vector instruction is one cycle per element plus 28 cycles of overhead common to all elements.

One of the nice features of vector processing is the ability to "section" a vector of arbitrary length into vectors of 128 elements. The 370/XA architecture provides instructions that simplify the process of fitting vectors of length unequal to 128 elements into registers. The

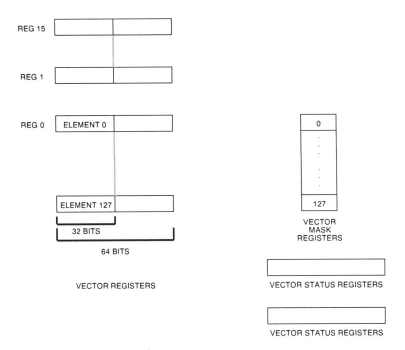

Figure 10-7 Vector facility.

length of the vector is placed in a register, and the processor automatically cuts up the vector into sections comprising 128 elements and processes a section at a time. If the size of the vector is smaller than 128 elements, the processor stops when the last element has been executed.

10.8 REVIEW OF THE 3090 DESIGN

The 3090 design is based on a pragmatic approach in improving the throughput of the 308X series, while keeping the 308X structure. We have seen how bottlenecks have been identified at a very detailed level, and engineering solutions have been proposed on a case-by-case basis. Two novel features, expanded storage and vector processing, also have been introduced. The former is a key feature of the new ESA/370 architecture.

REFERENCES

1. Tucker, S.G.: "The IBM 3090 System: An Overview," *IBM System Journal*, vol. 25, no. 1, 1986.

ADDITIONAL READING

An excellent description of the 3090 series is given in the following article:

Tucker, S.G.: "The IBM 3090 System: An Overview," *IBM System Journal*, vol. 25, no. 1, 1986.

The vector facilities are described in the article:

Buchholz, W.: "The IBM System 370 Vector Architecture," *IBM System Journal*, vol. 25, no. 1, 1986.

11

4381 Processor Design

The 4381 processor is not a mainstream processor, unlike the 308X and 309X series. Nevertheless, it is used in many installations that require a middle-range computer. The 4381 comes in two versions:

- A uniprocessor, operating on the 370 or 370/XA mode
- A dual processor, operating on the 370 or 370/XA mode.

A recent announcement has introduced a new model (4381 E) that is implemented under the ESA/370 architecture. Originally, the IBM 4381 was marketed by IBM as a growth machine for the IBM 4341 computers, which have since been discontinued. The 4341 supported 360 and 370 architectures but was not a mainstream processor because it was designed with the DOS/VSE operating system in mind. It had two modes of operation, a System 370 mode and a 4300 mode. The main difference between the two modes was that the 4300 mode used a different virtual addressing scheme and did not support multiprocessing. The 4300 architecture is not supported by the 4381 processors.

The reasons for including the 4381 in this book are the following:

- The 4381 has been given a new lease on life by IBM's decision to support it under the ESA/370 architecture.

• The 4381 is designed with different objectives than any of the computers discussed so far, namely, to satisfy data processing requirements for a small to medium-sized enterprise or department. It has very little in common with the 3033, 3081, or 3090 machines, even though it supports both 370 and 370/XA architectures.

11.1 TECHNOLOGY

The 4381 uses LSI technology, the same as the 3081. The TCM high circuit-density packaging technique improves performance and reduces floor space. The processor cycle time varies among models, with 68 nanoseconds for Model Group 3 and 56 nanoseconds for Model Group 14.

The 4381 is a heavily microcoded machine. The instruction sets for the 370 and 370/XA architectures are implemented using mostly microcode. The choice between microcodes for the two architectures is made by the operator by means of an initial microcode load (IML). Channels use microcode as well as hardware. They share control storage with the processor.

The 4381 is characterized by IBM as a scientific and engineering computer. Some models have high-speed multipliers for performing binary and floating-point applications. Assists for mathematical operations are available for many models. However, in practice the 4381 is used as a commercial machine in one of two roles, transaction processing or information center management.

11.2 OVERVIEW OF MACHINE ORGANIZATION

The major building blocks of the 4381 Uniprocessor (shown in Figure 11-1) are listed below:

• Instruction processor
• Cache
• Main storage
• Channels
• Control storage

These components are briefly described in the following paragraphs.

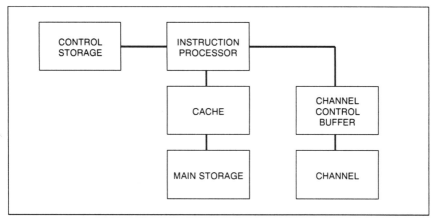

Figure 11-1 Schematic view of the IBM 4381 processsor.

11.3 INSTRUCTION PROCESSOR ORGANIZATION

The Instruction Processor is equivalent to the CPU in terms of the functions that it performs. It fetches, decodes, and executes instructions under microcode control. The cycle time varies among models. For the Model 13, it is 56 nanoseconds (as compared to 57 nanoseconds for the 3033 processor).

The Instruction Processor consists of the following elements (see Figure 11-2):

• Instruction buffer
• Local storage
• Arithmetic logical unit (ALU)
• Shifter.

The instruction buffer is used for storing prefetched instructions. The instruction fetching is overlapped with instruction execution activity.

The ALU executes decimal, binary, and floating-point instructions as well as logical instructions such as AND, OR and EXCLUSIVE OR. The shifter executes the shift instructions and also the PACK and UNPACK instructions for decimal arithmetic.

The local storage (not to be confused with the cache) is 8K bytes in length and is used as internal storage for the processor. It has a dedicated area as well as a nondedicated area. The dedicated area

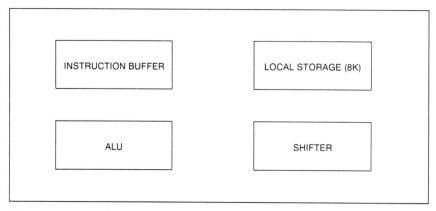

Figure 11-2   4381 instruction processor.

contains 16 general registers, 4 floating-point registers, 12 channel areas, and a branch and link save area.

The cache is of variable size, depending on the model. The smallest model (Model Group 1) has an 8K cache, and the largest (Model Group 13) has a 64K cache. The cache stores instructions and data. These are fetched from main storage in groups of 2 doublewords, i.e., the width of the data path from main storage to the cache is 16 bytes.

11.4   MAIN STORAGE

The size of supported main storage varies from 4 to 32 megabytes, depending on the model. The storage access is via the cache.

Error-checking and correction (ECC) hardware provides automatic detection and correction of errors pertaining to a single bit, and detection, but not correction, of double and multiple bit errors.

11.5   CONTROL STORAGE

Control storage contains microcode that is used for implementing the instruction set and the engineering/scientific assists, and for controlling channels. The channel control buffer holds two control words for each channel, as the channel is performing an, I/O operation. The microcode for a specific mode of operation (e.g., 370 or 370/XA) is loaded by the operator at initial microcode load (IML) time.

11.6 CHANNELS

The channels conform to the 370 architectural principles. There are two types of channels, byte multiplexer and block multiplexer. The byte multiplexer channel can be in the burst mode (used only by one I/O device during an I/O operation) or in a multiplex mode (several I/O operations can be done concurrently). The block multiplexer channels can be either in the multiplex mode or selector mode (the channel does not disconnect from an I/O device until the I/O operation is complete).

Data transfer between main storage and an I/O device is done via a channel data buffer. Each channel has 256 bytes in the channel data buffer. Data can be transferred in 64-byte blocks or in partial blocks.

In the 370 mode, the conventions regarding assignment of channels to CPUs as channel sets are followed. The 370 architecture specifies subchannels as being either shared between devices or unshared. The subchannel is implemented in the form of a unit control word (UCW) that contains the control information necessary for a channel to perform an I/O operation on a device that is attached to it. The UCWs are stored in the high area of main storage. In the 370 mode, the channel selection is done by the CPU (i.e., the operating system).

In the 370/XA mode, it is necessary to create an I/O configuration data set, which is loaded into main storage. A special program called I/O configuration program (IOCP) is available for this purpose. Path selection, in this mode, is done by channel microcode. Thus, even though the 4381 does not specifically have a channel subsystem (as in the case of the 3081, which has an EXDC), the functionality is still available.

11.7 MULTIPROCESSING

The IBM 4381 dual processor provides the capability of multiprocessing in the style provided by the 3033 machine. The 4381 dual processor is schematically illustrated in Figure 11-3. It consists of two 4381 uniprocessors combined to operate as a tightly-coupled multiprocessing system.

Two new components are added to affect the intercommunication between processors required by the multiprocessing capability. One is the Interprocessor Component (IPC), and the other is the Storage Control (SC). The IPC provides communication between the two

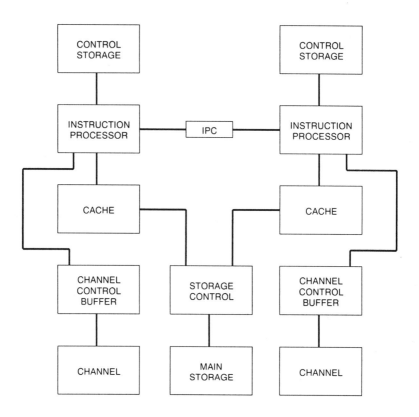

Figure 11-3 Processing in the 4381.

uniprocessors. The SC is used as an intermediary for all storage accesses.

The multiprocessing provided by the 4381 is not the true multi-processing specified in the 370/XA architecture and exemplified by the 308X or 3090. Instead, it is of a makeshift kind, with two uniprocessors strung together to form a dual processor.

11.8 REVIEW OF THE 4381

As mentioned before, the 4381 is not part of the mainstream IBM processors. Its architecture does not have the power or elegance of the 3033, 308X, and 3090 processors. It is not designed according to the 370/XA architecture and its future is doubtful, despite the new life given to it by the recent announcements that place it under the ESA/370 umbrella.

ADDITIONAL READING

Descriptions of the 4381 are available in the following IBM manuals:

"4381 Uniprocessor Functional Characteristics," Publication No. GA 24-39497.

"4381 Dual Processor Functional Characteristics," Publication No. GA 24-4021.

"A Guide to the IBM 4381 Processor," Publication No. GC 20-2021.

12

9370 Processor Design

The 9370 system is a family of small computers using the 370 architecture. Traditionally, the implementations of 370 architecture have been restricted to large-scale mainframes. There is, however, a need for smaller computers using the 370 architecture. The 9370 system is expected to address this need.

The 9370 system is intended for the needs of departmental computing as opposed to centralized corporate computing. Thus, the operating characteristics of the 9370 system are the following:

- It operates in an office environment.
- It does not require trained operational staff.
- It can be integrated with local area networks and with personal computers (PCs).
- It can be connected to a host via communication lines.
- User-friendly menus and help screens are available to the inexperienced user of the system to work with various programs and for problem determination.

The 9370 can be used as a stand-alone system. It can also be used as a node in a network hierarchy comprising mainframes running under IBM's Systems Network Architecture (SNA) at the highest level and the IBM PCs or 3270 terminals at the lowest level, as illustrated in Figure 12-1. SNA is briefly described in Chapter 14.

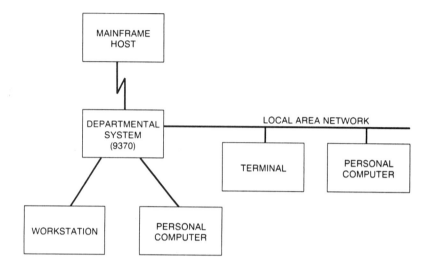

Figure 12-1 9370 in network configurations.

12.1 TECHNOLOGY

The technology used by the 9370 processors is very different from that used in mainframes. The 9370 processors are more like traditional minicomputers and use I/O buses for attaching devices. Physically, the lower end processors consist of sets of cards kept in a card enclosure — there are cards for I/O controllers, storage and processor logic.

The processors implement the 370 instruction set using mostly microcode. However, the higher models use high-speed circuitry in implementing arithmetic operations. Assists to the VM and IX operating systems are implemented on all processors and assists to MVS are implemented in the higher models. All models use translation look-aside buffers (TLB) of varying sizes, because of their critical nature in dynamic address translation. A cache is not used by the low-end models because of the cost involved.

12.2 OVERVIEW OF MACHINE ORGANIZATION

The logical components of the 9370 system are illustrated in Figure 12-2 and consist of the following:

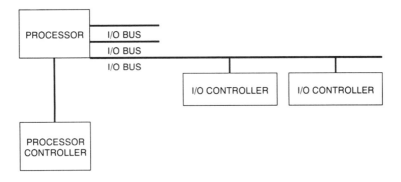

Figure 12-2 9370 machine configuration.

- 9370 Processor
- I/O Controllers
- Processor Console.

The 9370 processor supports the 370 instruction set (but not the 370/XA instruction set). It varies in packaging characteristics and in speed. The high-end processors support more I/O devices and are comparable in performance to the smaller mainframe models under the 370 architecture.

I/O controllers physically are cards that plug into the processor or into separate card units, depending on the type of processor. Logically, they function as control units that allow direct attachment of I/O devices.

One or more I/O buses connect the I/O controllers to the processor. The number of buses vary according to models. The cheapest model has only one bus, whereas the high-end model has six buses. Logically, the I/O bus, I/O controller, and device appear as a 370 channel-attached device.

The Processor Console enables trouble-shooting and problem determination and provides detailed displays on the course of action to be taken in case of system malfunction. The idea is to give the user a chance to diagnose and solve problems before calling for service. The information provided by the Processor Console is of use to the service engineer for remote identification of a malfunctioning unit. The Processor Console is also used for the initial loading of microcode required by the 9370 processor.

12.3 PROCESSOR ORGANIZATION

The 9370 processors are grouped into the following machine types:

- 9373 (Model 20)
- 9375 (Models 40 and 60)
- 9377 (Model 90).

The relative performance of these processors (using 9373 as the base, with value 1.0) are listed below:

9375/40: 1.0–1.4
9375/60: 2.2–3.0
9377/90: 4.5–5.2.

The basic building blocks of the processor are the following (see Figure 12-3):

- Main storage
- Control store
- Cache
- TLB
- Floating-point/high-accuracy arithmetic facilities.

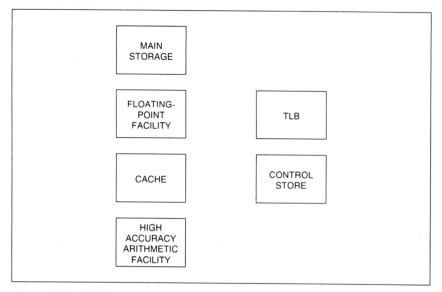

Figure 12-3 9370 processor components.

Main storage varies from 4 to 16 megabytes, depending on the model. In the cheaper models, it is plugged in as a separate card. The control store contains microcode and is about 8 KB in size. The higher-end models implement frequently used instructions in hardware. The cache is used for storing instructions and data. It is not available for the low-end models. A translation look-aside buffer (TLB) is implemented in all models, on account of its critical nature. The floating-point arithmetic facilities are available only in the high-end models.

A processor, in general, can be connected to the following I/O controllers (see Figure 12-4):

• Disk/Tape Subsystem Controllers
• Work Station Subsystem Controllers
• Communication Subsystem Controllers
• 370 Block Multiplexer Channel.

12.3.1   9373 Processor (Low-End Machine)

The 9373 processor is the entry-level processor of the 9370 series. It has a single I/O bus that can support up to four I/O controllers. These controllers can be chosen from the following mix:

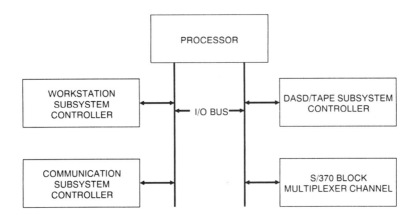

Figure 12-4 9370 machine organization.

- Up to two DASD or tape subsystem controllers to which 9332 or 9335 disk drives or 9347 magnetic tape units can be attached.
- Up to two work station controllers
- Up to two communications subsystems controllers
- One 370 block multiplexer channel.

The processor supports 4, 8, or 16 megabytes of main storage.

The processor has assists for VM and IX/370 operating systems. It has a floating-point facility that provides hardware support for floating-point operations, and also a small translation look-aside buffer (TLB) for storing translated addresses. The processor is physically contained in a card enclosure that has slots for cards for the CPU, storage, and I/O controllers.

12.3.2 9375 Processor (Midrange Machine)

The 9375 processor is an intermediate-level processor in the 9370 series. It comes in two models, Model 40 and Model 60.

The 9375 processor can have up to four I/O buses, which can support a maximum of 16 I/O controllers, as listed below:

- Up to four DASD/tape subsystem controllers
- Up to six work station subsystem controllers
- Up to four communication subsystem controllers
- Up to two 370 block multiplexers.

Both models support up to 16 megabytes of storage.

The processor of the Model 40 has a small translation look-aside buffer (TLB), assists for VM and IX operating systems, and a high-performance floating-point hardware unit, which has eight 64-bit registers and circuitry for multiplication, division, and square root functions. The processor of the Model 60 has, in addition to the above, the following capabilities:

- A 16-KB cache
- Assists for the MVS operating system.

Physically, the processor is housed in two card enclosures. One contains the CPU, storage, and five I/O controller cards; the other is an expansion unit for additional I/O controller cards.

12.3.3 9377 Processor (High-End Machine)

The 9377 processor is the high-end machine of the 9370 family.
The processor supports up to 16 I/O controllers, with the following allowable mix:

• Up to 12 DASD/tape subsystem controllers
• Up to 12 work station subsystem controllers
• Up to 12 communications subsystem controllers
• Up to 16 370 block multiplexer channels.

The processor supports up to 16 MB of storage. It has a 16-KB cache for storing data and instructions. A large TLB for holding translated addresses is provided. Floating-point operations are done on a high-performance floating-point accelerator, which uses special hardware circuits. Assists are provided for the VM, IX, and MVS operating systems.

12.4 I/O ORGANIZATION

An I/O controller is used to connect a device to the processor. An I/O controller plus the device(s) attached to it is called an I/O subsystem. An I/O controller consists of two functional units, namely:

• An I/O Processor (IOP), which communicates via an internal I/O bus with the central processing unit
• An I/O adapter (IOA), which communicates with a device over an external interface.

The IOP and IOA can reside in the same card or in separate cards. In Figure 12-5, the IOP and IOA are shown as residing in two cards.
A number of different types of I/O controllers are available for the 9370 system. Some of these are listed below:

• DASD/Tape Subsystem Controller
• Work Station Subsystem Controller
• 370 Block Multiplexer Channel
• Communication Subsystem Controller.

The DASD/Tape Subsystem Controller integrates the IOP and IOA functions in the same card. It interfaces with the 9332 and 9335 disk drives and the 9347 magnetic tape unit. The 9335 and 9332 are

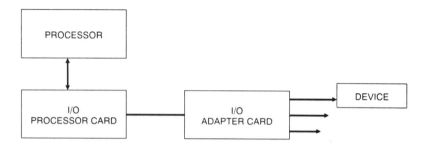

Figure 12-5 Organization of I/O controller.

high-performance moving-head disk storage units with storage capacity of 860 and 410 megabytes, respectively. These are not standard IBM mainframe disk drives. They are supported by the VM operating system but not by MVS.

The System 370 Block Multiplexer Channel is in the form of a card that plugs into an I/O slot. It conforms to the 370 architectural specifications. Up to eight control units can be attached to the channel, and I/O devices are attached to the control units. Frequently used mainframe disk drives (such as the 3380) can be attached to this channel via control units.

The Work Station Subsystem Controller is used for connecting terminals (3270 type devices), printers, and other devices. It needs two cards (an IOP and an IOA). There are six ports in an IOA, and each port can be connected to a device. A terminal multiplexer can also be attached to a port. The advantage of the terminal multiplexer is that up to eight devices can be attached to it and also longer cables can be used. A maximum of four terminal multiplexers is supported by each Work Station Subsystem Controller.

A number of different Communications Subsystems Controllers are available. Thus, a Telecommunications Subsystem Controller enables attachment to telephone lines using cards for a variety of protocols, such as BSC and HDLC. An ASCII Subsystem Controller enables attachment of ASCII devices. A Token Ring Subsystem Controller provides attachment to an IBM token ring network. An IEEE 802.3 Local Area Network (LAN) Subsystem Controller provides attachment to an IEEE 802.3 (ETHERNET) Local Area Network.

12.5 REVIEW OF THE 9370

The 9370 provides a user-friendly, network-oriented environment with System/370 program compatibility. It appears to be suitable for end-user computing because of its ease of operation and diagnostic capabilities. However, there are problems with the role that is assigned to the 9370 series. Its relatively small size combined with the 370 architecture makes it questionable to function in a moderately to highly active communication environment. In the meantime, the mainframe architecture is evolving to create more and more powerful processors. Where does this leave the 9370 series? The response from the user community has not been exactly overwhelming for these series, which is a pity because they are flexible, well-designed computers for the small user. There have been indications from IBM that newer models will be introduced at the high end of the series and that these will run under the 370/XA architecture. If it happens, the 9370 series may prove to be a success.

ADDITIONAL READING

An introduction to the 9370 series is available in the following IBM publication:

"Introducing the IBM 9370 Information System," Order No. GA 24-4030.

13

DASD Subsystems Implementation

This chapter deals with the implementation of I/O architectures for IBM mainframes, with special emphasis on Direct Access Storage Devices (DASD) and their control units. There has been an evolution in direct-access storage that parallels the evolution in mainframe architecture and has influenced the latter significantly. The 360 architecture and associated control programs recognized the practical importance of DASD in a data center as the repository of programs, catalogs, and files. The management of data became one of the key functions of a computer system. Two factors influenced the relationship between computer performance and data management: (a) the involvement of the CPU in data management should be kept to a minimum and (b) the time for I/O operations should be as brief as possible. The 360 architecture provided for two types of channels, the 370 provided for a third channel type, and the 370/XA came up with the channel subsystem in accordance with the first of these principles. The 3880 control units with caches were developed with relevance to the second principle.

The major milestones in DASD development in the IBM mainframe development are listed below:

- The introduction of the selector channel and the 2314 disk drives in the 360 architecture
- The introduction of the block multiplexer channel, disk drives with rotational positioning capability such as the 3330 and 3350, dedi-

cated channel sets, shared devices, and control units in the 370 architecture

• The introduction of the channel subsystem, and the 3380 disk drives with dynamic reconnection capability in the 370/XA architecture

• The introduction of the advanced models of the 3880 control unit with cache capability.

The DASDs of today hold large amounts of data, record at high density, and have microprogrammed controllers that perform a variety of functions. Their control units perform storage and multiple-path connection functions and are controlled by sophisticated microprocessors.

13.1 INTRODUCTORY MATERIAL

A disk subsystem consists of the following components:

• Control units usually called storage controls
• A string of disk drives attached to the control units.

Figure 13-1 shows a commonly used physical configuration of a disk system. The host is connected to a storage control via a block multiplexer channel. The storage control is connected to two strings of disk drives. A string is a set of disk drives, the first of which

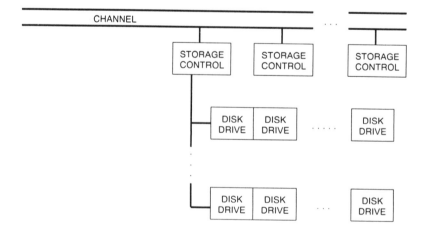

Figure 13-1 Hierarchical I/O configuration.

(called the head of string) has a controller. The controller is a microprocessor that is microprogrammed to perform functions associated with disk operations. A storage control also has a microprocessor (called storage director) associated with it. The storage director works with the controller in executing the CCWs in a channel program.

Figure 13-2 shows a configuration in which a string is attached to more than one control unit and control units are attached to more than one channel. Under this configuration, the device can be accessed by more than one I/O path.

A disk drive consists of a stack of recording disks. Each recording disk has two surfaces (called data surfaces) available for recording data. Each data surface is logically organized into concentric tracks. A track is divided into records. A set of tracks having the same radius resident on all data surfaces is called a cylinder. The hierarchy of data organization in a disk drive has the following levels:

• Disk drive
• Cylinder
• Track
• Record.

Logically, the data in a disk drive is composed of cylinders that consist of tracks; and tracks, in turn, are composed of records. Figures 13-3 and 13-4 illustrate the organization of data on a disk drive.

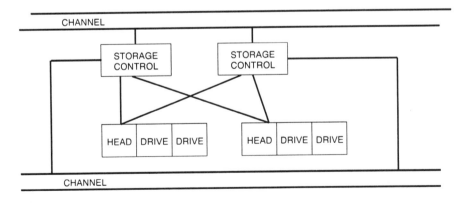

Figure 13-2 Network I/O configuration.

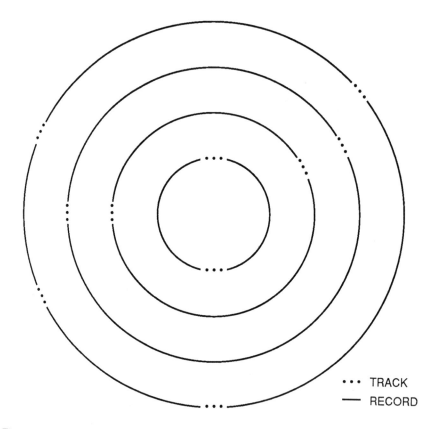

Figure 13-3 Variable length records on tracks.

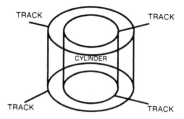

Figure 13-4 Cylinder/track relationship.

Read/write heads are used to access data from a data surface as the disk drive rotates about its axis with a constant speed. The read/write head can be either fixed or moving. In a fixed-head configuration, there is a read/write head corresponding to every track. Each read/write head is positioned immediately above a track and remains stationary while the disk drive rotates about its spindle. The delay associated with accessing a record in a track is caused by the rotation time required by the disk drive so that the record is positioned under the read/write head (this time is called rotational delay). In a moving head configuration, there is no longer a one-to-one correspondence between a track and a read/ write head. A read/write head is assigned to several tracks on a disk surface (e.g., in the case of the IBM 3350 two read/write heads are assigned per disk surface) and moves radially across the disk surface to reach a track. The delay associated with accessing a record on a track consists of the following elements:

1. The time required to position the read/write head over the addressed track, called seek time
2. The time required by the disk drive to position the addressed record under the read/write head, called rotational delay (same as for a fixed head configuration).

The precursor of today's disk drives is the magnetic storage drum, which is a rotating drum with parallel circular tracks (see Figure 13-5) with a read/write head assigned to each track. The read/write heads were costly and consequently drums were expensive. A cost-effective solution was found in a movable head that moved across concentric tracks on a disk surface or from disk to disk. The IBM 350 RAMAC, introduced in 1956, used this principle. The movable head concept was further modified so that each disk had one or more moving heads associated with it. The drawback of the movable head is the time required to move the head so that it is above a track (seek time). A solution is to have a fixed head for each track but, as mentioned before, this is expensive. The IBM 2305 is an example of a disk with fixed heads. This device was used to store critical data that had to be retrieved very quickly. Some disk drives, such as the IBM 3350, provided a small number of fixed heads in addition to moving heads.

13.2 EVOLUTION OF I/O ARCHITECTURE

The 360 architecture was the first architecture to stress the importance of DASD. This was because no prior computer system was as dependent on a single input/output device type for satisfactory system performance.

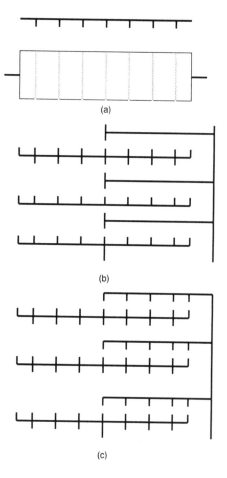

Figure 13-5 (a) Drum and head. (b) Disk with movable head. (c) Disk with fixed head.

"An assumption in the development of System 360 was that the attachment of direct access storage to the system would be highly desirable and almost universally accepted. This assumption was based on the fact that disk and drum technologies had sufficiently matured to make their use practical on all systems. Thus, IBM's major operating systems OS/360 and DOS/360 required at least one and preferably more direct access devices for external storage." (Brown [1])

Channels were introduced in the IBM 7090 (around 1960) and the I/O architectures of the 360 and 370 were heavily influenced by these. Prior to the introduction of channels, instructions for operating a device had to be a part of the instruction set for the CPU. Thus, the IBM 704, for example, had instructions for reading, writing, and rewinding a tape. The 360 architecture used the START I/O instruction to initiate a channel program, which was executed by the channel, leaving the CPU free to execute other instructions.

The trouble with the 360 I/O architecture was that it gave too much importance to the channel. Up to 256 channels were allowed, each capable of attaching up to 256 devices. In reality, it was impossible to implement 256 channels on a mainframe (normally 8 to 16 channels are used). The 370/XA architecture recognized that the role of the channel had to be downgraded and came up with the concept of the channel subsystem. In a way it was a recognition that the I/O operation was by its very nature a distributed operation and hence is best performed by distributed processors (the microprocessors contained in the channel subsystem, channel, control unit, and device). Thus we see the role of the channel changing from its original one in the 7090 to that of a path in the 3090.

The role of the control unit has changed, also. The earlier control units were single microprocessors that could control up to 32 disk drives. The control function consisted of device selection, status presentation, sending orders to the device, and other activities that were required for successfully initiating and completing an I/O operation. The current control units use multiple microprocessors and also support internal caches. They have become part of a storage hierarchy with four levels, namely processor cache, main storage, control unit cache and disk storage.

The disk drives themselves have evolved in two directions, namely by providing better price/performance ratios and more functionality. The price/performance ratio has improved because of increased density in recording and the availability of low cost microprocessors. The functionality has evolved in the direction of supporting multiprocessing by providing multiple paths, dynamic reconnection capability and other such functions.

13.3 CLASSIFICATION OF DASD

The classification of DASD in reference to IBM mainframes can be done in several ways, such as head movement, data format, etc.

On the basis of head movement, disks can be classified as fixed-head and movable-head units. The former do not have seek time and are considerably faster than the moving-head disks. But they are also expensive because of the cost per head. Hence fixed-head drives are used for storing data that should be retrieved quickly, such as pages in virtual storage.

The format of data stored in a disk drive can also be used as a basis of classification. The most commonly used format is the count-key-data format, which is implemented by the mainstream 3330, 3350, and 3380 devices. Under this format, records of variable length are allowed. A fixed-length field in the record can be defined as a key. A SEARCH KEY command is provided for comparing the key of a record with a given value. Another format, called the Fixed Block Architecture (FBA), was used by IBM in implementing the 3370 disk drives, which did not turn out to be as popular as the 3380. Under this format, a record is contained in a variable number of fixed blocks. The basic unit of transfer is a block, and a record comprising multiple blocks is assigned blocks in such a way that rotation and seek times in moving through the sequence of blocks is minimal.

A third basis of classification is by size. Large disk drives, such as the 3380s, are used by IBM mainframes. The 9370, on the other hand, can support smaller disk drives, such as the 9332, which has a capacity of 368 megabytes as compared to 2521 megabytes provided by a 3380 unit.

A fourth basis of classification is based on whether or not the disk is removable from the drive. The 3350 disks were removable. This meant that the disks could be physically carried from one installation to another and mounted on different drives. The 3380 disks are not removable and are permanently mounted for operation.

Another basis of classification is in terms of the functionality provided by the disk. A number of functions have been found to improve disk performance. These include features such as command retry, rotational position sensing, dynamic reconnection, etc., which are discussed in a subsequent section.

13.4 COUNT, KEY, DATA FORMAT

The general layout of a track is illustrated in Figure 13-6. An index point indicates the beginning of a track. A track is composed of records separated by gaps. A record consists of the following fields:

- Count area
- Key area
- Data area.

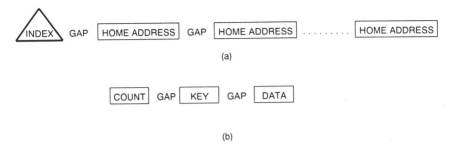

Figure 13-6   (a) Track format. (b) Record format.

These three fields contain the length (in bytes), the key (if present), and the data portion of a record.

The inter-record and intra-record gaps are used by channels and control units to perform their functions. For instance, command chaining requires that the channel fetch the next CCW from main storage, decode it, and pass it on to the control unit. The channel and control unit perform these operations during the time it takes for a gap to move under the read/write head.

The home address contains the physical address of the track and its condition (i.e., whether it is usable or defective). It is followed by record R0, which is called the track descriptor record. Its main function is to define the address of an alternate track for a defective track, and to provide the address of the defective track in the case of an alternate track.

A record can be uniquely specified by an address comprising a cylinder number, a track number (also called head) within the cylinder, and a record number (called record IDs) within the track. This address is represented as CC HH R, where CC represents the cylinder address, HH represents the track address, and R represents the record ID. A record can be located by using the CC HH R address or by specifying a key value, which is located in the key area of the record.

13.5   FIXED-BLOCK ARCHITECTURE

Fixed-Block Architecture (FBA) divides up the storage area into fixed blocks. Each block has a fixed length and is linearly addressable using a relative block address, ranging from 0 to $n - 1$, where n is the number of blocks in the device.

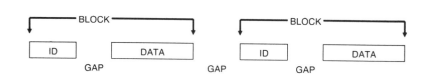

Figure 13-7 Fixed block format.

A block is the basic unit of transfer between the DASD and the processor. Physically, a track is divided into blocks. A block consists of two fields, an ID field and a data field, separated by gaps as shown in Figure 13-7. The ID field consists of a physical identifier of the block (i.e., cylinder number, head number, and block number), control information as to whether the block is primary or alternate, defective or operational, etc., and error-detection bytes. The data field consists of data and error-detection/error-correction bytes.

The fixed-block architecture was developed to simplify disk operations. The count, key, data format required "a significant amount of nonusable space or overhead for each record, depending on record length." (Nelson [2]) The number of commands is significantly reduced for FBA devices, by a factor of 5 (see discussion on 3370, later in this chapter). Channel programs are streamlined and the design of the disk controller is simplified. (Cho [3])

In spite of the advantages claimed for them, the FBA disk drives are not popular. The main reason is that users prefer the flexibility of the count, key, data format devices in file management.

13.6 DASD SUBSYSTEM FEATURES

The features of a storage control and disk controller vary according to implementation. In this chapter we are restricting ourselves to the more recent IBM storage control units (e.g., IBM 3880) and disk drives (e.g., 3380), which perform sophisticated data management functions. The following features are noteworthy and are explained briefly in the remainder of this section:

- Error detection and correction
- Command retry
- Multiple requesting
- Multitrack operation
- Record overflow
- Rotational position sensing

- Channel switching
- String switching (actually, a feature of the string)
- Dynamic reconnection
- Cache management.

Error Detection and Correction

These schemes vary from one storage control or device to another. An odd parity bit is used by the channel in transferring a byte to the storage control (i.e., the bit is set to 1 if there is an even number of one bits within a byte), and the storage control checks the parity bit for error detection. The storage control removes the parity bit and adds error correction code (ECC) bytes which are computed and written for each count, key, and data area in a track. During a read operation, the ECC bytes are recalculated and compared with the existing ECC bytes to detect errors. In case of errors, the instruction is re-executed using the Command Retry feature.

Command Retry

This feature pertains to the channel and/or storage control and enables the re-execution of a CCW in a channel program in case of error (e.g., timing, check, seek arrow). The retry is automatic and does not cause an interruption or the use of error recovery routines.

Multiple Track Operation

This feature enables the storage control to automatically select the next track (in ascending sequence of addresses) at the end of the track that is currently recorded. If a record cannot be found in a given track after a search operation, the next track is automatically scanned. Thus, the need for using another seek command in the channel program in order to position the read/write head the next track is eliminated.

Record Overflow

A record that is larger than a track spans more than one track. The portion of a record contained in a track is called a record segment.

Each track contains, in such a situation, an R0 record and the count, key and data of the record segment in that track. The tracks have to be formatted using a write special count, key, and data command. A flag byte in the count area indicates that the record is a record segment. Note that the size of a record cannot exceed a cylinder, and a record cannot span two cylinders.

Multiple Requesting

The multiple requesting capability allows a block multiplexer channel to perform concurrent I/O operations on disk drives that are in the same string. Assume that the channel is executing a channel program and that a SEEK or a SET SECTOR command is being executed. During the rotational delay necessary before the record appears under the read/write head, the disk drive is disconnected from the channel. If the multiple requesting capability is present in the storage control, an I/O operation on another drive can be initiated at the time.

Rotational Position Sensing

A disk surface is divided into equal sectors, as shown in Figure 13-8. Rotational position sensing (RPS) is the ability of the device to sense the arrival of a specified sector under the read/write head. We have seen that the block multiplexer channel can perform I/O operations on several devices concurrently. With RPS, a drive can disconnect from the block multiplexer channel during the rotational delay before the specified sector appears under the read/write head.

If RPS is not available and it is desired to read a record with a given cylinder, track, and record ID, every record in the track has to be examined to see if its ID matches with the given ID. This means that the channel has to be attached to the device for the entire search operation. When RPS is available, a sector corresponding to the record is specified by a SET SECTOR command in the channel program. The disk drive can disconnect from the channel until the sector appears under the read/write head. (An alert is issued to the channel) shortly before the sector appears under the read/write head. If the channel is not ready, the device goes through one more rotation and alerts the channel again before the sector appears under the read/write head.

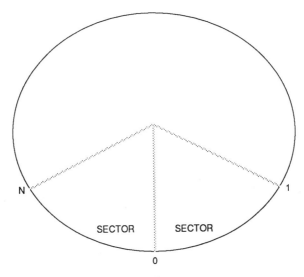

Figure 13-8   Disk sectors.

It should be pointed out that sectors are not physically marked out on data surfaces but are identified by the time that is required for a sector to be traversed by the read/write head as the disk rotates at constant speed. This time for a 3350, for example, is approximately 130 microseconds. It is obtained by dividing the time for a full revolution (16.7 milliseconds) by the number of sectors (128) on a data surface.

Channel Switching

Channel switching is the capability of attaching the storage control to more than one channel. By having this capability, the following advantages are obtained:

- Multiple I/O paths are available, and the start of an I/O operation does not have to be delayed if a channel is busy, since it can be started on another channel.
- If the dynamic reconnection facility is also available, the completion of an I/O operation does not have to be delayed because a channel is busy, since another channel can be used in its place.
- The availability of the I/O subsystem is enhanced because of multiple paths to the storage control.

Storage controls having two, four, and eight channel switches are available presently. For storage controls having two storage directors, it is possible to connect multiple channels to each storage director.

String Switching

String switching is a feature of the head of string and not of the storage control. A string of disk drives can be connected to more than one storage control if the head of string has the string-switching capability. As in the case of channel switching, the availability of the system is increased because multiple paths are provided between device and channel.

Dynamic Reconnection

This is the capability on the part of a device to reconnect to any available channel. In the absence of this capability, a device can reconnect only to the channel that originated the I/O operation.

End-of-File

The disk controller writes an end-of-file record consisting of a data area containing 20 bytes of zeros. The end-of-file record is useful in defining a set of sequential records.

13.7 CHANNEL PROGRAM EXECUTION

The channel commands pertaining to disk I/O operations can be divided into the following classes:

- SEARCH commands
- READ commands
- WRITE commands
- SENSE/TEST commands
- CONTROL commands.

The function of the SEARCH command is to locate a record satisfying given search criteria. The following are examples of search criteria:

- SEARCH ID EQUAL — A record address in the form (CC HH R) is given at the data address specified in the CCW and this record address is passed by the channel to the storage control which compares if for equality with the ID of the record most recently read by the device.
- SEARCH ID HIGH — The same as above, except that the most recently read record ID is checked to see if it is higher than the ID specified by the CCW.
- SEARCH KEY EQUAL — A key is given at the data address specified by the CCW and the storage control compares this value with the key area of the record most recently read by the device.

If the search criterion is satisfied, the storage control presents channel end, device end, and status modifier bits to the channel. If the search criterion is not satisfied, the storage control presents only channel end and device end bits to the channel. The status modifier bit indicates that the search has been satisfied and causes the channel to skip the next CCW and execute the succeeding CCW.

The READ commands are used to transfer count, key, or data from the device to the main storage. The data is transferred serially, bit by bit, from the device to the control unit, and one byte at a time from the control unit to the channel. The storage control or disk controller checks for the validity of data by examining error correction code (ECC) bytes. At the end of data transfer, the control unit presents an ending status byte containing channel end and device end.

The READ commands are also used to transfer addresses or sector numbers. For example, READ HOME ADDRESS transfers the home address area of the current track to main storage. READ SECTOR transfers the sector number of the most recent count area to main storage.

The WRITE commands are of two kinds, (1) for formatting tracks and records and (2) for updating an existing record.

The formatting write commands are used for initializing tracks and records and also for specifying the sizes of the various areas in a record, such as key area, data area, etc. During initialization, error correction code bytes are written after each area. The write update commands are used for data transfer from main storage to the device, and the tracks have to be formatted before using these commands.

The SENSE/TEST commands are used for ascertaining the status of a device; and this usually results in the control unit presenting a status byte to the channel.

The CONTROL commands are used for various seek operations and for setting sectors and file masks. A SEEK command positions the Read/write head at a track within a cylinder. It can be followed by a READ command to examine all the records in a track and to select a record that meets search criteria. The same result is obtained faster by using a SEARCH command, but in certain cases it may be preferable to SEEK and READ records sequentially. The SET SECTOR command specifies a sector number and is used with rotational position-sensing devices. The sector number for a record is obtained by means of a READ SECTOR command. The drive disconnects from the channel during the time it takes for the record to appear under the read/write head. The channel is alerted before the sector is due for appearance and is reconnected to perform operations like searching, reading, etc. In the event that a sector number corresponding to a record cannot be obtained easily, a sector address of zero can be specified that corresponds to the beginning of the track (positioned by the index). Another control command of interest is the SET FILE MASK, whose function is to specify subsequent permissible disk operations by means of a mask byte. The bits in the mask byte can specify admissible and nonadmissible commands.

We shall next give an example of a channel program for reading a record from a disk. Consider the following:

SEEK
SET SECTOR
SEARCH ID EQUAL
TRANSFER IN CHANNEL
READ

The foregoing is a sequence of commands whose functions are:

1. SEEK — The access mechanism is moved to the cylinder specified by the seek address and the head specified by the seek address is selected.
2. SET SECTOR — A sector number indicating the angular track position is specified, to be used in conjunction with the rotational position-sensing mechanism.
3. SEARCH ID EQUAL — This command attempts to locate a count area in a track having the matching CC HH R address.
4. READ — Transfers data area or record from disk to main storage.

13.8   EXAMPLES OF DISK DRIVES AND STORAGE CONTROLS

This paragraph describes various DASD and storage controls that were used (or are in use) in the IBM mainframes. It is not possible to include all the disk and storage controls that have been offered by IBM for use with their mainframes. A rough breakdown of devices that have been offered during the past 25 years is given below:

- The devices offered with the 360 were the 2305 fixed-head disks and the 2314, 2311, and 2319 moving-head disks. The 2314, 2311, and 2319 did not have the rotational position-sensing capability and were meant to be used with the selector channel.
- The devices initially offered with the 370 architecture were the 3330, 3340, and 3350 series. All three had rotational position sensing and were designed to be connected to block multiplexer channels.
- The 3380 devices were offered under the 370 architecture, but they have the dynamic reconnection capability and hence are suitable for operation under the 370/XA architecture, also.
- The devices discussed so far use the count, key, data format. The 3370 series offered under the 370 architecture use the Fixed-Block Architecture (FBA).

The 2305, 3350, 3380, and 3370 devices are briefly described in this section.

IBM 2305 Fixed-Head Disk Module and IBM Storage Control

The IBM 2305 (Model 2) fixed-head disk-drive module contains six recording disks. Each disk has two data surfaces (12 data surfaces in all). There are 72 tracks per data surface and one fixed read/write head (called a recording element) for each track. Thus there are 72 recording elements for each surface. Figure 13-9 illustrates the arrangement of tracks and recording elements. As shown in Figure 13-9, there are four access mechanisms, each carrying 18 recording elements. Of the 72 tracks, 64 are used for data recording and 8 are reserved as alternate tracks which are used as substitutes for defective recording tracks.

The 2305 (Model 2) can hold up to 11.25 MB of data. It was frequently used as a paging device in a virtual storage operating en-

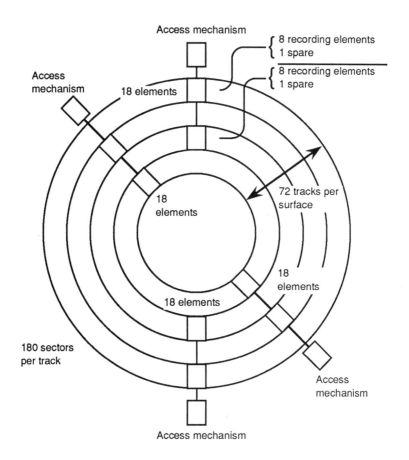

Figure 13-9 Top view of 2305 (Model 2) disk drive.

vironment because of its fast access time. Table 13-1 presents the functional capability of the 2305. The 2305 has the rotational position-sensing capability. Its control unit, IBM 2835, has multiple requesting and command retry features.

IBM 3350 Disk Drives and IBM 3830 Storage Control

The IBM 3350 disk drive was very popular a few years ago and has been superseded by the 3380. The 3350 has the following characteristics:

Table 13-1 Capability of IBM 2305 (Model 2) Disk Module

NUMBER OF ADDRESSABLE TRACKS	768
BYTES PER TRACK	14,660
BYTES PER MODULE	11,258,880
ROTATION TIME	10 milliseconds
ACCESS TIME (MAXIMUM)	10.25 milliseconds
ACCESS TIME (AVERAGE)	5.0 milliseconds
TRANSFER RATE	1.5 MB/sec

- It has 16 recording surfaces, one of which is used for servo information, data clocking, rotational position indication, and similar control data, plus fixed-head storage.
  The other fifteen recording surfaces are used for data storage. They are accessed by moving heads, and both sides of the surface can be used for data storage.
- The 3350 unit is logically organized into 555 cylinders, each cylinder having 30 tracks. Each track is capable of storing 19,069 bytes; 5 cylinders (150 tracks) are used as alternates, and one cylinder is for reserved use. The total capacity of the disk is 3175 MB.
- There are 128 sector marks that divide the surface of the disk into equal areas; their purpose is to aid in rotational sensing.
- The average seek time is 25 milliseconds. The average rotational delay is 8.3 milliseconds.

The 3350 units are attached to a channel using a 3830 storage control unit. A maximum of 32 physical drives can be connected to a single storage control unit. A string can contain up to four dual drives (two 3350 disk units). The first unit in each string has a controller, and if required, an alternate controller can be substituted for the last dual drive.

Table 13-2 presents the characteristics of the 3350.

Table 13-2 Disk Characteristics

PARAMETERS	3330	3340	3350	3380
AVERAGE SEEK TIME (MS)	30	25	25	16
FULL TRACK ROTATION TIME (MS)	16.7	20.2	16.7	20.2
DATA TRANSFER RATE (MB/SEC)	0.8	0.9	1.2	3.0
CAPACITY PER UNIT (MB)	400	140	635	2,521
CAPACITY PER DRIVE(MB)	200	70	317.5	1,260
CAPACITY PER ACCESS MECHANISM (MB)	200	70	317.5	630
CYLINDERS PER ACCESS MECHANISM	80	690	555	885
TRACK PER CYLINDER	19	12	30	15
BYTES PER TRACK	13,030	8,368	19,069	47,476

IBM 3380 Disk Drives and IBM 3830 Storage Control

The 3380 is the disk drive that is currently used with most IBM mainframes. It has a capacity of 2.5 GB, which is four times that of the IBM 3350.

The 3380 uses a new film head technology to access data recorded at densities higher than in the case of the earlier disk drives. The 3380 provides increased storage capacity without requiring additional floor space and its power consumption costs per stored byte are lesser.

There are three models of the 3380, A4, AA4, and B4. A4 or AA4 is designated as the head of a string. A4 has one disk controller and AA4 has two disk controllers. A string consists of one model A or AA and up to three model Bs. An AA has to be used in order to support dynamic reconnection. Each of the three models consists of two logical disk drives, each logical drive having two access mechanisms.

The 3380 Storage Control is used for attachment to 3830 disk drives. The 3880 comes in several models. Models 13 and 23 have caches and are controlled by sophisticated microprocessors. Here, we shall discuss only these two models.

The 3880 Model 23 consists of two microprocessors (each microprocessor is called a storage director) and a cache. The cache can be up to 64 megabytes in size. About 99 percent of the cache is used for storing 3380 tracks (each track is 47K bytes in size). A track is stored in a unit called a slot. A directory that translates cylinder and track information into slot locations is also kept in the cache.

The cache operates in three modes, normal, sequential, and bypass. In the normal mode, the 3880 stores the remainder of a track, i.e., the data starting from the requested record until the end of the track. This data is read concurrently to the 3880 cache and to processor storage. In a read operation, the cache is searched and when a read hit occurs (i.e., the record is found in the cache), the record is presented to the processor without accessing the disk. The format of the data record thus presented is identical to the one used by the disk, i.e., the cache operation is transparent. When a read miss occurs (the record is not found in the cache), the record is read from the DASD to the processor. At the same time, the record and the subsequent records to the end of the track are read into the 3880 cache. In the case of a write operation, the cache is searched. If the record appears in the cache, both DASD and cache are updated concurrently. If the record is not found in the cache, it is written directly to the DASD. In the sequential mode of operation, the 3830 reads the record and the remainder of the track. Subsequently, it does look-ahead reads. Thus, the next sequential track is read immediately after the first track. If a record from the second track is read by the processor, the third sequential track is read, and so forth. In the bypass mode of operation, the cache is not used at all.

IBM 3370 Disk Drives

The IBM 3370 is a movable-head fixed-block architecture (FBA) device, to be used in conjunction with the IBM 3380 storage control unit. Each block of data has a unique address and is individually accessible for read/write operations. It is also possible to access contiguous blocks, by specifying starting and ending addresses. The block position is sensed automatically, and the storage control can disconnect during seek time and rotational delay.

The 3370 comes in two models, A and B. Model A has an attached controller and should be the head of a string. A string can have up to four units; at least one A unit should be present in the string. Each unit has a capacity of 571 megabytes, a data transfer rate of 1.8 megabytes, and an average access time of 20 milliseconds.

The FBA architecture is noteworthy because of its simplicity. The command set for the 3370 consists of 16 commands as opposed to more than 70 commands for the operation of a disk using count, key, data format. The SEEK, SEARCH, and SET SECTOR commands are not used in the FBA architecture. Read/write operations use only four commands, namely READ, WRITE, DEFINE EXTENT, and LOCATE. The DEFINE EXTENT command specifies the high and low addresses that are used in a channel program. LOCATE specifies the address of the first data block to be accessed and the number of data blocks to be sequentially processed.

13.9 CONCLUDING REMARKS

It has not been possible to go into great detail regarding the structure of control units, devices, etc., because of space limitations. It is hoped that the reader gets a flavor of the variety and complexity of DASD and control unit implementations that are available.

REFERENCES

1. Brown, D.T., et al.: "Channel and Direct Access Device Architecture," *IBM Systems Journal*, vol. 11, no. 3, 1972.
2. Nelson, D.: "The Format of Fixed-Block Architecture in the IBM 3370 DAS," *IBM Disk Storage Technology*, 1980, Order No. GA 26-1665.
3. Cho, T.F.: "The Design Concept of the IBM 3880," *IBM Disk Storage Technology*, 1980, Order No. GA 26-1665.

ADDITIONAL READING

IBM manuals contain detailed descriptions of each DASD and storage control type. Overviews of DASD subsystems and I/O architectures are available in the following publications:

Matick, R.E.: "Impact of Memory Systems on Computer Architecture and System Organization," *IBM Systems Journal*, vol. 25, nos. 3/4, 1986.

Grossman C.P.: "Cache-DASD Storage Design for Improving System Performance," *IBM Systems Journal*, vol. 24, nos. 3/4, 1985.

Bohl M., "Introduction to IBM Direct Access Storage Devices," Science Research Associates, Chicago, 1981.

Prasad N., "Architecture and Implementation of Large Scale IBM Computer Systems," QED Press, 1981.

14

Communication Configurations

This chapter gives an overview of computer networking in an IBM environment. IBM's philosophy regarding networking is influenced by a number of factors, which we shall discuss briefly. One such factor is the organizational setup in data processing. A large, multi-site corporation, for example, has several levels of data processing. At the highest level is corporate data processing, which uses powerful mainframes such as the 3090 series for processing on-line transactions, managing large data bases, and for undertaking centralized functions such as payroll, human resources, and corporate management. At the next level is departmental computing, which embraces a wide variety of applications ranging from scientific or engineering to management of a local branch office. The computer used for the latter purpose can be a low-end mainframe (such as the IBM 4381 or 9370), an IBM small system (such as the System 38 or Series 1), or a non-IBM computer. At the next level are workstations that are personal computers (PCs), which may be tied together into local area networks (LANs) for wordprocessing and office automation. This setup is schematically shown in Figure 14-1. Another factor is the need to provide the communication requirements within IBM's own network architecture, Systems Network Architecture (SNA). A third factor is the need to accommodate international communication architectures such as the Open System Interconnection (OSI). None of those factors were even contemplated at the time of the design of the 360 machines, which were oriented initially toward batch processing.

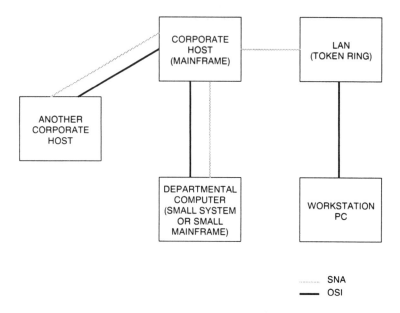

Figure 14-1 General communication plan in large enterprise.

14.1 HISTORICAL BACKGROUND AND EVOLUTION

The early computers used punched cards, paper tapes, magnetic tapes, and disks for input/output operations. Terminals grew out of the need of the user to interact with the computer. The early terminals were like typewriters and were attached directly to the computer in the same manner as a punched card reader or tape unit. As terminals gained widespread acceptance, there was a need for remote communication. This was provided by the use of telephone lines and a transmission control unit (TCU). The TCU was connected to a channel at one end and to telephone lines hooked to the terminals at the other end. The TCU was a microprocessor capable of providing two functions, (a) to appear like a control unit to the channel and CPU, and (b) to store and transmit data to the terminals. An access method for telecommunications, Basic Telecommunications Access Method (BTAM), and a teleprocessing system, Customer Information Control System (CICS), were developed at this time.

The early communication systems suffered from three drawbacks: (a) the TCU was not programmable (was hardwired) in many cases and consequently did not provide flexibility; (b) the CPU performed the bulk of communications-related functions, including polling; and (c) the lines and terminals could not be shared among different applications running on the same CPU. A significant step in the right direction was made in 1974, with a programmable communications controller (the IBM 3705) replacing the TCU. This was made possible by technological advances that enabled minicomputers to perform dedicated communication tasks. Systems Network Architecture (SNA) was also introduced at this time. The objective was to provide a layered architecture for management of end-to-end communication between users. An access method, Virtual Telecommunication Access Method (VTAM), and a Network Control Program (NCP) written for the communications controller were provided as part of the Advanced Communications Facilities (ACF). ACF is the implementation methodology for the part of SNA associated with the host. At a parallel level there was the emergence of an international architecture, Open Systems Interconnection (OSI). During the 1980s, both SNA and ISO have evolved significantly, as explained in subsequent paragraphs.

14.2 SMALL SYSTEMS COMPUTERS

The small systems computers do not use the 360, 370, or 370/XA architecture. Most of these have been developed as a one-of-a-kind computer, with its own architecture. Notable among the small system computers are the System 36, System 38, Series 1, and the PC/RT. Of these, the System 38 is very popular as a departmental machine or a small-enterprise machine. Its architecture has many noteworthy features, such as an instruction set that uses types (Soltis [1]). The PC/RT machine is a RISC computer that uses many recommendations made by the 801 project (Radin [2]). The Series 1 is used for communication and real time applications.

The small systems often need to communicate with mainframes or among themselves. When the mainframes perform centralized functions, the small systems use the host's files or send data to the host. The small system can have a software emulation package for emulating a terminal supported by the host, and the communication protocol is that of a host to a terminal. Alternately, the small system can be defined as a node under Systems Network Architecture (SNA).

The capabilities provided under SNA provide for peer-to-peer communication and small-system-to-host communication. Both are described in the section on SNA.

14.3 LOCAL AREA NETWORKS

A local area network (LAN) is a network of terminals or computers confined to a small area such as a building, or a floor within a building. It is distinguished from the networks used in remote communication (sometimes called long-haul networks), which use long-distance communication facilities such as telephone lines. LANs can be classified by the physical medium they use (e.g., coaxial cable, twisted pair of telephone wires) or by the methodology used in communication of messages (e.g., collision detection, token ring).

IBM's Token-Ring Network is a LAN that uses twisted pair (or optical fiber) for its physical medium and token passing for its communication methodology. It is based on IEEE standard 802.5 for a token-ring LAN. A token is a unique bit sequence that is passed through the LAN from one station to its neighbor. When a station has a message unit (called a frame) to send to another station, it modifies the bits in the token to a start-of-frame sequence. The entire frame is then transmitted. After the station has completed transmission, it inserts a new token into the ring, which is passed around for use by other stations. In the meantime, the transmitted data circulates around the ring until it is recognized and removed by the addressed station.

One station in the ring is elected as the token monitor. Its function is to ensure that a token is available in the ring as part of normal operation and also to detect error conditions.

A station can reserve a token for its use at a specified priority. In such a case, the next token will be issued at the highest priority specified. The idea is to allow a station to gain access to the ring for transmission of high-priority frames.

A bridge can be used to combine two token rings into one logical ring. A bridge is a physical device that copies a token from one ring and places it in the other. Bridges are useful when a token ring has reached its capacity and has to be split into two rings, or when stations in two physically separate rings have to send messages to each other.

The other local area network supported by some computers (e.g., 9370) is the IEEE 802.3 standard LAN, which uses coaxial cable. The Carrier Sense Multiple Access with Collision Detection

(CSMA/CD) protocol is used for message transmission. Under this protocol, each station can sense whether the cable is used for message transmission by another station. A station waits to transmit a message until the cable is free. The receiving station can detect an incoming message by its address. If two or more stations send messages concurrently, a collision is supposed to take place. In such a case, the stations resend the messages after waiting for a reasonable interval. The most widely known network using this methodology is the ETHERNET.

14.4 OPEN SYSTEMS INTERCONNECTION

Open Systems Interconnection (OSI) is an international standards activity for computer communication in a multivendor environment. This activity currently has strong support and commitment from computer vendors, including IBM (Sundstrom [3]), common carriers, and users. It was initiated in 1977 by the International Organization for Standardization (ISO). Its current scope includes the design of standards in relation to file transfer, job execution, and message handling in a multivendor communication environment.

The standards proposed by OSI are based on a reference model having seven layers (see Figure 14-2). A brief description of each layer is given below:

• The Physical Layer provides the physical ability to send or receive messages through a physical medium, such as telephone lines.

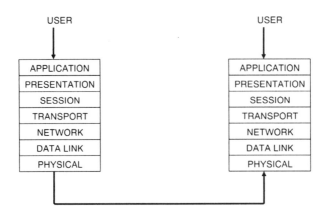

Figure 14-2 Seven-layered OSI basic reference model.

- The Data Link Layer provides protocols for transmission or reception of messages via the physical layer.
- The Network Layer provides sequencing and segmentation of messages.
- The Transport Layer provides end-to-end sequence control, blocking of messages, and error recovery procedures.
- The Session Layer provides services for establishing sessions between end users and for managing the sessions.
- The Presentation Layer provides data transfer and selecting of user data syntax.
- The Application Layer provides identification of the parties or subjects for establishing communications.

The status of development of standards for the various layers is the following:

- For the first three layers, standards are available and are implemented by many vendors, including IBM. The data link standard is the High-Level Data Link Control (HDLC) protocol. These standards will be supplemented by LAN (e.g., token ring, bus, etc.) protocols. The network layer standard is X.25, which is a protocol for packet-switching transmission of messages.
- The standards for the next two layers, the transport and session layers, have been completed and are approved.
- The standards for the next two layers are being defined and are expected to be complete by 1988.

X.25 is supported by a number of IBM systems. In 1980, IBM introduced a program product for the communication controller for X.25 support. The Series 1, System 38, and the IBM PC also support X.25.

IBM Europe has developed OSI software for the mainframes that support selected functions in the transport and sessions layers (levels 4 and 5) of the OSI model [3].

14.5 SYSTEMS NETWORK ARCHITECTURE (SNA)

Systems Network Architecture (SNA) is IBM's counterpart to the OSI architecture. Its beginnings were in 1974, when it was used to provide communication capabilities for a host connected to the IBM 3600 banking terminals. Initially, SNA was confined to tree-shaped communication networks with the host as the root of the tree. Multihost communication capabilities were introduced in 1977. During the 1980s, a number of capabilities were introduced, such as program-to-program communication (LU 6.2), low-entry (one hop) peer networking for small systems, and support of the token ring local area network. In this section we shall give a brief view of SNA's functions and capabilities.

SNA is a layered architecture with seven layers, as shown in Figure 14-3. The three lowest layers constitute SNA's transport network, implemented as VTAM/NCP. The four layers at the top constitute functions for a Logical Unit (LU). The logical unit is responsible for management of sessions between paired end users, via the transport network.

The transport network has the physical layer at the lowest level. This layer provides the interface for communication over media such as telephone lines, satellite systems, etc. The next layer, data-link control, provides the protocol for data communication. It is the Synchronous Data Link Control (SDLC) developed by IBM. SDLC is similar to the HDLC protocol in OSI. The next layer, path control, provides routing of the message to the addressed node.

The LUs are the interfaces with the end user in the network (see Figure 14-3). An end user can be an application program or a device. The LU handles the format of data that is presented to the end user (via the transaction and presentation services layer) and also the dataflow control of sessions (via the dataflow control and session layers). LUs are the ports (or addresses) through which users gain access to the path control network and conduct sessions with other end users. A session is a logical connection between two LUs. It is initiated by a BIND request, which binds a pair of LUs for the entirety of the session.

Logical units are classified by types. The early types 1, 2, 3 denote keyboard printers, work stations, terminals, and receive-only printers. These were primarily devices used for sending (or receiving) data from (or to) an application program at the host. The newer types reflect the need for program-to-program communication between hosts or between a host and a small system or LAN. A new LU type, 6.2, was introduced in 1982 as Advanced Program-to-Program Communication (APPC) to meet these requirements. The actual implementation covers a range of products, including CICS, small systems, and LAN. An interesting aspect about LU 6.2 is that it defines a set of generic commands (verbs) that are implemented by each LU 6.2 product in its own syntax. Users can have their programs execute LU 6.2 commands on CICS, System 38, and a PC that runs APPC/PC.

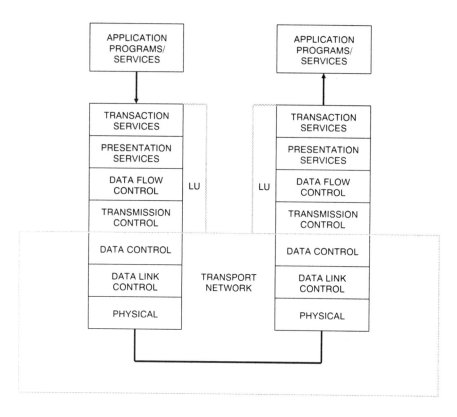

Figure 14-3 Systems network architecture schema.

In regard to LAN support, up to eight token rings can be connected to a host via the NCP program. The LAN requires only the functions of the two lowermost layers of SNA. The LAN uses physical and data link control layers that conform to the IEEE 802.2 recommendations. The first product that supported the token ring was the IBM PC. Subsequently, support has been extended to the communications controller 3725 and the IBM 9370. Also, the System 36 can be attached to a token ring via the IBM PC AT.

14.6 CONCLUDING REMARKS

We have given an overview of the current picture of communication requirements and IBM's approach toward an integrated solution that takes into account the factors mentioned in the beginning of the chapter.

REFERENCES

1. Soltis, F.G.: "Design of a Small Business Data Processing System," *Computer*, September 1981.
2. Radin, G.: "The 801 Minicomputer," *IBM Journal of Research and Development*, vol. 27, no. 3, May 1983.
3. Sundstrom, R.J., et. al.: "SNA: Current Requirements and Direction," *IBM Systems Journal*, vol. 26, no. 1, 1987.

ADDITIONAL READING

A number of books are available on communication networks and protocols. For a general introduction to the subject, the following are recommended:

Cypser, R.J.: "Communications Architecture for Distributed Systems," Addison-Wesley Publishing Company, 1978.

Tanenbaum, A.S.: "Computer Networks," Prentice-Hall, 1981.

The SNA architecture is described in detail in a set of IBM documents titled "SNA Format and Protocol Reference Manual."

15

Review and Concluding Remarks

We have attempted in this book to give an evolutionary picture of the architecture and design of IBM computers. It is truly amazing how the concepts introduced nearly a quarter of a century ago have managed to retain their hold in the ever-changing world of computer technology. To look for the reason for IBM's hold on the industry, we have to review first the concept of system architecture, which is a level higher than machine architecture.

15.1 REVIEW OF IBM SYSTEM ARCHITECTURE

Lorin [1] suggested the use of the phrase "system architecture" to describe the interacting components and layers that comprise a computing system. The system includes hardware and software located at various geographical points and connected by means of networks. In a broad sense, IBM has created a system architecture with the following goals:

- It should serve large-scale centralized enterprise functions, such as transaction processing, database management, batch processing, time-sharing, etc.
- It should satisfy network requirements imposed by external agencies (e.g., OSI) and by the vendor.
- It should provide capabilities for integration with other vendors' hardware or software products.

These goals have been met by a system architecture consisting of various subarchitectures, such as network architecture, software architecture, computer architecture, etc. The various subarchitectures have been developed over the past two decades and include products such as SNA, MVS, CICS, IMS, DB2, etc. Well-defined interfaces between the subarchitectures have also been developed. The success of IBM is in the strength of the system architectural concepts and implementation.

The main criticism often leveled at the system architecture is that software is not transportable between mainframe computers and midrange computers (e.g., System 38, Series 1, etc.) because they have different architectures. The question is asked, "Why can't IBM have a single computer architecture for all ranges?" By introducing the 9370 series IBM has taken a step in this direction. IBM also has been looking at the problem from another point of view, that of cooperative processing under the System Application Architecture (SAA). Cooperative processing is defined as the distribution of programming functions across machines with different architectures, using networking capabilities.

15.2   REVIEW OF IBM MAINFRAME ARCHITECTURE

In 1964, the 360 architects wrote specifications for a batch machine that combined scientific and commercial applications — a machine that did floating-point arithmetic as well as decimal arithmetic, a machine that was word-oriented as well as byte-oriented, a machine that viewed computing as consisting of layers and interfaces, a machine that was a member of a family of models and that interfaced in a uniform manner with peripheral devices having different characteristics. The specifications were subsequently extended to incorporate multiprogramming concepts and on-line transaction processing requirements and, in the process, grew indescribably complex. This complexity, in turn, made many critics (both inside and outside IBM) ask questions about fundamental issues, such as:

- What should the instruction set consist of? Should it be reduced in size and streamlined or should it continue the way it is now?
- Why should the cache and other implementation constructs not be part of the architecture also?

• Is the single-image multiprocessing concept going to be impractical when the number of processors is increased? Is there a better way for implementing multiprocessing?

We have seen that the architecture started as real storage uniprocessor architecture with some complex instructions and ended up as a multiprocessor virtual-storage architecture with a large number of very complex instructions. The only point that has not changed is that of the conceptual image of a unit of work that is executed in a serial manner corresponding to the von Neumann model.

We have seen the increasing complexity of the architecture, especially in relation to storage. The architectural resources needed for dynamic address translation and dual address spaces operations such as data movement and program calls are formidable, since special registers have to be dedicated for storing addresses of tables and other parameters needed for table look-ups.

We have also seen that many key constructs have been ignored in the architecture and relegated to implementation. One such construct is that of the cache. Cache coherence (the principle that the data in the multiple caches should be synchronized) is one of the fundamental principles of design of single-image multiprocessing computers. Yet this principle is not stated in the architecture. A second construct is that of microcode in control storage and its non-availability to users. It is implicitly assumed in the architecture that some or all of the instructions will be implemented in microcode. Yet there is no mention of an interface between the microcode layer and the user. A third construct has to do with the role of the operating system in multiprocessing. It is possible to present the single-image operation only because of the serialization performed by the operating system. The architecture does not mention this aspect of multiprocessing at all.

The basis for defining an instruction set and of specifying instructions has also been challenged. What functions should be performed by instructions and how an instruction should perform its functions are open issues. Should the assembly language provided by the 360, 370, and 370/XA architecture be the interface between the microcode level (or physical level) and the application developer or the compiler writer? Or should there be a different interface altogether? If the statistics shown in Chapter 3 are to be believed, the bulk of the instructions in the instruction set seems hardly to be used. The effect of providing these rarely used instructions on the instruction set as a whole has been a concern to computer architects, since the extra logical circuits needed for decoding instructions can result in overall delays.

"Most instruction frequency studies show a sharp skew in favor of high usage of primitive instructions (such as LOAD, STORE, BRANCH, COMPARE, ADD). If the presence of a more complex set adds just one logic level to a ten-level basic machine cycle (e.g., to fetch a microinstruction from ROS), the CPU has been slowed by 10 percent. The frequency and performance improvement of the complex functions must first overcome this 10 percent degradation and then justify the additional cost. If the presence of a complex function results in the CPU exceeding a packaging constraint on some level (e.g., a chip, a board), the performance degradation can be even more substantial." (Radin [2])

15.3 REVIEW OF IBM MAINFRAME DESIGN

We have reviewed a number of designs of IBM computers in the preceding chapters. In the large mainframe area, the design directions appear to be those set by the 3033 and 3081 computers, namely, pipelining, multiprocessing, and use of the cache. The 3090 has improved on the pipelining concepts introduced in the 3033 to the extent that there seems room for very little price/performance advantage in further improvement in that direction.

The multiprocessing is implemented using a number of related concepts. From the hardware point of view, the System Controller (SC) is the coordinator of multiprocessing activities. Its speed and streamlining are important from the performance point of view. This is an area of improvement that has been addressed in the 3090. The cross-interrogation of caches to preserve data integrity is an issue that is troublesome because of potential delays when the number of CPUs passes a certain threshold value. Right now, a CPU cross-interrogates the caches of other CPUs and concurrently issues a read to main storage. If the cross-interrogation shows that the cache line is not present in other caches, execution proceeds at the same speed. A unit of work, however, can use common areas of storage that are used by other units of work and this may result in potential delays. The 370 architects themselves are aware of this situation.

"Well, . . . there are things we would do differently if we were starting from scratch . . . . Maybe, if we were given today's technology without any precedents, we might have allowed private segments that would not provide cache coherence between CPUs. That would certainly have reduced cache cross-interrogation traffic between CPUs." (Gifford and Spector [3]])

The other point is that a unit of work is usually put on a waiting queue after it initiates an I/O operation. In such a case, a new unit of work is assigned to the CPU and the old unit of work may be assigned subsequently to a different CPU. This involves loading a different cache with the instructions and data pertaining to the task and consequent overhead.

15.4 FUTURE TRENDS

The ESA architecture is the most recent of mainframe architectures. Its primary emphasis is on making large volumes of data immediately available to the user. This is in line with the system architectural goals previously described, namely, to provide capability at a centralized level for data management in an on-line transaction-processing environment and to provide network functions at various levels, with the stress on the higher levels. The implementation of this concept is done via a three-level storage hierarchy, as described in Chapter 9.

It is highly probable that in the next few years the improvements in performance will be due to technology changes rather than design or architectural changes. By cutting down on cycle time and eliminating bottlenecks in the system controller, it will be possible to increase processing speed at a steady pace.

15.5 CONCLUDING REMARKS

We have attempted to capture approximately 25 years of architectural and implementation ideas pertaining to processing, memory, and input/output operations. We have stressed continuity in the concepts as we move from one architecture to another. Due to space limitations, we have not gone into detail in many areas, e.g., the design of the main operating systems such as MVS/SP, MVS/XA, etc., and I/O devices such as terminals, tape drives, etc. Our main interest has been to highlight critical aspects of the architecture and design.

REFERENCES

1. Lorin, H.: "Systems Architecture in Transition — An Overview," *IBM Systems Journal*, vol. 25, nos. 3/4, 1986

2. Radin, G.: "The 801 Minicomputer," *IBM Journal of Research and Development*, vol. 27, no. 3, May 1983.

3. Gifford, D., and A. Spector: "Case Study: IBM's System/360-370 Architecture," *Communications of the ACM*, vol. 30, no. 4, April 1987.

Index